£10-60
T 4/3

Library of
Davidson College

ROAD TO BABYLON
DEVELOPMENT OF U.S. ASSYRIOLOGY

ROAD TO BABYLON

DEVELOPMENT OF U.S. ASSYRIOLOGY

BY

C. WADE MEADE

With one folding map

LEIDEN
E. J. BRILL
1974

ISBN 90 04 03858 2

Copyright 1974 by E. J. Brill, Leiden, Netherlands

All rights reserved. No part of this book may be reproduced or
translated in any form, by print, photoprint, microfilm, microfiche
or any other means without written permission from the publisher

PRINTED IN THE NETHERLANDS

DEDICATED TO
"DOODLE"

CONTENTS

Preface IX
Abbreviations XII

I. Introduction 1
    Assyriology Defined 1
    Prolegomena 3

II. America takes Interest 17
    The Age of Romanticism 17
    Triumph of the Realists 23

III. The Curtain Rises 28
    Francis Brown and the Beginning 28
    David Lyon at Harvard 30
    Paul Haupt Comes to John Hopkins 32
    Hermann Hilprecht at Pennsylvania 34
    Assyriology at the Other Schools 37
    Societies and Publications 43

IV. The University of Pennsylvania Shows the Way 47
    Nippur 47
    Wolfe Expedition 49
    The First Babylonian Expedition 52
    Babylonian Expedition of 1890 56
    The Third Expedition, 1893-96 58
    The 1899-1900 Expedition 61
    Results 63

V. Assyriology comes of Age 64
    Robert F. Harper and the Assyrian Letters 64
    The Expedition to Adab 66
    Yale Joins the Ranks 71
    Peters-Hilprecht Controversy 72
    Institutions and Professional Societies 76
    Literature 80

VI. The War Years 83
    Literature 83
    Institutions and Professional Societies 86
    Founding of the Oriental Institute 90

VII.	OUT OF CHICAGO.	93
	The Breasted of Assyriology	93
	Luckenbill and the Assyrian Dictionary.	97
	Oriental Institute Museum.	102
	Publications of the Oriental Institute	103
VIII.	THE FIELD BECKONS.	105
	Penn and the British Museum.	105
	Tepe Gawra.	108
	Chicago Field Museum and Oxford.	110
	Other Joint Expeditions.	112
	The Iraq Expedition of the Oriental Institute	114
	The Persian Expedition	117
	European Expeditions	118
IX.	BLOOMING OF A SCIENCE.	120
	At the Institutions	120
	Learned Societies.	125
	Publications.	127
	Baghdad School.	131
X.	EPILOGUE.	134
	World War II and Assyriology.	134
	Since the War.	136

APPENDICES 139
    I. Chronology. 139
    II. Major U. S. Expeditons to Iraq and Iran Prior to 1973 141

BIBLIOGRAPHY 148
    U. S. Literature to 1940. 148
    Other Works Consulted 172

INDEX. 181

Map of Iraq and Iran . . . . at the end of the book

PREFACE

Today the United States is one of the leaders in the field of Assyriology, just as it is in Egyptology, Hittitology, and other areas of ancient Oriental studies. This has not been the case for any length of time, however. Americans did not embark into the sphere of cuneiform studies until less than one hundred years ago.

Babylon was never the site of any major excavation parties from the United States, but it was the leading city of Mesopotamia throughout much of that area's early history. In fact, Babylon is referred to as the "Queen City" of the ancient Near East. With this in mind, I have had no hesitation about using Babylon in the title of this book.

The first two chapters of this work set the stage for the development of Assyriology in the United States. In the first chapter, after defining Assyriology, I have attempted to sketch a brief outline of the birth of the discipline in the British Isles and on the continent of Europe. The intellectual atmosphere and interest in this European scholarship prevalent in the United States is the thesis of the second chapter.

American Assyriology can be divided into four distinct periods. These are:

(1) from Francis Brown's introduction of an Akkadian language course at Union Theological Seminary in 1880, with other institutions following this example, and the University of Pennsylvania sending out four expeditions to Babylonia, until 1900;

(2) from 1900 when American savants began to publish numerous scholarly works in cuneiform studies to the outbreak of World War I in 1914, after which all scholarly pursuit of academic knowledge is relegated to the background;

(3) the period between 1914 and 1920 when Assyriology consisted of writing and publishing, with no field research being carried out; and

(4) finally, the era from 1920, when the professional archaeologist takes over from the amateur and the Assyriological intelligentsia begin to specialize, until the start of World War II in 1939.

The period since 1939 is too recent to place the developments in their proper historical perspective, but I have sketched the highlights of this era in a brief epilogue.

The bibliography is not exhaustive, but it does include all significant books and articles published by American scholars through the year 1939. I have also listed other works consulted for this book.

In preparing this manuscript I have had the help of so many people that it is not feasible to mention them all. Some of these I will, of course, have to acknowledge, but my thanks go out to all those who have assisted me in any way, large or small.

I am deeply indebted to Mrs. Jean Herold, Mr. Charles Dwyer (formerly at UT), and Miss Kathleen Blow, librarians at The University of Texas at Austin, who aided me in my search for material and kept books flowing in on interlibrary loan;

to Professor M. E. L. Mallowan, London, Dr. A. R. Lewis, University of Massachusetts, Dr. Tom B. Jones, University of Minnesota, and Dr. Robert Braidwood, Oriental Institute, University of Chicago, for guiding my steps at the beginning of the research;

to Mr. G. E. Wright of the Harvard Semitic Museum and Mr. R. Dena Bulgaris, Harvard Alumni Office, who put me on the trail of the diaries of David G. Lyon, and Mr. Kimball C. Elkins and his staff of the Harvard Archives for allowing me to examine these diaries;

to Mr. Robert F. Beach and the library staff of Union Theological Seminary, New York, for making available to me the personal papers of Francis Brown;

to Mrs. Barbara Wilson, archivist, University Museum, University of Pennsylvania, who allowed me to examine the papers of the Nippur expeditions, along with Mr. Charley Detwiler and Dr. Samuel N. Kramer of the University Museum for their aid and advice as I studied these papers;

to Dr. Richard Storr of the University of Chicago, who guided me to the Harper papers, and to Mr. J. Richard Phillips and Miss Margaret McFadden of the Archives of the University of Chicago for making these papers available to me;

to Mrs. Ethel Schenk, Administrative-Secretary of the Oriental Institute, for answering my numerous inquiries, and Dr. John A. Wilson of the Institute for biographical information on E. J. Banks;

to Mrs. A. T. Olmstead, Kansas City, Missouri, and Dr. George G. Cameron of the University of Michigan for information on the career of Albert T. Olmstead;

to the late Dr. Ferris J. Stephens at Yale, who provided data on Albert T. Clay;

to Mr. Adolf Schrijver, Secretary of the New York Oriental Club, for providing information on that organization;

to the University of Chicago Press and the Oriental Institute for permission to quote from the *Journal of Near Eastern Studies*, and from Breasted's *The Oriental Institute, 1933*;

to the American Oriental Society for allowing me to use material and a photograph from the *Journal*;

to the American Schools of Oriental Research at Baghdad for permission to quote from the *Bulletin*;

to A. J. Holman Company for generously allowing me to quote from the *So-Called Peters-Hilprecht Controversy, 1908*:

to Dr. D. D. Van Tassel, Case Western Reserve University, Cleveland, Dr. W. H. Goetzmann, Dr. J. R. Wiseman, and Dr. G. G. Arnakis, of the University of Texas at Austin, and Dr. George Basalla of the University of Delaware, for aid in preparing the manuscript at the dissertation level;

to Mrs. Nell Hutchins of Louisiana Tech University, who typed the manuscript, my assistant Miss Joyce Johnson for proofreading it, and my secretary Miss Cindy Bamburg for preparing the index;

and, finally, to my wife and children, who endured it all.

To the above mentioned I am deeply grateful.

Ruston, Louisiana
January 3, 1973

C. WADE MEADE

ABBREVIATIONS

AASOR	Anual of the American Schools of Oriental Research
AJA	American Journal of Archaeology
AJSL	American Journal of Semitic Languages and Literature
AS	Assyriological Studies (Oriental Institute)
BASOR	Bulletin of the American Schools of Oriental Research
BZA	Beiträge zur Assyriologie
JAOS	Journal of the American Oriental Society
JCS	Journal of Cuneiform studies
JHUC	Johns Hopkins University Circular
JNES	Journal of Near Eastern Studies
JRAS	Journal of the Royal Asiatic Society
JSOR	Journal of the Society of Oriental Research
OIC	Oriental Institute Communications
OIP	Oriental Institute Publications
SAOC	Studies in Ancient Oriental Civilization (Or. Inst.)
ZFA	Zeitschrift für Assyriologie

CHAPTER ONE

INTRODUCTION

> The Assyrian came down like a wolf on the fold, And his cohorts were gleaming in purple and gold; And the sheen of their spears was like stars on the sea, When the blue wave rolls nightly on deep Galilee.[1]

These opening lines from Byron impress upon us the might of the Assyrian empire. The term Assyriology is derived from these people, but it is very misleading. In fact the Assyrians make up only a part of the science of Assyriology. What then does the word Assyriology mean? Before going any further it will be necessary to try to define this nebulous term.

Assyriology Defined

Ask ten Assyriologists to define Assyriology and, in all probability, you will get ten different answers. There is no doubt that they understand the term, but to put it into the form of a definition is another matter entirely. Over the past several years I have communicated, both orally and written, with the prominent workers in this field. To each the concept of Assyriology differs. A philologist maintains it is the decipherment of the cuneiform tablets. To the historian the science deals with the history of Mesopotamia and Persia. The archeologist is quick to say that it is the archeology of these areas. Each is right, but only partially. There is, however, no distinct line separating these disciplines. A competent ancient historian must be able to read the languages in his field. He must also be a fairly good archeologist, for much of early history is brought to light by archeology. The same holds true for the archeologist and the philologist. These three fields cannot be divorced, but work instead to complement each other.

---

[1] George G. (Lord) Byron, "The Destruction of Sennacherib," in *English Literature and its Backgrounds*, Bernard D. Grebannier, *et al.*, (eds.). (Shorter ed.; New York: Dryden Press, 1950), 791.

It might be wise to quickly examine why the term Assyriology came into use if it is not limited to the Assyrians. The first cuneiform tablets discovered in any quantity were in Assyria.[2] Later discoveries revealed that the people referred to their language as Akkadian. The northern dialect came to be known as Assyrian, and the southern one as Babylonian. In scholarly circles Akkadian has replaced the term Assyrian when speaking of the language, but the science remains Assyriology.[3]

Just after the turn of the century a British scholar attempted to broaden the definition of Assyriology as: "the study of the literature and antiquities of the Babylonians and Assyrians."[4] This is certainly true but is in no way an adequate definition. By "Babylonians" does he mean just the Old Babylonians, or does he include the Sumerians and Akkadians? It is not known whether or not he intended to include all the people throughout time that dwelled in that geographic area or limited it to the ethnic group called the Babylonians.

Gradually Assyriology began to embrace the study of the majority of the peoples of the ancient Near East who wrote in cuneiform. This included the Hittites until recently. Today most authorities tend to regard Hittitology as a separate field, now that more is known about them. One wonders if Sumerology will break away (some schools have chairs of Sumerology), but this is doubtful, as the Sumerians furnished the foundation for the culture of the Assyrians, Akkadians, and Babylonians. Persian studies may make the break when the knowledge of the field is enriched enough to do so.[5]

For the purpose of this essay Assyriology is defined as the study of the history, literature, and antiquities of ancient Mesopotamia, Persia, and the littoral regions. This includes all facets of their civilization from philology to architecture. Major groups of peoples coming under study are the Sumerians, Akkadians, Babylonians, Assyrians, Chaldeans, Kassites, Elamites, and Persians.

---

[2] Edward Chiera, *They Wrote on Clay: The Babylonian Tablets Speak Today* (Chicago: Univ. Chicago Press, 1938), vi.

[3] I. J. Gelb, *Assyrian Dictionary*, A. L. Oppenheim, editor-in-chief, Vol. I (Chicago: Univ. Chicago Press, 1964), vii.

[4] Theophilus G. Pinches, *The Old Testament in the Light of Historical Records and Legends of Assyria and Babylonia* (New York: E. & J. B. Young & Co., 1902), iii.

[5] For a fairly up-to-date discussion of the *status quo* of Assyriology see A. L. Oppenheim, "Assyriology—Why and How?" *Current Anthropology*, I (1960), 409-420; and *Ancient Mesopotamia* (Chicago: Univ. Chicago Press, 1964), 7-30.

INTRODUCTION 3

Prolegomena

Nineveh was the capital city of the Assyrian world during the closing decades of the empire. Sennacherib (704-681 B.C.), son of Sargon II, moved the seat of government there in the early seventh century B.C. After this Nineveh becomes one of the symbols of evil and wickedness in the Near East. From the Old Testament prophet after prophet thunders out against the city, foretelling its doom. The Lord speaks to Jonah, saying, "Arise, go unto Nineveh, that great city, and preach unto it the preaching that I bid thee."[6] Nahum said of it, "Woe to the bloody city! it is all full of lies and robbery; the prey departeth not";[7] making the prophecy "And it shall come to pass, that all they that look upon thee shall flee from thee, and say, Nineveh is laid waste: who will bemoan her? whence shall I seek comforters for thee?"[8]

This mighty city did fall in 612 B.C. to the combined onslaught of the Medes of Cyaxares and the Chaldeans under Nabopolassor. The hateful capital of the men of Ashur was completely destroyed, slipping from the pages of history and almost from the memory of man. There are a few references to Nineveh by Classical historians, but none have any suggestion of its location.[9] It was not until the middle of the nineteenth century that archeologists uncovered the ruins of Nineveh.

Babylon, queen city of the Near East for much of the ancient period, was also destroyed, but unlike Nineveh, its location was not completely forgotten until the medieval period. Like Nineveh, Babylon did not escape the wrath of the Hebrew prophets. Jeremiah records the words of the Lord, "And thou shalt say, Thus shall Babylon sink, and shall not rise from the evil that I will bring upon her: and they shall be weary."[10]

This prophecy came true, but not before a great deal of time had elapsed. Babylon was destroyed once by Sennacherib (689 B.C.). But, to ease tension with the Chaldeans, or for some other reason, the city was rebuilt by his son Esarhaddon (680-669 B.C.). Under Chaldean

---

[6] Jonah 3:2.
[7] Nahum 3:1.
[8] Nahum 3:7.
[9] S. A. Pallis, *The Antiquity of Iraq: A Handbook of Assyriology* (Copenhagen: Ejnar Munksgaard, Ltd., 1956), 19.
[10] Jeremiah 51:64.

and Persian rule Babylon survived many sieges without being destroyed. The great city did decline but was certainly still intact at the death of Alexander the Great there in 323 B.C. It received a blow from which it never recovered in 275 B.C. when Seleucia to the north was made capital of the Seleucid empire. Most of the residents of Babylon went to Seleucia to live.[11] After 93 B.C. there seems to be no record of life in Babylon.[12] Babylon was finally reduced to desolation, but her fate was different from that of Nineveh.

One of the earliest Classical historians to give an account of Assyrian history was Ctesias of Cnidus. Unfortunately his work has not survived, and it is only through Diodorus Siculus that we know such a work existed. Ctesias was a Greek physician, residing at the court of the Persian king Artaxerxes for a period of seventeen years. He returned to Greece about 390 B.C., where he wrote *Persica*.[13] This work consisted of twenty-three books, of which the first six dealt with Median and Assyrian history.

Diodorus Siculus, writing in the first century B.C., says quite frankly that his account is taken from Ctesias of Cnidus. In this work, Book II, chapters 1-29 deal with Assyrian history.[14]

During the long medieval period there were few written accounts of travel and exploration in Persia and Mesopotamia until the twelfth century. Benjamin de Tudela visited the site of Nineveh about 1173, and correctly identified it as such He was not as certain about Babylon, although he claimed to have seen the ruins of Nebuchadnezzar.[15] De Tudela, a Jewish rabbi from Navarre, was supposedly the first known European traveller in the Near East.

Other Europeans followed de Tudela in the Near East. In 1472, Giosafat Barbaro, the Venetian ambassador, viewed the Persian ruins at Takht-i-Jamshid (NE of Shiraz) and wrote a fairly good description of the scene.[16] More than a century elapsed before another European recorded his visit in the area. The Bavarian botanist, Leonhard

---

[11] Pallis, *The Antiquity of Iraq*, 30.

[12] *Ibid.*, 36.

[13] Diodorus Siculus, *Diodori Siculi Bibliothecae Historicae*, ed. Ludwig Dindorf (Paris: A. Firmin-Didot, 1855), Book 2, Chap. 2.

[14] Diod. Sic. 2. 1-29.

[15] Cyrus Adler, Review of *Les Langues de la Perse et de l'assyrie* by Joachim Menant, *Andover Review*, VIII (1887), 439; and Pallis, *The Antiquity of Iraq*, 41.

[16] E. A. Wallis Budge, *The Rise and Progress of Assyriology* (London: Martin Hopkinson & Co., 1925), 12; for a fuller description see Giosafat Barbaro and Ambrogio Contarini, *Travels to Tana and Persia*, trans. William Thomas and S. A. Roy (London: Hakluyt Soc., 1873) (a translation from the 1545 Italian edition).

Rauwolff, spent a few days at Mosul between 1573 and 1576, reporting that he recognized the ruins of Nineveh.[17] Rauwolff was followed by John Eldred, an Englishman, who visited the vicinity of Babylon in 1583.[18]

During the seventeenth century there are at least five European travellers that are worth mentioning. John Cartwright, another Englishman, not only described his travels in Persia in 1601 but actually gave some dimensions concerning the ruins of Nineveh.[19] Antoine de Gouvea, professor of theology at the College of Goa, travelled in Persia in 1602. He mentioned the strange writing that he saw in the Persian ruins.[20] First examples of cuneiform came back to Europe from the hand of the Italian Pietro della Valle, who visited the area of Mesopotamia and Persia between 1616 and 1621. His copies of the cuneiform were not accurate but were probably the first seen in Europe. Pietro also gets credit for being the first to actually point out the true location of Babylon.[21] Don Garcia de Silva Figueroa, Spanish ambassador to the court of Abbas I of Persia, described the ruins of Persepolis in 1617.[22] Last of the major seventeenth-century travellers was Jean Chardin. This Frenchman, who became a naturalized English citizen, visited Persia between the years of 1666 and 1674. He is credited with sending back the first accurate copies of the cuneiform from Persepolis.[23]

Englebert Kaempfer is usually given credit for naming the Persian script cuneiform. He used the term "cuneate," the Latin term meaning wedge.[24] Pallis maintains that Thomas Hyde should have the credit, as he used the term in his work published in 1700.[25]

---

[17] Joachim Menant, *Les Langues de la Perse et de l'Assyrie. Assyrie* (Paris: Ernest Leroux, 1886), 13-24.

[18] *Ibid.*

[19] Budge, *Rise and Progress*, 13; see also John Cartwright, *The Preacher's Travels* (London: W. Burre, 1611).

[20] Pallis, *Antiquity of Iraq*, 56; see also Antoine de Gouvea, *Relacam em que se trata das Guerras* (Lisbon: Pedro Craesbeek, 1611).

[21] R. W. Rogers, *A History of Babylonia and Assyria* (6th ed.; New York: Abingdon Press, 1915), I, 21; Pietro della Valle, *Viaggi* (Brighton: G. Garicia, 1843).

[22] A. J. Booth, *Discovery and Decipherment of the Trilingual Cuneiform Inscriptions* (London: Longmans, Green, & Co., 1902), 23; Garcia de Silva Figueroa, *L'Ambassade de D. Garcias de Silva Figueroa en Perse*, trans. M. de Wicqfort (Paris: Jean du Puis, 1667).

[23] Rogers, *History of Babylonia*, I, 30-31; Jean Chardin, *Sir John Chardin's Travels in Persia* (London: Argonaut Press, 1927) (taken from 1720 edition).

[24] Budge, *Rise and Progress*, 12.

[25] Pallis, *The Antiquity of Iraq*, 63; Thomas Hyde, *Historia Religionis Persarum* (Oxford Univ., 1700).

Kaempfer's book was not published until 1712.[26] The work of Kaempfer seems to be more widespread than that of Hyde; thus, most scholars thought that Kaempfer had derived the term. At any rate, the term cuneiform began to receive widespread use in the early eighteenth century.

Edward Ives visited Mosul in July of 1758.[27] He included a brief note about the ruins of Nineveh in his book.[28] This, however, added nothing new to what other travellers had already noted. The Danish explorer, Carsten Niebuhr, followed closely on the heels of Ives. He visited the area in 1764-65, and settled the question once and for all, concerning the true site of Nineveh.[29] Niebuhr gives a good account of his travels, not only in Mesopotamia but also in Persia.

One other eighteenth-century traveller worthy of note is G. A. Olivier, who visited the site of Nineveh and possibly Babylon in 1793.[30] He reproduced a Babylonian cylinder, but the copy was not very accurate.[31]

The list of travellers to Mesopotamia and Persia comes to an end with two early nineteenth-century explorers. J. McDonald Kinneir visited in the vicinity of Mosul in 1813, and described several of the mounds around Nineveh.[32] Three years later James Silk Buckingham investigated the ruins of Nineveh. He also described the area around Babylon but thought the city took in more territory than it actually did.[33]

Egypt left to view many gigantic monuments, covered with hieroglyphs, that aroused the interest of scholars and laymen alike. For this reason the hieroglyphs of the Nileland were deciphered earlier than was the cuneiform script. Most of the monuments of ancient Mesopotamia had long since been covered with heaps of dirt and sand, forming large mounds. The cuneiform script was not

---

[26] Engelbert Kaempfer, *Amoenitates Exoticae* Lemgo: H. W. Meyer, 1712).

[27] R. C. Thompson and R. W. Hutchinson, *A Century of Exploration at Nineveh* (London: Luzac & Co., 1929), 17.

[28] Edward Ives, *A Voyage from England to India* (London: E. & C. Dilly, 1773).

[29] Rogers, *History of Babylonia*, I, 43-45; Carsten Niebuhr, *Travels Through Arabia and other Countries in the East*, trans. Robert Heron (Edinburgh: R. Morrison & Son, 1892) (taken from the 1774 edition).

[30] Thompson and Hutchinson, *Century of Exploration*, 17; Pallis, *Antiquity of Iraq*, 43.

[31] Pallis, *Antiquity of Iraq*, 78.

[32] Thompson and Hutchinson, *Century of Exploration*, 17; J. M. Kinneir, *Journey Through Asia Minor* (London: J. Murray, 1818).

[33] Thompson and Hutchinson, *Century of Exploration*, 17; J. S. Buckingham, *Travels in Mesopotamia* (London: H. Colburn, 1827).

exposed to view as were the hieroglyphs of Egypt. Only in Persia were there monuments that could readily be seen without excavation. It is only natural, therefore, that the first attempts to decipher the cuneiform took place in Persia.

Many of the travellers already mentioned had sent back to Europe descriptions of the strange-looking script they found at Persepolis and at Behistun.[34] Persepolis, one of the four capitals of the Achaemenids, was built by Darius the Great (522-486 B.C.) between 513 and 497 B.C. On the cliffs behind the great palace are the inscriptions of Darius and his son Xerxes (486-465 B.C.), carved out of the solid rock. These inscriptions are in Old Persian, Elamite, and Akkadian.[35] The other major site of the cuneiform inscriptions is at Behistun, located about twenty-two miles west of Kermanshah. Here on the sheer wall of an escarpment were copied the feats of Darius. Each text is written in Old Persian, Elamite, and Akkadian.[36]

One of the earliest accounts in modern times of the Behistun inscriptions is given by Ambrogio Bembo, a Venetian merchant, travelling in Persia between 1675 and 1700.[37] Pietro della Valle had already ascertained the fact that the Persepolitan script must be read from left to right.[38] The next important contribution was made by Carsten Niebuhr (1778). Niebuhr noted that the inscriptions at Persepolis contained three kinds of script. He also drew up an alphabet of Old Persian, containing forty-two characters. Today, thirty-two of these are still valid.[39]

In 1798 Oluf Gerhard Tyschen continued the work of della Valle and Niebuhr. He established, quite correctly, that one of Niebuhr's characters was not a letter, but a stop to separate words.[40] Frederik Munter in the same year submitted two papers on the Persepolitan inscriptions to the Royal Danish Society of Sciences. These were not published until 1800. Munter, independently of Tyschen, had also recognized the cuneiform divisor.[41]

---

[34] A very good study of the decipherment is carried in A. J. Booth, *Discovery and Decipherment.*

[35] A. T. Olmstead, *History of the Persian Empire* (Chicago: Univ. Chicago Press, 1948), 173-175.

[36] Budge, *Rise and Progress*, 25-29.

[37] *Ibid.*, 29-30; see also Jacopo Morelli, *Dissertazione Intorno ad Alcuni Viaggiatori Eruditi Venezioni*.... (Venice: Stamperia di A. Zotta, 1803).

[38] Pallis, *Antiquity of Iraq*, 94.

[39] Budge, *Rise and Progress*, 39.

[40] Pallis, *Antiquity of Iraq*, 98.

[41] Rogers, *History of Babylonia*, I, 52-55.

Georg Friederich Grotefend (1775-1853) made the first giant step towards deciphering the Persian script. Using the texts of Niebuhr and others, he detected the word for king.[42] Next he assigned the correct phonetic values to twelve of the Persian characters. Finally, he identified the names of Hystaspes, Darius, and Xerxes. Besides this original work, accomplished for the most part between 1802 and 1815, Grotefend corroborated the works of Niebuhr, Tyschen, and Munter.[43]

Although these earlier attempts at decipherment were made with the Persepolitan script, it was the Behistun inscriptions that finally provided the key. This was due probably to the fact that the inscriptions at Behistun were quite long, while those at Persepolis were very short with small vocabularies. The first attempts were probably not made at Behistun because the inscriptions are about three hundred feet above ground and extremely difficult to reach.[44]

Henry Creswicke Rawlinson (1810-1895) first made the hazardous climb to copy part of the Behistun inscriptions. Rawlinson was born at Chadlington, Oxford, April 11, 1810, son of Abram and Eliza Rawlinson.[45] After completing his education at Wrington and Ealing, Rawlinson accepted an appointment as military cadet in service of the East India Company, and set sail for Bombay in July 1827. While in India he quickly mastered the Persian and Indian vernacular. In 1833 he was transferred to Persia, where from then until 1839 he helped reorganize the Persian army.

The spring of 1835 saw Rawlinson at Behistun, looking at the famous inscriptions he had heard of so often. Rawlinson was aware of the work done by Grotefend but maintains that he was unable to obtain a copy of the professor's alphabet.[46] Thus, quite independently of Grotefend, Rawlinson deciphered the names Hystaspes, Darius,

---

[42] Morris Jastrow, Jr., *The Civilization of Babylonia and Assyria* (Philadelphia: J. B. Lippincott Co., 1915), 69-80.

[43] Pallis, *Antiquity of Iraq,* 99-103.

[44] According to Roland G. Kent, "Cameron's New Reading of the Old Persian at Behistan," *Jour. Amer. Oriental Soc.,* LXXII (1952), 9-20, five modern scholars have made the perilous climb to examine these inscriptions. They are Henry C. Rawlinson, A. V. Williams Jackson (1903), L. W. King and R. C. Thompson of the British Museum (1904), and George G. Cameron (1948).

[45] Biographical material on Rawlinson is taken from George Rawlinson, *A Memoir of Major-General Sir Henry Creswicke Rawlinson* (London: Longmans, Green, & Co., 1898); and *Dictionary of National Biography,* XLVII, 328-331.

[46] Sir Henry C. Rawlinson, "The Persian Cuneiform Inscriptions at Behistun," *Jour. Royal Asiatic Soc.,* X (1847), 2-13.

and Xerxes. During the spring and fall of 1835, with the use of ropes and ladders, Rawlinson began to copy the Persian portion of the inscriptions. Work was continued throughout the summer and fall of 1836. By the spring of 1837 he had copied about two hundred lines of the Persian text. For most of the year of 1838 Rawlinson remained in Baghdad perfecting his copies. Then in 1839 the Afghan War broke out and Rawlinson's scholarly pursuits were put aside for the time being.

Before participating in the Afghan War Rawlinson had translated the first two paragraphs of the Behistun inscriptions. In 1836 he had finally seen a copy of the work of Grotefend but tells us that it added nothing to his knowledge.[47] Rawlinson's manuscript of the translation was sent to the Royal Asiatic Society in London on January 1, 1838. The Royal Society forwarded the manuscript on to Paris to the Société Asiatique where it was favorably received. From this time on the scholars in London and Paris kept Rawlinson supplied with the work of Lassen (1800-1876), the Norwegian scholar, and other Europeans who had worked and were working currently on the inscriptions from Behistun.[48]

Rawlinson was given the post of political agent to Turkish Arabia by the East India Company in 1843. The following year on March 5 Rawlinson was made British consul at Baghdad. He finished the task of copying the text at Behistun in the summer of 1844. Rawlinson also copied the Elamite version and tried without success to copy the Akkadian version.[49] In 1847 Rawlinson returned and made a paper cast of the Akkadian version.[50] The Royal Asiatic Society received the manuscript for Rawlinson's translation of the Persian script in 1846 and published it in 1847. Two years later this was followed by a vocabulary of the ancient Persian language.[51] The work was complete with text, translation, comments, and notes.

While Rawlinson was working on the Behistun inscriptions, another scholar was pursuing independent research on the Persepolitan script. This was the Irish scholar Edward Hincks (1792-

---

[47] Ibid., 7-9.
[48] Pallis, *Antiquity of Iraq*, 112.
[49] Sir Henry C. Rawlinson, "The Behistun Inscription," *Archaeologia*, XXXIV (1852), 74.
[50] Ibid., 75.
[51] Rawlinson, "The Persian Cuneiform Inscriptions at Behistun," *Jour. Royal Asiatic Soc.*, X (1847), 1-349; and XI (1849), 1-192.

1866).⁵² Hincks, born in Cork, August 19, 1972, received his education at Trinity College, Dublin. After graduation in 1811 he was appointed rector at Killyleagh, Down County, a position he held until his death.

Hincks made a decipherment of the Persepolitan inscriptions. He described this in his paper written in May of 1846. It was read before the Royal Irish Academy in June of the same year but was not published until 1848.⁵³ Edwin Norris sent this report to Rawlinson in August of 1846, and within a few days Rawlinson sent a report to London that contained the same discovery as that of Hincks. These two reports passed each other in the mail; thus, Rawlinson and Hincks reached the same conclusions quite independently of each other.⁵⁴

Across the channel in France, a young scholar had arrived at some independent conclusions regarding the Old Persian inscriptions. They turned out to be essentially the same as those reached by Hincks and Rawlinson. This twenty-two year old scholar was Jules Oppert (1825-1905), born July 9, 1825, at Hamburg, Germany, and received his Ph. D. degree from the University of Berlin in 1847.⁵⁵ In this same year he moved to Paris and became a teacher of German. Oppert would remain a French citizen for the rest of his life. His contribution of 1847 was a thorough discussion of the Old Persian vowel system. Later Oppert would revise some of the grammar set up by Rawlinson.

By 1850 most scholars felt that the Old Persian language had now been deciphered. As all of the Achaemenid inscriptions were trilingual, philologists now had a key to unlock the other two forms of cuneiform script. The second type of script, known variously as Susian, Median, Elamite, and Scythian, had drawn attempts to decipher it almost as early as had the Old Persian script. Grotefend had begun to work on it in 1802. In 1837 he discovered that before the word for king there always appeared a peculiar shaped wedge. This led to the decipherment of the Achaemenid proper names.⁵⁶

---

⁵² Biographical material on Hincks is taken from *Dict. National Biog.*, XXVI, 438; and *Jour. Roy. As. Soc.*, III (1867), xix-xxiii.

⁵³ Edward Hincks, "On the First and Second Kinds of Persepolitan Writing," *Trans. Royal Irish Academy*, XXI (1848), 114-131.

⁵⁴ Pallis, *Antiquity of Iraq*, 121.

⁵⁵ Biographical material taken from *Wer ist's*, 1905, 620; and *Nouvelle Biographie Generale*, XXXVIII (1862), 714.

⁵⁶ Adler, *Andover Review*, VIII (1887), 439.

After Rawlinson finished his work with the Old Persian he turned his attention to the Elamite, but here he found Hincks and Westergaard already ahead of him.[57]

Niels Ludwig Westergaard (1815-1878) visited the site of Naksh-i-Rustam and copied the trilingual inscriptions of Darius. Building on the earlier work of Lassen, he deciphered eighteen consonants and six vowels. Within two years he had pushed his total number of signs to eighty-two. Although a great many of the signs were later proven to be inaccurate (only one vowel was finally accepted), this was the foundation for the final decipherment.[58]

Edward Hincks disapproved of the methods of Westergaard and proved him wrong on several occasions. In 1846 Hincks translated the text from Naksh-i-Rustam.[59] Of the signs he established, about half of them were accepted by later scholars. Although the work of Hincks was not final, it was a giant step in the right direction.

The next contribution was made by an Englishman, Edwin Norris (1795-1872). Since 1838 Norris had kept Rawlinson in touch with cuneiform research in Europe. Rawlinson sent Norris his Elamite version of the Behistun inscriptions. Norris then produced a work composed not only of an introduction, text, transliteration, translation, and vocabulary but an extensive discussion of the grammar.[60] In 1859 Jules Oppert rounded out the work of Norris and completed the decipherment of the Elamite script.[61]

Shortly after the turn of the nineteenth century Grotefend had made attempts to decipher the Akkadian version of the Behistun inscriptions. This script proved much more difficult to translate than the other two. Chevalier Isidore Lowenstern in the year 1847 made the correct observation that the language was Semitic. Two other Frenchmen also made contributions in this same year. Henri Longperier identified the name of Sargon. L. F. de Saulcy followed this up by identifying more of the Akkadian characters.[62]

Once again the linguistic ability of Edward Hincks proved to be up to the task of decipherment. In November and December of 1846

---

[57] Budge, *Rise and Progress*, 57-58.
[58] Pallis, *Antiquity of Iraq*, 126-129.
[59] Hincks, *Trans, Royal Irish Acad.*, XXI (1848), 125-130.
[60] Edwin Norris, "Memoir on the Scythic Version of the Behistun Inscription," *Jour. Royal Asiatic Soc.*, XV (1855), 1-213.
[61] Jules Oppert, "Syllabaire Medo-scythique," *Expedition Scientifique en Mesopotamie*, II (1859), 71-77.
[62] Adler, *Andover Review*, VIII (1887), 439.

Hincks made significant contributions in papers read before the Royal Irish Academy.[63] This is followed within a short time by another paper.[64] He was the first to decipher a Babylonian word that was not a proper name. Two more papers in 1848 and 1850 established a correct analysis of the Akkadian numeral system, and added more signs.[65] With this the decipherment was almost complete, but not quite.

Meanwhile, Rawlinson, since 1847, had also been working on the Akkadian script. At meetings in January and February of 1850, Rawlinson read before the Royal Asiatic Society papers which indicated he knew the meaning of about five hundred Babylonian words.[66] He had essentially arrived at the same conclusions concerning the language as had Hincks. Rawlinson picked up some ideas from Hincks and then in 1851 published one of his most significant contributions.[67] In this work he gives a list of Assyrian and Babylonian characters, an alphabet, an analysis, text, transliteration, and translation.

Hincks rounded out the decipherment in 1853 with another important paper.[68] Despite all of this, many of Europe's leading scholars were not ready to accept the fact that the language had been deciphered. With this in mind, the Royal Asiatic Society invited Hincks, Rawlinson, Oppert, and Fox to take part in a conference scheduled for London. Jules Oppert, no stranger to us, had been doing independent work on the Babylonian language. W. H. Fox Talbot (1800-1877), an eminent British mathematician and amateur Orientalist, had followed closely the works of Hincks and Rawlinson, and had actually published an Akkadian grammar.[69] Each of these men was sent a copy of the same inscription to work on. These scholars worked independently, then sealed their results in an

---

[63] Edward Hincks, "On the Three Kinds of Persepolitan Writing, and on The Babylonia Lapidary Characters," *Trans. Royal Irish Acad.*, XXI (1848), 233-248.

[64] Hincks, "On the Third Persepolitan Writing," *Trans. Royal Irish Acad.*, XXI (1848), 249-256.

[65] Hincks, "On the Inscriptions at Van," *Jour. Royal Asiatic Soc.*, IX (1848), 387-422; and "On the Khorsabad Inscriptions," *Trans. Royal Irish Acad.*, XXII (1850), 3-72.

[66] Budge, *Rise and Progress*, 73; Sir Henry C. Rawlinson, "On the Inscriptions of Assyria and Babylonia," *Jour. Royal Asiatic Soc.*, XII (1850), 401-483.

[67] Rawlinson, "Memoir on the Babylonian and Assyrian Inscriptions," *Jour. Royal Asiatic Soc.*, XIV (1851), 1-246.

[68] Edward Hincks, "On the Assyrio-Babylonian Phonetic Characters," *Trans. Royal Irish Acad.*, XXII (1853), 293-370.

[69] Pallis, *Antiquity of Iraq.*, 159-161.

envelope. The sealed envelopes were taken to the meeting held in London on May 25, 1857, where a committee of five examined the results. Although there were some minor differences, the translations of all four were very similar.[70] The committee, and later most of the scholarly world, accepted the fact that the Babylonian script had been deciphered.

During the time that scholars had been working on the decipherment of the cuneiform, archeologists had begun to make excavations in Mesopotamia. In fact the translation of Akkadian had been helped along by the addition of tablets dug up in the 1840's. The work of exploration with regard to excavation really began in 1811 when the Englishman (born in France) Claudius James Rich spent about ten days mapping the ruins of Babylon.[71] He went back to Babylon in 1817 and rechecked his observations. In October of 1820 Rich spent four months at Mosul and made a significant description of the ruins of Nineveh.[72] This survey would form the foundation for the later excavations of Botta and Layard.

Sir Robert Ker Porter arrived in Baghdad from England in 1818. His interesting sketches of the ruins of Babylon aroused interest in England and France which eventually led to excavation parties being sent out. France was the first western country to begin excavations in Mesopotamia. Paul Emile Botta, an Italian, was appointed French vice-consul to Mosul in 1842. On March 20, 1843, Botta began digging at Khorsabad. In less than a year he had opened numerous chambers, corridors, and halls—all speaking mutely of the wonders of the ancient Assyrians.[73]

The person who did the most to popularize archeology in the nineteenth century was probably A. H. Layard. Austen Henry Layard was born March 5, 1817, in Paris, son of Henry Peter and Marianne Layard.[74] His parents were English, but he spent most of his early childhood travelling on the continent. Layard arrived in Mosul in

---

[70] "Inscription of Tiglath Pileser I, King of Assyria, B.C. 1150, as translated by Sir Henry Rawlinson, Fox Talbot Esq., Dr. Hincks, and Dr. Oppert," *Jour. Royal Asiatic Soc.*, XVIII (1861), 164-219.

[71] Adler, *Andover Review*, VIII (1887), 439.

[72] Thompson and Hutchinson, *Century of Exploration*, 18-21.

[73] Budge, *Rise and Progress*, 196; for more details see Paul E. Botta, *The Buried City of the East: Nineveh* (London: National Illustrated Library, 1851).

[74] Biographical material was obtained from A. H. Layard, *Autobiography and Letters from his Childhood until his Appointment as H. M. Ambassador at Madrid*, ed. by Hon. William N. Bruce (2 vols.; London: John Murray, 1903); and Nora B. Kubie, *Road to Nineveh* (Garden City, N. Y.: Doubleday, 1964).

October of 1845 to begin digging at Nineveh. In the period from 1845 to 1850 Layard exposed to the view of the world the wonders of the last capital of the Assyrians. His book describing the lost city aroused interest in Mesopotamia all over the world.[75]

The French continued their work at Khorsabad under the direction of Victor Place (1818-1875). Place arrived in Mosul on January 12, 1852, as the new consul. He continued the work begun by Botta, and in the period from January 1852 to April 1855 he successfully excavated parts of a great palace, along with portions of the ancient city wall.[76] While Place was carrying on his excavations at Khorsabad, the philologist Jules Oppert carried on some excavations at Babylon that lasted from 1852 to 1854.[77]

Meanwhile the English had not stopped their excavations in the area. At Nineveh the work started by Layard was continued by H. C. Rawlinson (1852-54), William K. Loftus (1854), and George Smith (1873-74).[78] At Ur in 1854 J. E. Taylor made the first trial trenches in the area of that ancient city.[79]

By 1860 the science of Assyriology was established. Sired by philologists, it was now nurtured by archeologists. Next the historian would begin his task of recording the ebb and flow of the ancient civilizations that flourished in this area, one of the cradles of civilization. As to whom can be dubbed the "Father" of Assyriology, there is much controversy. Some scholars say Rawlinson. Others cry out in favor of Hincks. Still others tell us not to forget Oppert. In all fairness it must be pointed out that there can be no one "Father." Three people must share the title equally. They are Edward Hincks, Jules Oppert, and Sir Henry C. Rawlinson.

Great Britain had played a very prominent role in the development of Assyriology. One has only to recall Hincks and Rawlinson to be reminded of this. Layard probably did more than any other Englishman at making Assyriology known to the world. George Smith, mentioned before, cannot be omitted from the list. A great injustice would be perpetuated if Edwin Norris weren't mentioned

---

[75] A. H. Layard, *Nineveh and its Remains* (New York: G. P. Putnam, 1850); and *Discoveries in the Ruins of Nineveh and Babylon* (London: John Murray, 1853).

[76] Rogers, *History of Babylonia*, I, 199.

[77] H. V. Hilprecht (ed.), *Exploration in Bible Lands During the 19th Century* (Philadelphia: A. J. Holman, 1903), 163-171.

[78] Jastrow, *Civilization of Babylonia*, 28-35.

[79] J. E. Taylor, "Notes on the ruins of Muqeyer," *Jour. Royal Asiatic Soc.*, XV (1855), 260-276.

INTRODUCTION   15

not only for his independent work on the Elamite script but for his invaluable aid rendered to Rawlinson.[80]

New faces were appearing on the Assyriological scene. E. A. Wallis Budge had continued excavations at Nineveh in 1888-89 and again in 1890-91.[81] After the turn of the century the books of Budge kept alive the interest in Assyriology that had been aroused by Layard. Oddly enough England did not possess a chair of Assyriology until 1890, when one was established at Oxford with Archibald Henry Sayce as the first holder. Sayce is noted for his translations, work with Akkadian grammar, and finally for social histories of Mesopotamia.[82]

Across the channel France had been an active partner in the founding of Assyriology with the great contributions of Oppert. At first the French looked with some suspicion upon the works of Oppert. Later there was a change of heart and Oppert was made Professor of Assyriology at the College de France in 1869.[83] He is credited with being the first to propose the name Sumerian.[84] Hincks had recognized that the Semitic Akkadian had an Indo-European origin. Rawlinson had also been aware of an older language and gradually an older civilization. The Akkadian language had been built on this older language.[85] Sayce made contributions to Sumerian grammar, but it was the French who integrated Sumerian studies into Assyriology.[86]

The giant of Sumerology is a Frenchman by the name of François Lenormant (1837-1883). In a series of works between 1873 and 1879 he produced a grammar which would remain the foundation for future Sumerian grammars. His work was aided by the fact that the Akkadians, Babylonians, and Assyrians had compiled Sumerian dictionaries.[87] Despite all this another French scholar, Joseph

---

[80] Layard, *Nineveh and its Remains*; and *Discoveries in the Ruins*.

[81] Thompson and Hutchinson, *Century of Exploration*, 55-56.

[82] A. H. Sayce, *Social Life Among the Assyrians and Babylonians* (New York: Fleming H. Revell Co., 1893); *A Primer of Assyriology* (New York: Fleming H. Revell Co., 1894); and *Babylonians and Assyrians: Life and Customs* (New York: C. Scribner's Sons, 1899).

[83] *Nouvelle Biographie Generale*, XXXVIII (1862), 74.

[84] Rogers, *History of Babylonia*, I, 250-251.

[85] For a brief but good look at the decipherment of Sumerian see Rogers, *History of Babylonia*, I, 247-272.

[86] For the development of Assyriology in France see Budge, *Rise and Progress*, 206-213; and Menant, *Les Langues*, 230-265.

[87] François Lenormant, *Lettres Assyriologiques, Seconde Série: Etudes Accadiennes* (3 vols.; Paris: Maisonneuve, 1873-79).

Halévy, denied the existence of a Sumerian language, or even a civilization. He maintained in the 1870's that Sumerian was simply an artificial language created by the Semites for esoteric purposes.[88] Excavations in the following twenty years, plus the work of Schrader, Delitzsch, and others proved him wrong. By 1889 the scholarly world accepted the fact that the Sumerians had been a distinct group of people, both ethnically and politically.

Before leaving France one should, in all fairness, say a word about Joachim Menant (1820-1899). Menant, a lawyer by trade, was an excellent philologist. He continued cuneiform studies in the same scholarly line as Oppert. It was the writings of Menant that really made Assyriology a well-founded science in France.[89]

According to Adler the center of study for Assyriology passed from England and France to Germany about the year 1869.[90] By this time a lot of independent work in Assyriology had been accomplished, but it had not all been tied together. Eberhard Schrader (1836-1908), Professor of Theology at Jena, began to synthesize this work and bring it into focus. It was really his pupil Friedrich Delitzsch, who put Germany on the Assyriological map. Delitzsch (1850-1922) created the first school of Assyriology in Germany.[91] He established himself as a privatdocent in Leipzig in 1874 to teach Assyrian, where he turned out first-rate scholars. Delitzsch also published the first really good Assyrian grammar book.[92] Other Assyriologists who would rise to prominence in Germany were Carl Bezold (1859-1922) and Hugo Winckler (1863-1913).[93]

Great Britain and France had furnished the triumvirate that had given birth to Assyriology. By 1880 Germany had taken the lead in this new science. The spread was not limited to Germany but took in Switzerland, Spain, Italy, Denmark, and Belgium.[94] In the closing decades of the nineteenth century Europe was sold on Assyriology. Would this interest spread to the United States?

---

[88] Samuel N. Kramer, *The Sumerians: Their History and Culture* (Chicago: Univ. Chicago Press, 1963), 21.
[89] Budge, *Rise and Progress*, 208-209.
[90] Adler, *Andover Review*, VIII (1887), 240.
[91] Morris Jastrow, Jr. in *Thirty Years of Oriental Studies*, ed. R. G. Kent (Philadelphia: Oriental Club of Philadelphia, 1918), 60.
[92] *Ibid.*
[93] Budge, *Rise and Progress*, 226, 234.
[94] Menant, *Les Langues*, 309-315.

CHAPTER TWO

AMERICA TAKES INTEREST

By 1880 the scholars of Europe were devoting as much of their efforts to Assyriology as they were to the older sister field of Egyptology. In the preceding chapter one noted that this interest was not confined to a few countries but had spread over most of western Europe. This interest was eventually felt in the United States, with the development beginning in this country in 1880. Before a discipline is born there usually has to be a certain amount of general interest in the subject. This interest was cultivated in that period of American literary history known as the Age of the Romantics.

The Age of Romanticism

The Neo-Classic Age in the United States had run its course shortly after the turn of the nineteenth century, just as it had done in Europe. This dying age of human reason and natural order gave way to the Age of Romanticism, a period that lasted roughly from 1830 (although some scholars begin it shortly after the War of 1812) to about 1860.[1] Among the intellectuals in the United States there was a feeling of pride in the youthful vigor of a new and growing nation. It is true that Europe was also undergoing a feeling of romanticism, no doubt communicating this spirit to the young republic. Youth walks hand in hand with the spirit of romanticism; thus, this romantic spirit was typified by the new breed of American writers. This romantic view of life portrays a mood of individualism in feeling and imagination of the intellectual. Gone are the Age of Reason, and the ideas set in motion by the Renaissance and the Reformation.

This new age of popular exotica was characterized by the works of Washington Irving, who reveals his love of life and desire to please in *The Sketch Book* and *The Alhambra*. James Fenimore Cooper portrays the idea of rugged American individualism in the *Last of the Mohicans, The Deerslayer,* and others. These feelings of a new era were reflected also in the poetry of William Cullen Bryant, and even

---

[1] For a detailed look at this period see Tremaine McDowell (ed.), *The Romantic Triumph: American Literature from 1830 to 1860* (rev. ed.; New York: Macmillan Co., 1949).

in the tortured writings of Edgar Allen Poe. The list of Romanticists is lengthy, indeed, including Ralph Waldo Emerson, Nathaniel Hawthorne, Herman Melville, John Greenleaf Whittier, Henry Wadsworth Longfellow, James Russell Lowell, Oliver Wendell Holmes, and Walt Whitman, to mention a few. It should come then as no surprise that some writers of this period should delve into the ancient past of Mesopotamia and Persia, seeking material to present to an eager public, for after all what is more romantic than the mist-shrouded cultures of a long-dead age.

James Baillie Fraser (1783-1856) wrote one of the first books of an Assyriological nature to be published in the United States. Fraser, an English traveller who spent a great deal of time in the Near East, drew upon his travels in the area to write this work entitled *Historical and Descriptive Account of Persia From the Earliest Ages to the Present Time*.[2] The book was published in 1843 in the United States, although it had previously been published in Edinburgh in 1834. Fraser's book is not completely devoted to history but also gives fairly good anthropological, biological, geographical, and geological accounts of Persia. Chapters III through V are concerned with history, religion, and antiquities of ancient Persia. Fraser makes no mention of the cuneiform language. His next work, *Mesopotamia and Assyria*, appeared in the United States in 1845, having first been published by Oliver and Boyd of Edinburgh in 1842.[3] The American edition sold so well that Harper reissued it in 1865. Fraser tries to deal with Mesopotamia as he had with Persia; consequently, the book follows the same pattern as the earlier one. Both books were of the popular type, appealing more to the general public than to the historian or other specialist.

Reverend James Phillips Fletcher (1819-1872) published the next book in America concerned with Mesopotamia. Fletcher was an English clergyman sent by the church to Mosul in 1842.[4] His work, *Notes From Nineveh*, was published in two volumes in 1850 by H. Colburn of London. Within the same year the American edition was released, consisting of one volume.[5] His book was for the most part a travelogue dealing with the area of Mesopotamia and Syria. Although

---

[2] (New York: Harper and Bros., 1843).
[3] *Mesopotamia and Assyria, From the Earliest Ages to the Present Time; With Illustrations of Their Natural History* (New York: Harper and Bros., 1845).
[4] *Manchester Guardian*, November 6, 1872, 1388.
[5] (Philadelphia: Lea and Blanchard, 1850).

chiefly a travel sketch, the book did contain a description of the work of Paul E. Botta at Khorsabad. Fletcher also attempted a short sketch of Assyrian history, taken mainly from the works of Classical authors.

The first scholarly book to appear on the American market was by A. H. Layard. *Nineveh and its Remains* appeared in two volumes in 1850.[6] This work stimulated the first real interest in the archeology of Mesopotamia. In an introductory note Edward Robinson of Union Theological Seminary declared that this work was not only of "high interest and importance" but predicted that it would "mark an epoch in the wonderful progress of knowledge...."[7] Volume I describes early travel in the vicinity of Nineveh, plus a description of the events leading up to the excavations. Layard also speaks of the Classical historians who deal with the history of Assyria. The rest of this first volume is concerned with geography and anthropology. Students of Assyriology find more of value in the second volume which contains a description of the excavations at Nineveh, and a sketch of the history of Assyria.

Jacob Abbott (1803-1879) was one of the first to write and publish biographies of the Achaemenid kings. Abbott was such a prolific writer that he deserves more than just a word in passing. He was born November 14, 1803, in Hallowell, Maine. After graduation from Bowdoin College in 1820, Abbott studied theology at Andover Seminary. In his lifetime Abbott wrote over one hundred and eighty books, all of a popular nature. During 1850 he published three popularized biographies of Persian kings. His work entitled *Cyrus the Great* was published by Harper.[8] The book was so popular that the publishing company put out later editions in 1879 and 1900. His other two biographies of this same year, *Darius the Great* and *History of Xerxes the Great*, enjoyed the same popularity.[9] Harper published two more editions of *Xerxes* in 1878 and 1900, and *Darius* in 1906. All of these biographies were based on secondary works and did not represent scholarly research.

An American clergyman, Daniel P. Kidder (1815-1891), who had travelled in the Near East, published *Nineveh and The River Tigris* in 1851.[10] This work was a geographical study, mainly of the

---

[6] See above Chap. I.
[7] *Nineveh and its Remains*, I, 1.
[8] (New York: Harper and Bros., 1850).
[9] (New York: The St. Hubert Guild, 1850); (New York: Harper and Bros., 1850).
[10] (New York: Lane & Scott, 1851).

travelogue type, but contained a description of some of the ruins in the vicinity of Nineveh. Asahel Davis summarized archeological activity in the Near East up to the year 1852 in a small sixteen-page booklet that he published in the same year.[11]

A. H. Layard came out with another book in 1853. This work, *Discoveries in the Ruins of Nineveh and Babylon*, was published first in London.[12] Publishers in this country recognized the fact that the American public had taken a fancy to reading about archeological discoveries, and not one, but two companies released the book in the United States before the year was out.[13] Not only did Layard describe the antiquities uncovered, but he also spoke of the results of the decipherment of the cuneiform. Layard was evidently arousing some interest in the United States, or at least the publishing companies thought so.

In 1857 another book by an Englishman reached the American market. *Travels and Researches in Chaldaea and Susiana*, written by William Kenneth Loftus (1821?-1858), was published first in England.[14] Within the same year it was released in the United States by a New York firm.[15] Loftus was a traveller and archeologist who spent a great deal of time in the Near East. This book, bordering between a popular and a scholarly work, gives an account of excavation in the area of southern Mesopotamia and western Persia between 1849 and 1852.

Several articles that could be described as having a bearing on Assyriology appeared from time to time in the period from 1830 to 1860. One of the first was by Azariah Smith (1817-1851), an American clergyman and missionary who lived in the Near East from 1842 until his death in 1851. This paper, describing the results of the excavations at Nineveh, appeared in a scholarly journal in the year 1845.[16]

Three articles appeared in the 1850's. A book review by an anonymous author summarizing Layard's book *Discoveries in the Ruins of Nineveh and Babylon* (1853) can be found in *The New*

---

[11] *Lectures on the Remarkable Discoveries Lately Made in the East: As Those of Nineveh, Persia, Etc.* (Buffalo, New York: Phinney & Co., 1852).
[12] See above Chap. I.
[13] (G. P. Putnam's Sons, and Harper and Bros.).
[14] (London: J. Nisbet & Co., 1857).
[15] (New York: R. Carter & Bros., 1857).
[16] "Ruins of Nineveh: Description of the Discoveries Made in 1843 and 1844," *American Journal of Science and Arts*, XLIX (1845), 113-128.

Englander in 1853.[17] This review states that the book is a very good work. Also appearing in this same year was an article by David Brewster (1781-1868), the Scottish natural philosopher, giving a short description of a rock-crystal lens from Nineveh.[18] Brewster's article was somewhat on the technical side, of interest mostly to the geologist, chemist, and physicist. In 1859 the New York Historical Society announced the arrival in the United States of some antiquities from Nineveh.[19] These were gifts from James Lenox (1800-1880), the bibliophile philanthropist who gave his library to New York City which later became the New York Public Library. This shows that a popular interest in ancient Mesopotamia had been cultivated by the books that appeared in the 1840's and 1850's.

Many relics from Mesopotamia, such as inscribed bricks, statuettes, pottery, etc., began to arrive in the United States between 1851 and 1860. A record of these relics or antiquities was given by Reverend Selah Merrill (1837-1907), writing in 1875.[20] Merrill was born May 2, 1837, at Canton Centre, Connecticut. He entered Yale with the class of 63 but did not graduate. Merrill was a student at New Haven Theological Seminary and was ordained in 1864. He spent two years in Germany between 1868 and 1870, where he studied the ancient Hebrew language. At various intervals he spent the years from 1882 to 1907 as U.S. Consul at Jerusalem. Merrill took part in some of the excavations carried on around the holy city.

These antiquities were sent to the United States by missionaries residing in the Near East, such as Reverend Dwight W. Marsh, Rev. W. F. Williams, Dr. Austin H. Wright, Rev. Wilson A. Farnsworth, Rev. Daniel A. Goodsell, Dr. H. B. Haskell, and Rev. Leonard W. Bacon, to name a few. Most of these antiquities came from the reign of Ashurnasirpal and went to Andover Theological Seminary, Andover, Massachusetts; Bowdoin College, Brunswick, Maine; Episcopal Seminary, Alexandria, Virginia; Middlebury College, Middlebury, Vermont; Auburn Theological Seminary, Auburn, New York; Mercantile Library Association, St. Louis; Amherst College, Amherst, Massachusetts; Union College, Schenectady, New York; Yale; and Williams College, Williamstown, Massachusetts. Add to this

---

[17] "Layard's Discoveries," *The New Englander*, XI (1853), 457-470.
[18] "Nineveh Lens and Glass," *The American Polytechnic Journal*, II (1853), 157.
[19] "Announcement and Arrival in this Country of Some Nineveh Marbles at New York, April 5, 1859," *Historical Magazine*, III (1859), 146.
[20] "Assyrian and Babylonia Monuments," *Bibliotheca Sacra*, XXXII (1857), 320-349.

the shipment sent by Lenox to the New York Historical Society in 1859, and the collection becomes impressive for a country only beginning to take an interest in the ancient civilizations.

Prior to 1880 the American Oriental Society seems to be the only learned society in the United States pursuing an active interest in Assyriology. This society was founded in Boston in the year 1842. The first meeting was an informal one, held in August. On September 7 another meeting was held in which a constitution was adopted and officers were elected. Officers elected for the year 1842-43 included John Pickering of Boston, President; William Jenks of Boston, Moses Stuart of Andover, and Edward Robinson of New York, Vice-Presidents; William W. Greenough of Boston, Corresponding Secretary; and Francis Gardner of Boston, Treasurer. Additional members were elected on October 13, the constitution was amended, and by-laws were adopted.[21]

The society was incorporated by the Commonwealth of Massachusetts on March 22, 1843. In May of 1843 the first annual meeting was held in Boston. From the very beginning the American Oriental Society began to add manuscripts and books to their library. The list from 1842 until January 1847 was very impressive. It was not until May 24, 1847, that the next meeting was held, but after this the society usually met at least twice per year. The spring meeting was called the Annual Meeting, and the one in the fall was the Semiannual Meeting.[22] Volume I of the *Journal* appeared in 1849, but there was no regular interval of time specified for it to appear.[23] At the meetings of 1847-48 some of the topics discussed were the chronology of the Near East, letters from travellers in the Near East, the Druze-Maronite problem, decipherment of the cuneiform, and Layard's work at Nineveh.[24]

Discussion of Assyriological topics was sporadic in the 1850's. At times this topic dominated the program; at other times it was not even on the agenda. At the Annual Meeting, held May 24, 1850, in Boston, the program dealt with the decipherment completed by Rawlinson, plus travelogue descriptions of Mesopotamia and Persia.[25]

---

[21] "Proceedings," *Journal American Oriental Society* (hereafter referred to as *JAOS*), I (1849), ii-v.

[22] *JAOS* (Proc.), I (1849), xxv-lxv.

[23] II — 1851; III — 1853; IV — 1854; V — 1856; VI — 1860; VII — 1862; VIII — 1866; IX — 1871; X — 1880.

[24] *JAOS* (Proc.), I (1849), xxv-lxv.

[25] *Ibid.*, II (1851), ix-xviii.

The next meeting was not held until the spring of 1853, but Assyriology was not on the program. In the fall at the Semiannual Meeting, held in New Haven, October 26-27, 1853, several letters were read, describing the archeological activity taking place near Nineveh.[26] The society also held a lengthy discussion of the ancient Persian language.[27] Reverend H. Lobdell, one of the missionaries from Mosul, spoke to the society at the fall meeting of 1854, describing some of the Assyrian inscriptions at Nineveh.[28] The following spring at the Annual Meeting in Boston, Professor E. E. Salisbury of Yale presented a paper dealing with two Assyrian cylinders from Nineveh.[29] At Boston in May of 1858 Reverend Alger read a paper concerned with the Persian doctrine of future life.[30]

Toward the close of the Romantic Age the interest in Assyriology, at least the popular interest, begins to slacken, probably due to the idea that the Civil War was inevitable. One scholar states that only two books of an Assyriological nature were published in the United States prior to the Civil War.[31] A close examination of the literature, however, shows at least ten books published during the period, indicating that Layard and others did have some impact upon the intellectual strata of American society. The problems of slavery and the impending war did put a damper on Assyriological interest, at least at the popular level. Popular exotica was giving away to scholarly writing, as the Age of Romanticism had had its day and a new period, the Age of the Realists, was taking over.

Triumph of the Realists

Just as the Neo-Classic Age gave way to the Romantic Age, the Romantic Age yielded in turn to the Age of Realism. Or as many social historians put it, the Golden Age had been replaced by the Gilded Age. This new age, beginning around 1860, or some would place it as late as 1865, did not put aside the idea of "rugged" individualism but tended to emphasize it even more. By 1865 the Civil War was coming to a bitter end, so that the nation could turn

---
[26] *Ibid.*, IV (1854), xxvi.
[27] *JAOS*, IV (1854), 462-464, 472-480.
[28] *JAOS* (Proc.), V (1856), i-ii.
[29] *Ibid.*, ii-iv.
[30] *Ibid.*, VI (1860), 577-587.
[31] Phillip Andrew Kildahl, *British and American Reactions to Layard's Discoveries in Assyria (1845-1860)* (unpublished Ph. D. dissertation, University of Minnesota, 1959).

itself to the task of rebuilding, and reevaluating its ideas and concepts. Another name that could be applied to this new era would be the Age of Materialism. Science and technology advanced, wider use was made of machinery, and the day of the self-made millionaire had arrived. As the people moved westward, settling the nation, they no longer had time for the romantic thoughts and ideas of the earlier period; the theme of the time was practicality. According to some authorities, literary and artistic tastes had been vulgarized and debased.[32]

In this new society the rich tended to become wealthier, while the numbers of poor people increased rapidly. The forces that shaped this new society also contributed toward a change in literature. Literature was no longer poetic nor artistic but reflects the spirit of realism. Writers of this period tend to be more detached and scientific, writing with logic and analysis and not from the heart. Among this new school of writers was Samuel L. Clemens (1835-1910), writing under the name of Mark Twain, who bridged the gap between the Romanticists and the Realists. Twain was certainly a Realist but wrote with a certain amount of romanticism added to his realism. Another American writer who tempered realism with a dash of romanticism was Bret Harte (1836-1902), who made the West the number one topic for local color fiction. Other prominent authors of this period, to mention a few, are Joel Chandler Harris (1848-1908), William Dean Howells (1837-1920), Henry James (1843-1916), and Emily Dickinson (1830-1886). Would this new style of writing carry over into the field of Assyriology?

During the 1860's no books of an Assyriological nature were published by American publishing houses, probably because of the Civil War and its aftermath. George Smith, an Englishman mentioned before, published two works in the 1870's. Smith came out first with *Assyrian Discoveries*, published in London.[33] An American firm made arrangements, and before the year 1875 had come to an end had released it on the U.S. market.[34] His other book, *The Chaldean Account of Genesis*, was actually in its fourth English edition before being released by an American firm. Finally in 1876, it

---

[32] For a fuller look at this era from a literary viewpoint see Foerster, *American Poetry and Prose*.

[33] *Assyrian Discoveries; An Account of Exploration and Discoveries on the Site of Nineveh, During 1873 and 1874* (London: S. Low, Marston, Low & Searle, 1875).

[34] (New York: Scribner, Armstrong & Co., 1875).

was published in the United States.³⁵ This work enjoyed enough popularity that Scribner put out another edition in 1880. These works were not the popular exotica of the earlier era, but tended to be more along scholarly lines.

On the other hand a book published by another Englishman, John Philip Newman (1826-1899), in 1876 resembled the works of the earlier era. Newman, a clergyman, spent some time studying and travelling in the Near East. His book, *The Thrones and Palaces of Babylon and Nineveh*, was actually of little value to the serious scholar.³⁶ It was simply a personal account of travel through the region on horseback.

Several articles appeared in the 1870's that dealt with cuneiform studies. William H. Ward, editor of the *New York Independent* (of whom more will be said in Chapter IV), summarized the development of Assyriology in 1870. His article in the biblical studies journal *Bibliotheca Sacra*, "Assyrian Studies—Text-Books," was a little more comprehensive than the title indicated.³⁷ Not only did he list the major books dealing with Assyrian philology, but he also summarized the development of the knowledge of Assyrian grammar between 1855 and 1868. Continuing in this same vein, Otis Tufton Mason (1838-1908), an ethnologist at the National Museum, described the historical development of the decipherment of cuneiform in 1874.³⁸ The following year Reverend Selah Merrill published a list of all the antiquities from Mesopotamia in the United States, and where they were located.³⁹

In 1878 the *American Antiquarian*, a quarterly journal that carried some articles on the Near East, was born. This journal was devoted to early American history, ethnology, and archeology; the first part coming out in April. Volume I (April 1878—June 1879) contained articles and book reviews on the ancient Near East. Volume II contained three Assyriological articles. One of these briefly described the expedition of Hormuzd Rassam to Nineveh and Nimrod in 1878-79 on behalf of the British Museum.⁴⁰ Orlando Dana Miller (1821-

---

³⁵ (New York: Scribner, Armstrong & Co., 1876).
³⁶ (New York: Harper and Bros., 1876).
³⁷ *Bibliotheca Sacra*, XXVII (1870), 184-191.
³⁸ "Progress and Result of Cueniform Decipherment," *Baptist Quarterly*, VIII (1874), 191-208.
³⁹ *Bibliotheca Sacra*, XXXII (1875), 320-349.
⁴⁰ Anonymous, "A Buried Temple and Palace," *American Antiquarian*, II (1879-80), 297-298.

1888), American clergyman and archeologist, penned another of the articles in which he discussed some of the sacred cuneiform writings of Mesopotamia.[41] A. H. Sayce wrote the other article, entitled, "The Latest Cuneiform Discovery," and discussed the translation of a cylinder and a tablet.[42] Both of these objects dealt with the conquests of Cyrus the Great (549-529 B.C.). The tablet described his conquest of Media and Babylonia, while the cylinder told of the capture of Babylon (539 B.C.).

In the 1870's few scholars in the United States had a reading knowledge of Akkadian. Merrill states that the person with the best knowledge of Akkadian in this country was Gustaf Adolph Fidelio Van Rhyn, a professor of English at one of the colleges in New York City.[43] One of the first scholars in the United States to translate a cuneiform document was Edward C. Taintor.[44] Evidently, Taintor learned Akkadian on his own, although he corresponded with Rawlinson. He graduated from Union College in 1863. During this year Taintor translated an Assyrian document with the help of Layard and Rawlinson, by correspondence.

Four papers relating to Assyriological subjects were presented at the meetings of the American Oriental Society in the 1860's. Professor James Hadley of Yale discussed "Remains of Ancient Babylonian Literature in Arabic Translation," at the October 1860 meeting at New Haven.[45] At the Annual Meeting the following spring Professor William D. Whitney of Yale presented "Ancient and Modern Dialects of the Persian Language."[46] A continuation by Hadley of his earlier paper was carried on in May 1862, when he presented "More on the Remains of Ancient Babylonian Literature in Arabic Translation."[47] Mr. Hyde Clark of Smyrna discussed "Lydo-Assyrian Monuments at Smyrna," at a meeting held October 24-25, 1866.[48]

During the 1870's five papers of an Assyriological nature were read before the society. Three of these were by the Reverend Selah Merrill.

---

[41] "The Antiquity of Sacred Writings in the Valley of the Euphrates," *Amer. Antiq.*, II (1879-80), 290-295.
[42] *Amer. Antiq.*, II (1879-80), 287-289.
[43] *Bibliotheca Sacra*, XXXII (1875), 348.
[44] *Ibid.*
[45] *JAOS* (Proc.), VII (1862), i-lxxii.
[46] *Ibid.*
[47] *Ibid.*
[48] *Ibid.*

At the October 1873 meeting in New Haven, Merrill gave a description of an inscription from the reign of Ashurnasirpal.[49] One year later he described the Assyrian and Babylonia relics that could be found in the United States.[50] Merrill shared the spotlight with W. H. Ward at the Boston meeting held in May of 1879. The title of Merrill's paper was "On the Use of Gold and Silver Among the Assyrians," which was slanted toward the philologist rather than the metallurgist.[51] Ward described a Babylonian seal cylinder and at the fall meeting presented a paper entitled "The Dragon and Serpent in Chaldaean Mythology."[52]

At the beginning of 1880 there was a certain amount of interest in Assyriology present in the United States. The American Oriental Society was doing a great deal toward promoting this interest. As the age of Realism grows older, the Assyriological works become more scholarly, but this is after 1880, and brings this work into another era in American Assyriology.

---

[49] "On the Assyrian Inscription at Andover, Mass.," *Ibid.*, X (1880), lxxiii.
[50] "On the Assyrian and Babylonia Monuments in America," *Ibid.*, xcix-c.
[51] *Ibid.*, XI (1885), x-xi.
[52] *Ibid.*, xi-xx.

CHAPTER THREE

THE CURTAIN RISES

Assyriology had taken root in Europe by 1880, but this did not hold true for the United States. The stage was set, however, for the establishment of the field in this country. Assyriology began in the fall of 1880 when Francis Brown introduced a course in Akkadian (referred to then as Assyrian) at Union Theological Seminary. From this humble beginning the discipline began to grow, so that by 1899 this country could be considered an equal partner with England, Germany, and France in Assyriological studies. This rapid growth of Assyriology over a period of twenty years will be the subject of this chapter.

Francis Brown and the Beginning

Francis Brown (1849-1916) was born December 26, 1849, at Hanover, New Hampshire, son of Professor Samuel and Sarah Brown.[1] After receiving an A.B. from Dartmouth in 1870, and an A.M. in 1873, Brown enrolled at Union Theological Seminary, where he became avidly interested in Hebrew, graduating in 1877. He realized that in order to get a solid background in Ancient Hebrew, it would be necessary to study in Germany. Brown attended the University of Berlin from 1877 to 1879. While at Berlin he studied Assyrian under Eberhard Schrader.[2]

Upon returning to the United States, Brown was appointed Instructor of Biblical Philology at Union Theological Seminary. One year later he taught a course in Assyrian (Akkadian), the first to be taught in this country.[3] For this language course Brown used a series

---

[1] Biographical information on Francis Brown was obtained from various sources, including *Dict. American Biography*, III, (1929), 115-116; *Who's Who in America*, IX (1916-17), 304; *New York Times*, October 16, 1916; Henry Preserved Smith, "Francis Brown—An Appreciation," *American Journal of Semitic Languages and Literature* (hereafter referred to as AJSL), XXXIII (1916-17), 75-88; and personal papers in the archives of the library of Union Theological Seminary.

[2] See above Chap. I.

[3] Francis Brown, "Semitic Studies in America," *Johns Hopkins Univ. Circular*, No. 3 (1909), 240-259.

of texts excavated from Assyria, the same used by Schrader at Berlin.[4] A promotion came in 1881 when Brown moved up the ladder to Associate Professor. Besides Assyrian, he taught Hebrew, Greek, and Aramaic. Brown became Professor of Hebrew and Cognate Languages in 1890, a rank he held until his death in 1916. Despite the fact that Brown taught Assyrian and published quite a few Assyriological articles, his first love was Hebrew.[5] The fact that he devoted more time to Hebrew than to Assyrian is probably the reason he is not usually referred to as the "Father of American Assyriology."

At Union it was customary to inaugurate the year of study with a lecture by one of the faculty members to his colleagues and members of the public. On September 18, 1884, Francis Brown was the speaker in Adams Chapel. He chose Assyriology as his topic and entitled his speech, *Assyriology: Its Use and Abuse in Old Testament Study*. Brown appended an introductory note and a short annotated bibliography, and published it in book form the following year.[6] By today's standards there are some who would not consider this a scholarly book, but at the time it made a definite contribution to the science. Its main value was probably Brown's warning to theologians to accept the clear facts displayed by Assyriology, and not to shade them to fit corresponding statements from the Bible.[7]

Brown also published several articles of an Assyriological nature. In 1881 he made a survey of recent books in Assyriology, and noted the current work of some of the leading European scholars.[8] The following year Brown contributed an article that was more of interest to the layman than to the scholar,[9] but in 1884-85 he listed the major contributions to the field of Assyrian philology.[10] In 1886 Brown wrote another article, describing the Wolfe Expedition to Babylonia (more will be said of this expedition in the next chapter).[11] In 1888

---

[4] Brown tells of the introduction of this course in a handwritten note included in his personal papers at Union.

[5] This can readily be discerned by looking at the records of the Hebrew Seminar kept by Brown between 1893 and 1906 (consisting of eleven handwritten notebooks in the archives of the Union Library).

[6] (New York: Chas. Scribner's Sons, 1885).

[7] *Ibid.*, 23-28.

[8] "Recent Work in Assyriology," *American Journal of Philology*, II (1881), 225-230.

[9] "The Sabbath in the Cuneiform Records," *Presbyterian Review*, III (1882), 688-700.

[10] "Assyriological Notes," *Hebraica*, I (1884-85), 182-183.

[11] "The Wolfe Exploring Expedition to Babylonia," *Presbyterian Review*, VII (1886), 155-159.

he contributed three more articles, none of them of any great scholarly value.¹² An article that did have value for the Assyriologist as well as the theologian was published by Brown in 1888-89. In a brief note he wrote of Semitic studies in the Theological Seminary, stressing the importance of Assyro-Babylonian language as a background for the study of Hebrew.¹³

Shortly after 1880 the United States had a scholar, who not only taught Akkadian but published in the field of Assyriology. He not only published a standard text in the field but inspired students to take their training in this discipline.

David Lyon at Harvard

Harvard followed closely on the heels of Union by initiating the teaching of Akkadian in the year 1882. The person responsible for this was David Gordon Lyon (1852-1935), the scholar most often referred to as the "Father of American Assyriology." ¹⁴ Lyon, a native of Benton, Alabama, was born May 24, 1852.¹⁵ He obtained his undergraduate training at Howard College, Birmingham, Alabama, receiving an A. B. degree from there in 1875. Young Lyon was fortunate enough to be able to make a trip to England during summer vacation between his sophomore and junior years. He left Benton on July 7, 1873, and returned on September 20.¹⁶ Lyon's interest in Assyriological topics is reflected by the many lecture notes on Babylonia and Assyria from Howard College recopied into one of his diaries.¹⁷

In order to pursue his interest in Oriental studies, Lyon realized that he would have to go to Germany to continue his education. The young American arrived in Leipzig on August 16, 1879, and spent the intervening days until September 2 engrossed in the routine of

---

¹² "The Religious Poetry of Babylonia," *Ibid.*, IX (1888), 69-86; "The Babylonian 'List of Kings' and 'Chronicle,'" *Ibid.*, 293-299; and "Babylon and Egypt," *Ibid.*, 476-481.

¹³ "Semitic Study in the Theological Seminary," *Hebraica*, V (1888-89), 86-88.

¹⁴ Budge, *Rise and Progress of Assyriology*, 244.

¹⁵ Biographical information for D. G. Lyon was taken from forty volumes of his personal diaries; two biographical sketches written by Robert H. Pfeiffer, *Proceedings of the American Academy of Arts and Sciences*, LXX (1936), 552-554, and *Dict. Amer. Biog.*, Supplement 1, 518-519; and a memoriam sketch by G. A. Barton, *Bulletin of the American Schools of Oriental Research* (hereafter referred to as *BASOR*), No. 62 (1936), 2-4.

¹⁶ *Personal Diaries*, III, 151-175.

¹⁷ *Ibid.*, 65-72.

finding a room and settling down to prepare for the ensuing academic year.[18] Lyon spent the next four years studying Akkadian, Hebrew, and other related Oriental languages. This effort was rewarded in the spring of 1882 with the Ph. D. degree from the University of Leipzig.

Upon returning to the United States in the summer of 1882, Lyon accepted the position of Hollis Professor of Divinity at Harvard, beginning in September.[19] Unlike Francis Brown, whose main interest was Hebrew, Lyon was devoted to Assyriology. For the academic year of 1882-83 he organized two Assyriological courses, one devoted to Assyrian archeology, and the other to Akkadian grammar.[20]

Lyon was not content to devote his efforts solely to classroom teaching but carried out research, also. In 1885 he published two articles in the *Journal of the American Oriental Society*. The first was a review of foreign books covering the field of Assyriology, while the other dealt with Akkadian philology.[21] His main contribution, however, was a book of Akkadian grammar. This work, entitled *An Assyrian Manual*, was the first Assyriological grammar published by an American scholar.[22] The book, published in 1886, was written for the student not having access to oral instruction. Lyon recommended the use of Volume V of The *Cuneiform Inscriptions of Western Asia* by Rawlinson to supplement the work.[23] The book is organized into three parts. Grammar comprises the first section, part two is composed of transliterated texts, and the last portion contains copies of the original cuneiform texts. Later on with new excavations bringing more documents to light, the work eventually was outdated, but for the 1880's it was probably one of the best works on Assyrian grammar to be found in Europe or the United States.

In 1889 Harvard began to collect material for a Semitic museum. A committee was selected to solicit funds and a donation of $10,000 made to buy objects for the collection. This collection was housed in

---

[18] *Ibid.*, IV, 202-207.

[19] *Ibid.*, 3-28.

[20] *Annual Reports of the President and Treasurer of Harvard College, 1882-83* (Cambridge, Mass.: Harvard Univ. Press, 1883), 60.

[21] "On Some Recent Assyrian Publications," *JAOS*, XI (1885), ccii; and "Was There at the Head of the Babylonian Pantheon a Deity Bearing the Name of El?" clxiv-clxviii.

[22] *An Assyrian Manual, for the Use of Beginners in the Study of the Assyrian Language* (Chicago: The American Publication Society of Hebrew, 1886).

[23] (London: British Museum, 1861-1880).

a room in Peabody Museum in 1891.[24] Lyon was chosen as the first curator in this same year of 1891, a task he devoted himself to untiringly.

The work of D. G. Lyon does not come to an end in the 1890's but continues on; however, the study of this work after 1899 is reserved for another chapter. David Gordon Lyon can, without a shadow of doubt, be considered the American trailblazer for Assyriology, as he taught Akkadian in the classroom, conducted research, published books and articles, and was developing the Harvard Semitic Museum.

Paul Haupt Comes to Johns Hopkins

Johns Hopkins quickly followed Harvard in establishing Assyriology, but unlike Harvard and Union, hired a German scholar already established in the field. Paul Haupt (1858-1926) was the man who initiated Assyriology at Johns Hopkins University, Baltimore, Maryland.[25] Hugo Hermann Paul Haupt was born November 25, 1858, at Görlitz, Germany. He studied the Oriental languages at the University of Leipzig, receiving his Ph. D. from there in 1878. Before coming to the United States Haupt spent five years doing post-doctoral work in the Semitic languages at the University of Leipzig, University of Berlin, and the British Museum. He arrived in Baltimore in the summer of 1883, ready to begin the school year as Professor of Semitic Languages at Johns Hopkins.[26]

Haupt started the school year of 1883-84 by organizing language courses in Sumerian and Akkadian.[27] This was probably the first Sumerian course taught in the United States. Beginning in the fall of 1884, Haupt received help from Cyrus Adler (1863-1940), the first student in Haupt's Semitic Seminar, initiated in this same year. Adler, born September 13, 1863, at Van Buren, Arkansas, received his A.B. from the University of Pennsylvania in 1883.[28] While

---

[24] Harvard Univ., *Addresses Delivered at the Formal Opening of the Semitic Museum of Harvard University, February 5, 1903* (Cambridge, Mass.: Harvard Univ. Press, 1903), 8-9.

[25] Biographical information for Paul Haupt taken from a memoriam sketch by Cyrus Adler in *JAOS*, XLVII (1927), 1-2; an obituary notice in the "Proceedings for Dec. 1926," *Jour. of the Society of Biblical Literature*, XLVI (1927), i; and *W. W. in Amer.*, XIV, 1926-27, 909.

[26] *The Johns Hopkins Univ. Register, 1882-83* (Baltimore: John Murphy for Johns Hopkins Press, 1883), 3.

[27] Cyrus Adler, *Andover Review*, VIII (1887), 441.

[28] Biographical information on Cyrus Adler taken from James A. Montgomery,

working on a master's degree at Pennsylvania, Adler came to Johns Hopkins where he was appointed a Fellow in 1884. Pensylvania awarded him the A.M. degree in 1886, and Johns Hopkins gave him the rank of Instructor of Semitic Languages.

A special course in Assyriology was organized by Professor Haupt in January of 1887. It was designed for scholars and professors from other institutions. The course not only covered the Akkadian language but dealt heavily with the history and art of the area.[29] This course started January 3 and continued until January 31, no tuition charged to the scholars. Out of the eleven scholars who attended, besides Adler, there were some who would make a name for themselves later, notably Rev. John Phelps Taylor and Robert W. Rogers. One missionary, Edgar P. Allen, came all the way from Shanghai, China, to attend the class. The course was repeated again in January of 1888.[30]

Adler's assistance to Haupt increased in the spring of 1887 when John Hopkins conferred upon him the Ph.D. degree and promoted him to Associate Professor of Semitic Languages. Adler became the first recipient of the Ph. D. in Semitic Languages granted by a U. S. school.[31] This assistance was shown in the fall courses for 1887-88. Adler taught "Assyrian for Beginners" and the "History of Babylonia and Assyria," while Haupt taught "Babylonian Inscriptions" and the "Cuneiform Account of the Deluge."[32] By 1888 Adler was teaching "Third Year Assyrian," giving Haupt more time to devote to publication.

This practice of educating one's own scholars continued at Johns Hopkins. Christopher Johnston, Jr. (1856-1914) began to lend a hand with the elementary Assyrian courses for 1889.[33] Johnston, a native of Baltimore, was born December 8, 1856.[34] He received a Bachelor of Literature from the University of Virginia in 1878, and an M.A. in 1879. In 1880 Johnston received the M.D. degree from the University of Maryland. After practicing medicine in Baltimore

"Cyrus Adler, 1863-1940," *JAOS*, LXI (1941), 193; and a memoriam sketch by W. F. Albright, *BASOR*, No. 78 (1940), 2-3.

[29] *Johns Hopkins University Circular* (hereafter referred to as *JHUC*), No. 56 (1887), 71.

[30] *Ibid.*, No. 60 (1887), 4.

[31] J. A. Montgomery, *JAOS*, LXI (1941), 193.

[32] *JHUC*, No. 60 (1887), 4.

[33] *Ibid.*, No. 76 (1889), 11.

[34] Biographical information on Christopher Johnston, Jr. taken from Paul Haupt, "Christopher Johnston," *JAOS*, XXXVI (1916), 339-341.

for eight years, he entered Johns Hopkins to study under Haupt, and was made a Fellow for 1888-89. The following year Johnston was promoted to Instructor of Semitic Languages, thus helping Haupt and Adler with the basic Assyrian courses.

Another scholar came to Johns Hopkins in the fall of 1891. This was John Dyneley Prince (1868-1945), who was appointed a Fellow of Semitic Languages for the school year 1891-92.[35] Haupt was in need of more help because he had branched out and was teaching courses in Hebrew, Aramaic, Ethiopic, and Arabic.[36] Adler was on leave, travelling in the Near East for the fall and early winter of 1891-92.[37] After his return in January of 1892, he restricted himself to the teaching of Hebrew.[38] Prince received his Ph.D. from Johns Hopkins in the spring of 1892 and moved on to New York University.[39] Meanwhile the load remained on Johnston and Haupt, as Adler became Librarian of the Smithsonian Institution in 1893. Johnston earned his doctorate in 1894 and stayed on as Associate Professor of Semitic Languages.[40] The staff was back to two members.

Despite the large teaching loads of the two scholars, they managed to write a few significant articles. Between 1884 and 1891 Paul Haupt published seven major articles of an Assyriological nature.[41] Professor Haupt also found time to serve as one of the editors of the new journals, *Hebraica* which was begun in 1884, and *Beiträge zur Assyriologie* established in 1889.[42] His partner, Johnston, published five major articles between 1893 and 1899.[43] The work of these two, plus the valuable contributions of Adler and Prince, made Johns Hopkins University a first-rate school, Assyriologically speaking, by the close of 1899.

Hermann Hilprecht at Pennsylvania

In Philadelphia the administration at the University of Pennsylvania began to see the need for developing Assyriological courses at the university, just as had been done at Union and

---

[35] *JHUC*, No. 98 (1892), 93.
[36] *Ibid.*, 98.
[37] *Ibid.*
[38] *Ibid.*
[39] *Ibid.*, No. 100 (1892), 118.
[40] P. Haupt, *JAOS*, XXXVI (1916), 339-340.
[41] See bibliography.
[42] *Hebraica*, I (1884), preface; and *JHUC*, No. 76 (1889), 16.
[43] See bibliography.

Harvard. During the academic year of 1886-87, public lectures were given at the university by Peters and Jastrow.[44] John Punnet Peters (1852-1921) gave lectures on "Ancient Civilization of Babylon."[45] Morris Jastrow, Jr. (1861-1921) lectured on "Assyrian Literature and its Bearing on the Old Testament."[46] Jastrow was born August 13, 1861, in Warsaw, Poland. After earning his A.B. from the University of Pennsylvania in 1881, Jastrow went to Germany to study the Semitic languages. The University of Leipzig granted him the Ph. D. in 1884. He spent several months studying in France before returning to the United States.

As shown by the lectures on Assyriology, one can see that there was an interest in cuneiform studies in Philadelphia before it was cultivated at the university. The person chosen for the Pennsylvania faculty to begin Assyriology at the school was not Jastrow, who was still engaged in independent study and research, but a German scholar, Hermann Vollrath Hilprecht (1859-1925). Hilprecht was a native of Hohenerxleben, Germany, born there July 28, 1859.[47] After earning the Ph.D. degree from the University of Leipzig in 1883, Hilprecht taught Old Testament Theology at the University of Erlangen. He came to Philadelphia early in 1886 to become editor of the *Sunday School Times.* Edward W. Clark of the prominent Philadelphia banking family endowed a chair at Pennsylvania. This chair, known as the Clark Research Professorship of Assyriology and Semitic Philology, was offered to Hilprecht in the summer of 1886. He accepted and began his duties in the fall of the same year.[48]

Hilprecht proceeded to push Penn to the top of the Assyriological scholastic world. Many scholars have questioned the true abilities of Hilprecht as an Assyriologist.[49] Despite doubts raised about his abilities as a scholar, Hilprecht did bring recognition to the university

---

[44] *Univ. Penn. Catalogue and Announcements, 1886-87* (Philadelphia: Univ. Penn. Press, 1886), 35-36.

[45] The work of Peters will be examined later, see Chapter IV.

[46] Biographical material on Jastrow taken from J. A. Montgomery, "Morris Jastrow, Jr.," *American Journal of Semitic Languages and Literature* (hereafter referred to as *AJSL*), XXXVIII (1921-22), 1-11; A. T. Clay, "Prof. Jastrow as an Assyriologist," *JAOS*, XLI (1921), 333-336; and a biographical sketch by A. T. Clay in *Proc. of Amer. Philosophical Soc.*, LX (1921), x-xviii.

[47] Biographical information on Hilprecht taken from "Proceedings for Dec. 1925," *Journal Soc. Biblical Literature*, XLV (1926), iii-iv; and *Dict. Amer. Biog.*, IX, (1932), 59.

[48] *Univ. Penn. Catalog, 1886-87*, 19.

[49] See the Peters-Hilprecht Controversy in Chapter V.

as a topnotch school in Assyriological circles. He had the ability to attract donors for the archeological expeditions launched by the University of Pennsylvania. In 1887 Hilprecht was appointed Curator of the Semitic section of the University Museum.[50] Professor Hilprecht had a hand in all four of the expeditions sent to Nippur by Pennsylvania, but this story is reserved for Chapter IV. With Hilprecht away on the Nippur Expedition in 1888-89, Jastrow was invited in to teach Hilprecht's two Akkadian courses.[51] In 1890-91 when Hilprecht returned he offered three courses in Akkadian: "Assyrian Grammar," "Selected Babylonia Texts," and "Cursive Reading of Assyrian Texts."[52] The offerings in Assyriology were increased to seven courses in 1892-93.[53] In the fall of 1892 Morris Jastrow, Jr. was hired as a Professor of Semitic Languages.[54] Although Jastrow helped Hilprecht somewhat with the Assyriology courses, he concentrated mainly on teaching Arabic; he and Hilprecht did not get along too well, as will be seen later. The department was very proud of the fact that they could claim in 1893 three majors and two minors in Assyriology at the undergraduate level.[55]

Like Haupt at Johns Hopkins, Hilprecht found the time, despite his heavy teaching load, to publish in his field. Between 1889 and 1894 he published six scholarly articles, and many others of the travelogue type.[56] He also was selected as editor of the *Babylonian Expedition Series* to publish the documents and tablets unearthed by the Nippur Expedition.[57] In this same series he and Albert Tobias Clay published some business documents from Nippur, dated between 464 and 424 B.C.[58] Earlier he had edited a book dealing with excavation in Mesopotamia, Egypt, Palestine, and Asia Minor.[59]

---

[50] For the growth and development of the University Museum see Percy C. Madeira, Jr., *Men in Search of Man* (Philadelphia: Univ. Penn. Press, 1963).

[51] *Univ. Penn. Catalog, 1888-89* (1888), 178.

[52] *Ibid., 1890-91* (1890), 131-132.

[53] *Ibid., 1892-93* (1892), 182-183.

[54] *Ibid.*

[55] *Report of the Provost of the University of Pennsylvania for the Three Years Ending Oct. 1, 1892* (Philadelphia: Univ. Penn. Press, 1893), 63.

[56] See bibliography.

[57] More will be said of this later, see below Chap. V.

[58] H. V. Hilprecht and A. T. Clay, *Business Documents of Murashu Sons of Nippur, Dated in the Reign of Artaxerxes I*, Vol. IX of *Babylonian Expedition of Univ. Penn.*, ed. by H. V. Hilprecht, Series A (Philadelphia: Univ. Penn. Press, 1898).

[59] H. V. Hilprecht (ed.), *Recent Researches in Bible Lands* (Philadelphia: J. D. Wattles, 1896).

Despite all this writing, editing, and translating, Hilprecht managed to increase the offerings at the University of Pennsylvania. For the 1898-99 school year he added a course in Sumerian, the first to be taught at the school.[60] Jastrow could give very little help as he was appointed Librarian in 1898, and could only devote himself to Arabic and Hebrew on the teaching side of the ledger. Hilprecht did get help in 1899 from a former student, Albert T. Clay, who was appointed Lecturer of Assyriology in this year.[61] With this welcome help from Clay, Hilprecht added a second Sumerian course for the 1899-1900 academic year.[62] As the nineteenth century came to a close, Pennsylvania looked forward to even bigger and better things in the field of Assyriology.

Assyriology at the Other Schools

Assyriology was not limited to the four institutions on the preceding pages. By the end of the nineteenth century the discipline had spread to at least fifteen other universities, colleges, and seminaries. The University of Missouri, at Columbia, offered an Assyrian course before Pennsylvania had hired Hilprecht. A postgraduate course in the Akkadian language was offered by Professor James Shannon Blackwell (1844-1911?) of the School of Hebrew and Semitic Literature in the fall of 1885.[63] Blackwell was one of those gifted individuals to whom languages come easily.[64] By the 1888-89 academic year Akkadian had been dropped from the university offerings.[65] Blackwell's departure from Missouri in 1894 put an end to the teaching of Semitic languages at the school for the rest of the century.[66]

Princeton managed to inaugurate Assyriology, even if only for a

---

[60] *Univ. Penn. Catalog, 1898-99* (1898), 191.

[61] *Ibid.*, 1901-02 (1901), 208-209; more will be said of Clay in Chapter V.

[62] *Univ. Penn. Catalog, 1899-1900* (1899), 203.

[63] *Annual Catalogue of the Missouri Agricultural College and University, 1885-86* (Jefferson City, Mo.: Tribune Printing Co., 1886), 81-82.

[64] According to the *National Cyclopedia of Amer. Biog.*, VIII, 187-188, Blackwell could read and write German, French, Greek, Latin, Hebrew, Arabic, Ethiopic, Syriac, Assyrian, Egyptian, Sanskrit, Pali, Persian, Russian, Spanish, Italian, Portuguese, Old Slavonic, modern Greek, Dutch, Swedish, Danish, Icelandic, and Anglo-Saxon.

[65] *Annual Catalogue of the University of the State of Missouri, 1888-89* (Jefferson City: Tribune Printing Co., 1889), 54.

[66] *Catalogue of the University of the State of Missouri, 1894-95* (Columbia: Univ. Mo. Press, 1895), 41.

brief period. John F. MacCurdy taught a course entitled "Cuneiform Inscriptions and the Old Testament," during the school Year for 1885-86.[67] After this brief attempt, Assyriology seems to have faded out at Princeton until the 1930's.

Nathaniel Schmidt (1862-1939) initiated Assyriology at Colgate University. Schmidt, born May 22, 1862, at Hudiksvall, Sweden, studied at Stockholm University from 1882 to 1884.[68] He came to the United States in 1884, where he entered Madison University (Colgate), receiving an A.M. from there in 1887. He became a Professor of Semitic Languages and Literature at Colgate in 1888. His main task was the teaching of Hebrew, but in 1888 he organized a two-hour course in the history of Babylonia and Assyria that he offered every year. After studying at the University of Berlin in 1890, Schmidt was awarded the Doctor of Hebrew Literature by the Jewish Institute of Religion. In 1896 Schmidt left Colgate and went to Cornell.

Assyriology did not die out at Colgate after the departure of Schmidt but was continued by his successor George Ricker Berry (1865-1945). Berry was a native of West Sumner, Maine. After receiving an A.B. degree from Colby College, Waterville, Maine, in 1885, and graduating from Newton Theological Institution in 1889, he went to the University of Chicago as soon as the new school opened its doors in 1892 to study the Semitic languages. Berry earned his Ph.D. in 1895, stayed on a year as an instructor at Chicago, then in 1896 was appointed Instructor of Semitic Languages at Colgate. He continued the history course begun by Schmidt.[69] In the fall of 1897 Berry was promoted to Professor.[70] After the turn of the century he would expand the Assyriological offerings even more.

The teaching of Akkadian was begun at Boston University by Hinckley Gilbert Mitchell (1846-1920) in the fall of 1887.[71] Mitchell was born February 22, 1846, in the small village of Lee, Oneida County, New York. He took an A.B. at Wesleyan University, Middletown, Conn., in 1875, and an A.M. in 1876. After receiving a Bachelor of Sacred Theology (S.T.B.) from Boston University in 1876,

---

[67] Adler, *Andover Review*, VIII (1887), 441. The writer has been unable to find any biographical information on MacCurdy.

[68] Memoriam sketch by Millar Burrows, *BASOR*, No. 75 (1939), 7-8.

[69] *Colgate Univ. Catalogue, 1896-97* (Hamilton, N. Y.: Colgate Univ. Press, 1896), 16.

[70] *Ibid., 1898-99* (1898), 10.

[71] Adler, *Andover Review*, VIII (1887), 441.

he went on to the University of Leipzig, earning the doctorate in 1879. Mitchell returned to Wesleyan where he taught Latin and Hebrew from 1880-83. He was hired by Boston University in 1883 as a Professor of Hebrew and Old Testament Exegesis. In 1887 Mitchell began to teach a language course in Akkadian. The following year he started a course in the ancient history of the Near East, in which a great deal of time was devoted to the study of the civilizations of Mesopotamia.[72] After 1895 the history course was taught by various members of the History Department, but Mitchell continued to teach Akkadian.[73]

George Aaron Barton (1859-1942) inaugurated Assyriology at Bryn Mawr College (located just outside Philadelphia) in the last decade of the nineteenth century. Barton, a native of Farnham, Canada, attended Haverford College (Philadelphia area), earning an A.B. degree in 1882, and an A.M. in 1885.[74] Barton moved next to Harvard where he studied with David Lyon. He received an A.M. degree from Harvard in 1890 and the Ph.D. in 1891. Bryn Mawr hired him as Associate Professor of Biblical Literature and Semitic Languages in the fall of 1891.[75] Barton's Assyriological offerings, begun in 1891, consisted of an elementary Akkadian language course and cuneiform inscriptions that related to the Old Testament, both at the graduate level.[76] In 1894 an advanced Akkadian grammar course was added.[77] Then in 1898 Barton added another course in Assyrian literature and dropped the course relating to the Old Testament.[78]

At the brand new University of Chicago, Assyrian studies were initiated by Robert Francis Harper (1864-1914), the younger brother of the president of the school, William Rainey Harper.[79] Before the school had even opened its doors, scholars seemed to sense that Chicago would enter into the field of Assyriology. In 1891 Hilprecht asked President Harper to bear some of the expenses of the Babylonian Expedition, giving the new school the right to share in

---

[72] *Boston Univ. Year Book for 1889-90* (Boston: Boston Univ. Press, 1890), 57
[73] *Ibid., 1895-96* (1896), 69.
[74] Biographical material on Barton taken from a memoriam sketch by E. A. Speiser, *BASOR*, No. 87 (1942), 2-4; "Necrology," *American Jour. Archaeology*, XLVI (1942), 546.
[75] Barton also served as a lecturer at Haverford College, 1891-95.
[76] *Bryn Mawr College Program, 1891-92* (Bryn Mawr: College Press, 1891), 67.
[77] *Ibid., 1894-95* (1894), 96.
[78] *Ibid., 1898-99* (1898), 124.
[79] More will be said of R. F. Harper in Chapter V.

the tablets excavated at Nippur.[80] David G. Lyon inquired about a position as professor of Assyriology on the Chicago faculty in this same year.[81] Harper, however, had his brother Robert in mind for the job and hired him, beginning the academic year of 1892-93 to handle Assyrian and Babylonian studies.[82] This was perhaps nepotism, but the younger Harper had begun to show scholarly promise.

Robert Harper received help in the teaching of Assyriology from his friend and schoolmate Ira Maurice Price (1856-1939). Price was born April 29, 1856, at Newark, Ohio. He earned a B.A. degree from Denison University, Granville, Ohio, in 1879, and an M.A. in 1882. Price received the Bachelor of Divinity from Baptist Union Theological Seminary, Morgan Park, Illinois, also in 1882. He then sailed for Germany where he earned the M.A. from the University of Leipzig in 1886, and the Ph.D. in 1887. Price taught various languages at several schools until hired by President Harper in 1892 as Associate Professor of Semitic Languages and Literature. By 1896 Robert F. Harper and Price were offering nine courses in the Akkadian language and three in social life and geography of Mesopotamia.[83] As the nineteenth century drew to a close, Chicago was making her bid for a frontrunning position among the universities, where Assyriology was concerned.

At the University of Michigan, Carl William Belser (1848?-1895) taught the first Akkadian courses. Belser, a native of Ann Arbor, studied at the University of Leipzig under Friedrich Delitzsch, earning the Ph.D. in 1889. He was hired as Instructor of German and Hebrew in the fall of 1890, where he immediately initiated two courses in the Akkadian language for 1890-91.[84] He was promoted to Assistant Professor of Oriental Languages in 1891, a position he held until ill health forced him to retire at the end of the first semester of 1892-93. Wilhelm Muss-Arnolt (Ph.D., Johns Hopkins, 1888) was

---

[80] Letter of 1891 (no specific date) from Hilprecht to W. R. Harper, Folder 19, Personal Papers of W. R. Harper, Archives, University of Chicago Library.

[81] D. G. Lyon, Cambridge, Mass., June 20, 1891, letter to W. R. Harper, Univ. Chicago, Folder 17, Personal Papers of W. R. Harper.

[82] *The President's Report of the University of Chicago, July, 1892 to July, 1902* (Chicago: Univ. Chicago Press, 1904), 40-41; and R. F. Harper, Chicago, June 12, 1892, letter to brother Frank, R. F. Harper Folder, President's File, Archives, University of Chicago Library.

[83] *Univ. Chicago Annual Register for 1896-97* (Chicago: Univ. Chicago Press, 1897), 221.

[84] *Univ. Michigan Catalogue for 1890* (Ann Arbor: Univ. Mich. Press, 1890), 46.

brought in to finish out the school year for Belser. In the fall of 1893 James Alexander Craig (1860?-1932) was hired as Professor of Oriental Languages.[85] Beginning in the 1893-94 school year Craig took over the Akkadian courses.[86] In 1894 he added another Akkadian language course, and two history courses dealing with the area of Babylonia and Assyria.[87] Craig had earned his Ph.D. at Leipzig in 1886 under Delitzsch. Later scholars have challenged his work as an Assyriologist.[88]

At Columbia University, Assyriology was initiated by Richard James Horatio Gottheil (1862-1936). Gottheil was born October 13, 1862, in Manchester, England.[89] The family moved to New York City in 1873. After earning the A.B. degree from Columbia in 1881, Gottheil went to study in Germany. He received the Ph.D. from the University of Leipzig in 1886, graduating *summa cum laude*. Gottheil returned to Columbia in 1886 as Instructor of Syriac Languages and Literature.[90] By 1892 he was Professor of Rabbinical Literature and Semitic Languages.[91] Gottheil offered two elementary and one advanced Akkadian course for the academic year of 1895-96.[92]

Columbia did not restrict itself to the teaching of Akkadian alone but branched out and offered Old Persian. Abraham Valentine Williams Jackson (1862-1937) was the founder of Iranian studies at Columbia in 1896. Jackson, a product of Columbia, was also a native of New York City.[93] All of his degrees were earned at Columbia. After earning the Ph.D. in 1886, he stayed on as an assistant and then instructor in English. In the fall of 1895 he was appointed Professor of Indo-Iranian Languages.[94] The following year Jackson organized three courses—"Old Persian Cuneiform Inscriptions,"

---

[85] *Univ. Mich. Catalogue for 1893-94* (1894), 11.
[86] *Ibid.*
[87] *Ibid., 1894-95* (1895), 57.
[88] T. J Meek, "The Challenge of Oriental Studies to American Scholarship," *JAOS*, LXIII (1943), 87.
[89] Memoriam sketch by Samuel Rosenblatt, *BASOR*, XLVI (1936), 4/2-479.
[90] *Catalogue of Officers and Graduates of Columbia University, 1754-1906* (New York: Columbia Univ. Press, 1906), 41.
[91] *Ibid.*
[92] *Columbia Univ. Catalogue, 1895-96* (New York: Columbia Univ. Press, 1896) 107.
[93] Biographical information on Jackson extracted from a memoriam sketch by Louis H. Gray in *BASOR*, No. 68 (1937), 5-7; and Edw. D. Perry, "Abraham Valentine Williams Jackson," *JAOS*, LVIII (1938), 221-224.
[94] *Catalogue of Columbia Univ., 1754-1906* (1906), 45.

"Zoroaster and his Teachings," and "Comparative Iranian Grammar."[95] Thus, Columbia closed out the century by offering not only Akkadian but Persian as well.

Nathaniel Schmidt, who had begun Assyriology at Colgate, was also the founder of the discipline at Cornell University. He arrived at Cornell in 1896 as Professor of Semitic Languages and Oriental History.[96] Schmidt's departure from Colgate had not been under happy circumstances, as he had been put on trial for heresy by the Colgate Divinity School, since many of his Assyriological translations and interpretations ran contrary to the Old Testament.[97] At any rate, Colgate's loss was Cornell's gain. Schmidt immediately organized some Assyriological offerings. Prior to the turn of the century, he did not teach any language courses but offered instead the history of Babylonia and Assyria, history of Persia, and a course in Semitic literature that was predominantly of an Assyriological nature.[98]

John Prince, who has been mentioned before, introduced Assyrian studies at New York University.[99] He had studied under Paul Haupt and lost no time in organizing a basic Akkadian language course upon his arrival at NYU in 1892 as Professor of Semitic Language.[100] Prince was appointed Dean of the Graduate School in 1895.[101] Despite this increase in administrative load, he was teaching four Akkadian courses at the graduate level by the autumn of 1896.[102] As the century ended, Prince was still offering these courses at New York University.

At Vanderbilt University, Nashville, Tennessee, the architect for cuneiform studies was James Henry Stevenson (1860-1919). Stevenson was born April 16, 1860, at Petersborough, Ontario, Canada. After earning the A.B. from McGill University in 1889, and graduating from Wesleyan Theological College, Montreal, in 1891, Stevenson went to the University of Chicago to study Hebrew under William R. Harper. Before he completed his doctorate, which he

---

[95] *Col. Univ. Catalogue, 1896-97* (1897), 109.
[96] *Fourth Annual Report of President Schurman, 1895-96* (Ithaca, N. Y.: Cornell Univ. Press, 1896), 11-12.
[97] Morris Bishop, *A History of Cornell* (Ithaca: Cornell Univ. Press., 1962), 327.
[98] *Pres. Rept., 1896-97* (1897), lxii.
[99] Biographical information on Prince will be given in Chapter IV.
[100] *New York Univ. Catalogue for 1892-93* (New York: New York Univ. Press, 1892), 119.
[101] *Ibid., 1896-97* (1896), 109.
[102] *Ibid.*, 121.

finally earned in 1897, he accepted a position as Professor of Hebrew at Vanderbilt for the fall of 1893.[103] Beginning with the school year of 1895-96, Stevenson taught two courses in the Akkadian language.[104] These courses were still being offered without change in format as the year 1899 came to a close.

Since Assyriology began at a Theological Seminary, it seems reasonable to assume that the other theological schools would make offerings in the new discipline. According to Cyrus Adler, Assyrian language courses were offered in 1887 at Andover Theological Seminary, Andover, Mass., by John Phelps Taylor (1841-1915); at Baptist Theological Seminary, Newton Centre, Mass., by Charles Rufus Brown (1849-1914); at Protestant Episcopal Seminary, Philadelphia, by John P. Peters; and at the Summer School of Hebrew, Chicago, by James A. Craig and Robert F. Harper.[105]

By the turn of the century at least nineteen institutions offered instruction in Assyriology, in one form or the other, although it was for the most part language studies. For some the interest in cuneiform studies would decline; for others this interest would become even greater in the future.

Societies and Publications

This interest in cuneiform studies shown by its expansion in the institutions is also reflected in the programs of several learned societies. The American Oriental Society (already mentioned in Chapter II) continued to propagate the new discipline of Assyriology. One has only to check the *Proceedings* of the society to be impressed with the number of papers containing Assyriological subject matter presented at the two yearly meetings, between 1880 and 1900. By the writer's count, at least seventy-eight Assyriological papers were read, ranging from syntactical studies to the work of the expeditions in the field. Longer papers were presented as articles in *JAOS*, and there were at least ten of these.[106] By 1899 Assyriology had become one of the dominant topics on the programs of the American Oriental Society.

---

[103] *Register for Vanderbilt Univ. for 1893-94* (Nashville: Vanderbilt Univ. Press, 1894), 62.
[104] *Ibid., 1895-96* (1896), 55.
[105] Adler, *Andover Review*, VIII (1887), 441.
[106] See bibliography.

Other societies were showing a vague interest in Assyriological studies. The American Philosophical Society was concerned mainly with Egyptology, at least as far as their interest in the Near East went. Daniel G. Brinton did read a paper on April 19, 1895, entitled "The Protohistoric Ethnography of Western Asia," in which he discussed the Sumerians and Semites of Mesopotamia.[107] The society also published some of Hilprecht's discoveries at Nippur, between 1893 and 1896.[108] Assyriology would not really creep into the program of the society until after 1900.

In Philadelphia an Oriental Club was founded in 1888 by a group of professors, amateur archeologists, and other interested persons to promote the cause of Oriental studies. The first task the new club set for itself was the preparation of a card catalogue of Oriental manuscripts and texts, located in the libraries of Philadelphia, both public and private.[109] With such founding members on the rolls as John P. Peters, H. V. Hilprecht, Morris Jastrow, Jr., and the later addition of Cyrus Adler, Paul Haupt, and R. W. Rogers, it was natural to have a major portion of their programs devoted to Assyriology. The atmosphere of the meetings was very relaxed, and the proceedings were much more informal than in the larger societies. Some of the longer papers, such as the ones by Jastrow, Hilprecht, and others were published later in book form.[110] This club, like the educational institutions of Philadelphia, was doing much to promote interest in Assyriology. Its nineteen members were promoting public lectures and making Assyriological literature known to the citizens of Philadelphia.

Another club similar to that at Philadelphia was formed in New York City in 1896. The New York Oriental Club was organized on February 27, 1896, by scholars living in the vicinity of New York City. No formal papers were presented, but dinner was served and informal discussions of Assyriological, Egyptological, and other Near Eastern topics were discussed.[111]

Turning to literature one could not even hope to enumerate the

---

[107] *Proc. Amer. Philosophical Soc.*, XXXIV (1895), 71-102.

[108] H. V. Hilprecht, "Old Babylonian Inscriptions, Chiefly from Nippur," *Trans. Amer. Philosophical Soc.*, XVIII, n.s., Pt. 1 (1893), 5-54; Pt. 2 (1896), 221-282.

[109] Oriental Club of Philadelphia, *Oriental Studies* (Boston: Ginn & Co., 1894), 9.

[110] H. V. Hilprecht, "A Numerical Fragment from Nippur," in *Oriental Studies* by the Oriental Club of Philadelphia, 137-140; and M. Jastrow, Jr., "A Legal Document of Babylon," 116-136.

[111] Personal correspondence with Adolf Schrijver, Sec.-Treas., June 4, 1968.

hundreds and even thousands of articles published on Assyriology between the years 1880 and 1900. The writer has used hundreds of these in this work, and has only made a dent in the total number. Books, on the other hand, are not nearly so copius. There seems to be not many more than twenty-five significant books covering cuneiform studies, published in the period under discussion. Many of these have already been mentioned.

James A. Craig copied one hundred and four religious text from the British Museum, and published them in two volumes, between 1895 and 1897.[112] Morris Jastrow, Jr. published a very good survey of the religions of Mesopotamia in 1898.[113] A. V. Williams Jackson was fast becoming the leading authority on the religions of ancient Persia. In 1898 he released a book dealing with the life of Zoroaster.[114] Although this work made use of traditional material, it was, nevertheless well written, and a contribution to the field.

Social and cultural studies of Mesopotamia were dominated by Archibald H. Sayce. It is true that Sayce was not an American, but several of his books were published in the United States. His *Social Life Among the Assyrians and Babylonians* appeared in 1893, and *Babylonia and Assyria: Life and Customs* came out in 1899.[115]

On the popular side there are several books worth noting. One popular writer, Zenoide A. Ragozin, turned out three semi-popular historical books. Her first work, *The Story of Chaldea*, was published in 1886, proving so popular that Putnam's put out a second edition in 1898.[116] This was followed up with *The Story of Assyria* in 1887, and a second edition in 1893.[117] The following year she published *The Story of Media, Babylon, and Persia*.[118]

Herbert Cushing Tolman (1865-1923) was working in the field of Persian philology at Vanderbilt. Tolman, a native of South Scituate, Mass., received his education at Yale; an A.B. in 1888, and the Ph.D. in 1890. In 1894 Tolman became Professor of Greek at Vanderbilt University. Although he taught no Persian language courses, he conducted research and published in the field. In 1892 Tolman

---

[112] *Assyrian and Babylonian Religious Texts* (Leipzig: J. C.Hinrichs, 1895-97).
[113] *The Religion of Babylonia and Assyria*, Vol. II of *Handbooks of the History of Religions* (Boston: Ginn & Co., 1898).
[114] *Zoroaster the Prophet of Ancient Iran* (New York: Macmillan Co., 1898).
[115] See above Chap. I.
[116] (New York: G. P. Putnam's Sons).
[117] (Putnam's).
[118] (Putnam's, 1888).

published *A Grammar of the Old Persian Language*[119] and *A Guide to the Old Persian Inscriptions* in 1893.[120]

Several journals were founded during this period from 1880 to 1900 that would carry Assyriological articles. The Archaeological Institute of America inaugurated the *American Journal of Archaeology* in 1885.[121] One of the most important periodicals, at least as far as Assyriology was concerned, had its beginning in July of 1884. This was the journal *Hebraica*, published by The American Publication Society of Hebrew, Chicago. In 1896 the title was changed to *The American Journal of Semitic Languages and Literature*. Shortly after the title was changed, the University of Chicago took charge of publication. *Beiträge zur Assyriologie* was begun in 1889 as an Assyriological journal.[122] It was published by J. C. Hinrich of Leipzig, but with the cooperation of Johns Hopkins. This journal was the brainchild of Paul Haupt, and he and Friedrich Delitzsch served as editors of the new journal.[123]

By 1900 Assyriology was being taught in the institutions of higher education in the United States. Many journals now carried articles of an Assyriological nature, and there was an increase of books dealing with the topic. Assyriology now had achieved outstanding academic status which would train future scholars. These professional journals could act as periodical outlets for the results of scholarly research. All the tangible ingredients necessary to make possible the production of original works of the first order of importance in the field were now present in U. S. scholarly circles.

---

[119] (Boston: Ginn & Co.).
[120] (New York: American Book Co.).
[121] I, First Series (1885), 1.
[122] *Beiträge zur Assyriologie und Semitschen Sprachwissenschaft (Contributions to Assyriology and Comparative Semitic Philology)*.
[123] *JHUC*, No. 76 (1889), 16.

CHAPTER FOUR

THE UNIVERSITY OF PENNSYLVANIA SHOWS THE WAY

In Chapter III one could see how Assyriology evolved and developed at many institutions of higher learning in the United States. The literature in this field was very prolific, and interest was being shown in the learned societies. Up to this point we have talked only in terms of what could be called "armchair Assyriology." To broaden the scope of its Assyriological interests, the United States would have to send scholars to the field to engage in archeological excavations. In this category the University of Pennsylvania stepped forward in the 1880's and 90's to provide the necessary leadership. Between 1889 and 1900 Pennsylvania sent out four archeological expeditions to the site of the ancient city of Nippur.

Nippur

The city of Nippur, located approximately one hundred miles southeast of Baghdad, was a city-state founded and inhabited by a group of people known as the Sumerians. From whence the Sumerians came is still a question today among ancient historians and archeologists. Many scholars favor the theory that they had their origins around the Caspian Sea. Unlike other peoples who migrated into the area, the Sumerians were a non-Semitic group. They probably arrived in the lower part of the Tigris-Euphrates valley between 4500 and 4000 B.C.[1] Seemingly they were not the first people to settle the area, as evidence indicates that the Ubaids were there prior to the Sumerian arrival. At any rate by the middle of the fourth millenium B.C. these migrants began to dominate the southern part of the valley, the area that came to be known as Sumer.

By 3000 B.C. the Sumerians had established a flourishing civilization, attaining a high degree of cultural life. Sumer, however, was not united, but was made up of a series of independent city-states, bound together by a common core of language, religion, and

---

[1] For a good study of Sumerian political history see Kramer, *The Sumerians*.

customs. There is some evidence that Etana of Kish may have brought Sumer under his control, but this is highly debatable. Some of the more important of these city-states or urban centers were Nippur, Kish, Ur, Larsa, Eridu, Isin, Adab, and Lagash. The rulers of these city-states were known as *ensis* and later took the title of *lugal* or king.

Nippur was founded early in the fourth millenium B.C., and perhaps as early as 4000. It quickly became important as a religious and intellectual center. From the cuneiform tablets there is evidence to indicate that shortly after 3000 B.C. the air-god, Enlil, replaced An, the heaven-god, as chief deity in the Sumerian pantheon. Enlil's home was in Nippur, thus, this city became a seat of worship for all Sumer. Coronation ceremonies for kings of all the city-states usually took place in the temple of Enlil in Nippur.

About 2350 B.C. the Semitic king Sargon, later known as Sargon the Great, from the land of Akkad to the north conquered all of Sumer and brought it under his sway, building up a large empire. Under Akkadian rule Nippur remained the religious center, as Sargon and his successors continued to support the Enlil temple. One source tells us that Sargon's grandson, Naram-Sin, desecrated the temple of Enlil, and for this was punished by the Gutian invasion.[2] These Guti were a fierce barbaric people who overran the land of Sumer and Akkad about 2250 B.C. During the confusion of this period the city of Ur became very powerful and aggressive and by 2100 B.C. had thrown off the yoke of the Guti and started to establish a Sumerian empire. This was under their able king Ur-Nammu. Although Ur was the seat of political power, Nippur remained the chief religious center.

With the conquest of the land by the Amorites and the destruction of Ur by the Elamites about 2000 B.C. we pass into the period of the Old Babylonians and Kassites, during which time Nippur suffered no loss of religious prestige. In the 10th century B.C. with the Assyrian conquest of Babylonia the seat of political power shifted to the north, but Nippur remained an important seat of worship and culture. Records reveal that Ashurbanipal (668-627 B.C.) rebuilt portions of the Ekur temple of Enlil.

After the Persian conquest of Mesopotamia in 539 B.C., Nippur began to be neglected as a religious center, but still retained an air of

---

[2] *Ibid.*, 65-66.

prosperity as there were numerous houses of business there during the Persian period (539-330 B.C.). Under Seleucid rule (323-126 B.C.) the city began to sink into stagnation and was finally abandoned in Parthian times toward the middle of the 3rd century B.C.

Drifting sands covered the city, forming a large mound that remained forgotten until Layard began to excavate there in early 1851.[3] How did the University of Pennsylvania come to choose Nippur as a likely excavation site? The locality was chosen on the recommendation of an exploratory survey known as the Wolfe Expedition.

Wolfe Expedition

Several members of the American Oriental Society began to discuss the idea of an expedition to Babylonia in the spring and summer of 1884. They were acting on their own and not as official representatives of the society. Those taking part in the discussion were William H. Ward, David G. Lyon, Charles H. Toy, John P. Peters, I. H. Hall, and Francis Brown.[4] These scholars were all interested in cuneiform studies, some of them anxious to find material in Mesopotamia that would support the Old Testament. They obtained the backing of the Archaeological Institute of America by describing the excavations of the British, French, and Germans in the area under discussion. The next step was to plan a preliminary expedition to select a good excavation site.

The group decided that this preliminary expedition should not take more than six months, with the expense not exceeding $ 5,000. Committees were appointed in New York, Boston, and Philadelphia to solicit funds for the expedition. It turned out that these committees were not needed, as Miss Catherine Lorillard Wolfe of New York contributed the entire $ 5,000. William Ward was named director of this expedition, now called the Wolfe Expedition for its benefactress.[5]

William Hayes Ward (1835-1916) was born June 25, 1835, at Abington, Massachusetts.[6] He began his college education at

---

[3] Layard, *Discoveries in the Ruins*, 556.
[4] William H. Ward, *Report on the Wolfe Expedition to Babylonia, 1884-85* (Boston: Archaeological Institute of America, 1886), 5.
[5] *Ibid.*, 5-6.
[6] Biographical material on Ward taken from M. Jastrow, Jr., "In Memoriam, W. H.

Amherst, receiving an A.B. in 1856, and in 1857 he attended Union Theological Seminary. In 1859 he graduated from Andover Theological Seminary and the following year was ordained a Congregational minister. After several teaching jobs at small schools and colleges, Ward became Associate Editor of the *New York Independent* in 1865. He was with the *Independent* until 1913, eventually rising to the position of Editor. During the 60's and 70's Ward began to study the Assyrian grammars out of Europe and taught himself to read the Akkadian language. As editor of the *Independent* Ward constantly described archeological activity in Mesopotamia, and from time to time offered translations of cuneiform texts. This brought him to the attention of President Charles Eliot of Harvard, who offered the Chair of Semitic Languages to Ward in 1879, but Ward felt that he could not handle the job due to his lack of formal study, and declined it.

After accepting the directorship of the Wolfe Expedition, Ward devoted all his time to the study of cuneiform inscriptions and read all geographical accounts of Mesopotamia that he could obtain. On September 6, 1884, Ward sailed from New York, bound for London. After arriving in London, Ward studied the cuneiform tablets in the British Museum and held conferences with Budge, Sayce, and Theophilus Pinches, all prominent British Assyriologists. Ward journeyed next to France where he looked at the Assyrian material in the Louvre and Bibliotheque Nationale and interviewed the French scholar Joachim Menant. He continued his journey, stopping briefly at museums in Munich, Vienna, and Budapest.[7]

After Ward arrived in Constantinople in the latter part of October, John Henry Haynes (1849-1910) joined him; a native of Massachusetts and at that time a professor at Central Turkey College in Aintab. With the help of Haynes, Ward applied for a permit from the Ottoman government to explore Mesopotamia. The pair spent several weeks in fruitless waiting, because government officials took the word explore to mean excavate, a considerably more serious proposition that required a great deal of deliberation. Finally toward the middle of November after the misunderstanding was straightened out, the government granted the permit (ferman) as well as letters to the governors of Aleppo, Baghdad, and Mosul, asking them to assist

---

Ward," *JAOS*, XXXVI (1917), 233-241; *Amer. Dict. Biog.*, XIX, 442-443; and an obituary notice in the *New York Times*, Aug. 29, 1916.

[7] Ward, *Report on the Wolfe Expedition*, 5-7.

THE UNIVERSITY OF PENNSYLVANIA SHOWS THE WAY 51

the Americans.[8] This was the American archeologist's first contact with the tremendous amount of delay and red tape that was common in the Ottoman empire.

Haynes and Ward left Constantinople by steamer after receiving the ferman granting them permission to explore. They were joined in Smyrna by the third member of this expedition, John Robert Sitlington Sterrett (1851-1914). Sterrett had a keen interest in archeology, his training having been at the University of Munich where he earned the Ph.D. degree. He had been doing independent study in Athens prior to joining the expedition. Later Sterrett attained fame as the editor of the Loeb Classical Library. The party travelled overland by horse and carriage from Smyrna, looking superficially at ancient ruins as they went. They finally arrived in Baghdad late on the night of December 31.[9]

The party remained in the city of Harun al-Rashid for about two weeks, making plans for a more detailed study of the terrain than was made on the trip into Baghdad. Also, the time was used by Sterrett to recuperate; he had fallen ill at Erbil and had to have medical attention immediately upon his arrival in the city of Baghdad.[10] At this point the fourth member of the expedition, Daniel Z. Noorian, who was to act as interpreter, joined the group.[11]

On Monday, January 12, 1885, the expediton left Baghdad at about 10:30 a.m., along with Arab bearers and servants.[12] Important sites visited by the expedition were Borsippa, Nippur, Fara, Bismya, Jasm, and Telloh.[13] As Ward and the party came to the site of an ancient ruin they looked first at the surface of the ground to see how many archeological objects could be found without digging. They also measured the size of the mound to estimate the size of the ancient city. In areas that had been excavated by other expeditions Ward had small trial trenches dug to see what could be exposed easily. Members of the party also talked to the native Arabs in the vicinity to see what they could reveal about the archeology of the site. In this manner

---

[8] *Ibid.*, 8.
[9] *Ibid.*, 9-16.
[10] *Ibid.*, 16.
[11] Diary of W. H. Ward, found in J. P. Peters, *Nippur; or, Exploration and Adventures on the Euphrates* (New York: G. P. Putnam's Sons, 1897), Vol. I, Appendix F, 318.
[12] Unless otherwise noted the events of the expedition are taken from Ward's diary, 318-375.
[13] According to Ward's diary (p. 351) Jasm was the site of the Garden of Eden.

Ward felt he could determine if a locality was suitable for excavation. The party arrived back in Baghdad on Thursday, March 5, where they remained for about two weeks. After this rejuvenating rest, Ward and the others left the city on Wednesday, March 18. This time the party explored to the west and north of Baghdad, as opposed to the south and east the first time. Finally, on Saturday, April 18 the exploration came to an end with the party's arrival in Palmyra. From there they went to Beirut and on to London by way of Alexandria. Ward arrived in New York on June 20, 1885.

After his arrival in New York, Ward set about the task of drawing up his recommendations concerning the archeological exploration of Mesopotamia. It was his opinion that the site of ancient Nippur was one of the largest cities of Mesopotamia that had undergone the least excavation. He also felt that the city was very ancient and according to classical accounts had been a very important city. Ward stated that many valuable antiquities could be recovered without digging, merely by walking over the ruins. This would be a very cheap way to fill museums of the United States with antiquities from ancient Mesopotamia. For these and other reasons Ward recommended that an American expedition should be sent to Nippur at once.[14]

The First Babylonian Expedition

At the semiannual meeting of the American Oriental Society held October 28-29, 1885, in New York, Professor C. A. Briggs of Union Theological Seminary proposed a resolution. This resolution that was passed by the society stated:

> *Resolved,* That this Society expresses its gratification at the valuable discoveries made by the Wolfe Expedition; that we regard it as highly important that the ruins discovered by Dr. Ward in ancient Babylonia be thoroughly explored as soon as possible; and that we recommend to the American public this object as one worthy of liberal contributions, in order that a second expedition may be sent out at an early date to make the excavations, and that the Assyrian and Babylonian antiquities may be acquired by American museums.[15]

John Punnett Peters (1852-1921), who had been one of the instigators of the Wolfe Expedition, stepped forward to devote his energies to seeing that this resolution was carried out.

---

[14] Ward, *Report on the Wolfe Expedition*, 27-33.
[15] "Proceedings," *JAOS*, XIII (1889), lxxxi.

John Peters was born December 16, 1852, in New York City. After earning an A.B. degree at Yale in 1873, he stayed on and received the Ph.D. in 1876. Peters continued his education at the University of Berlin between 1879 and 1883, where he studied Semitic languages. In 1885 he was appointed Professor of Hebrew at the University of Pennsylvania, a position he held until 1893.

Upon the advice of Peters, the provost of the University of Pennsylvania, William Pepper, called a meeting at his home on the evening of November 30, 1887. About thirty people were present, including Peters, Ward, and Hermann Hilprecht.[16] Peters spoke of the need for an American expedition to Babylonia, telling his interested audience that a three-year expedition could be financed for $15,000. Hilprecht disagreed with this, saying that one year would cost about $19,200.[17] This disagreement seemed trivial at the time but gave an indication of the feud that would arise between the two at a later date. Before the meeting ended the Babylonian Exploration Fund had been organized. From those present about $7,500 was subscribed to the new fund, and an executive committee was formed.[18] Provost Pepper was named president, Hilprecht was elected secretary, Mr. Edward W. Clark of a prominent Philadelphia banking family acted as treasurer, Peters was named director of the expedition, and Clarence H. Clark, brother of E. W. Clark, was made chairman of the publication committee. Besides these officers, there were ten other members of the executive committee.[19]

The Babylonian Exploration Fund was incorporated on March 17, 1888, Prior to this date the committee had made an application to the Ottoman government for permission to excavate in Mesopotamia. Ambassador Straus, the American consul at Constantinople, had filed the request in February.[20] Final organization of the expedition was completed during the spring of 1888. Accompanying Peters would be Robert Francis Harper, acting as Assyriologist, Perez Hastings Field was the architect and surveyor, John Henry Haynes was photographer and business manager, Daniel Noorian was interpreter and director of workmen, and John Dynely Prince was named secretary to the director.[21] Prince, another native of New York City,

---

[16] Peters, *Nippur*, Vol. I, 4.
[17] Hilprecht, *Exploration in Bible Lands*, 297-298.
[18] *Ibid.*, 299.
[19] *Ibid.*
[20] Peters, *Nippur*, Vol. I, 7-8.
[21] Hilprecht, *Exploration in Bible Lands*. 300.

was born April 17, 1868. After earning an A.B. degree at Columbia in 1888, he went to the University of Berlin where he studied between 1888 and 1890. In 1892 he received the Ph.D. from Johns Hopkins.[22] On April 4, 1888, Provost Pepper requested that Hilprecht be allowed to accompany the expedition as a second Assyriologist. Hilprecht agreed to serve without pay, but Pepper and H. Clay Trumbull, editor of the *Sunday School Times*, paid his expenses.[23] Field and Harper were also serving without salary.

Expedition sponsors shipped the provisions for the field team early in the summer of 1888. Most of these went to Baghdad, with the exception of the tents, bridles, and saddles, which went to Alexandretta. Harper, Peters, and Prince sailed for London on June 23, arriving there the first week in July. There they were joined by Field. Some time was spent in London talking with Sayce and Rawlinson, getting valuable advice for the expedition. This advice included the best methods to excavate and how to handle an Arab work crew. A small portion of the funds was used to purchase Assyrian antiquities in London, which were shipped back to Philadelphia. By mid-October most of the members of the expedition had arrived in Alexandretta, with the exception of Peters, who had been in Constantinople since September 6. Due mainly to the efforts of Hamdy Bey, the director of the Imperial Mueseum in Constantinople, a permit to excavate at El-Birs and Nippur was issued to Peters on December 1. Peters joined the party at Alexandretta, and after a slow exploratory journey they arrived in Baghdad around noon on Tuesday, January 8, 1889.[24]

Prince had the misfortune of falling ill on the way to Baghdad, as Sterrett had on the Wolfe Expedition. He was much more unfortunate than Sterrett, however, in that he did not recover right away, and had to be sent back to the United States without really taking part in the expedition.[25] While in Baghdad the group purchased antiquities from the Arab dealers. Funds ran low and it became necessary for them to telegraph the Babylonian Exploration Fund for extra money to carry out these transactions. The executive committee obliged them by sending about $6,500 with which to do

---

[22] See above Chap. III.
[23] Hilprecht, *Exploration in Bible Lands*, 300-301.
[24] Peters, *Nippur*, Vol. I, 11-190.
[25] Hilprecht, *Exploration in Bible Lands*, 300.

the purchasing.²⁶ Before leaving Baghdad, the party made a quick sightseeing tour of the ruins of Ctesiphon.²⁷

Preparations were finally completed, and the party left Baghdad at 10:00 a.m. Wednesday, January 23. The government required an Ottoman official present on all excavating expeditions to see that all archeological objects were reported. On this expedition Bedry Bey was the Ottoman commissioner.²⁸ They reached the site of Babylon on Friday, where they spent a few hours poking through the ruins. On this journey Harper formed a very low opinion of the native muleteers. He states that they contract to carry your goods and equipment, and then about halfway to your destination they will threaten to dump your load upon the ground unless you pay them more money. The best way to deal with this situation, says Harper, "is to give the good for nothing fellow a good beating with a whip, and he will agree to the original price." ²⁹ The expedition reached Nippur about dark on Thursday, January 31.³⁰

The construction of a permanent camp began the following day. On Wednesday, February 6, 1889, the excavation officially began. For the digging they used an Arab labor force about two hundred strong.³¹ Peters and Hilprecht began to have problems immediately. Hilprecht felt that Peters did not carry out the excavation in a scientific manner but was more interested in finding objects that would quickly fill a museum.³² Hilprecht believed in excavating slowly and methodically in order to establish an archeological sequence. Another problem was finances. Peters quickly became aware that the $15,000 would not last much longer than about two months.³³ Despite these troubles the excavations continued, and by April more than 2,000 cuneiform documents had been uncovered.³⁴

These problems paled into insignificance, eclipsed by a new and more dangerous problem. The workers were creating this new problem by constantly pilfering from the camp. Then on the night of

---

[26] *Ibid.*, 301.
[27] Peters, *Nippur*, Vol. I, 197.
[28] Hilprecht, *Trans. Amer. Philosophical Soc.*, XVIII, n.s., Pt. 2 (1896), 222.
[29] Robert F. Harper, "The Expedition of the Babylonian Exploration Fund," *The Old and New Testament Student*, XIV (1892), 214.
[30] Peters, *Nippur*, Vol. I, 231.
[31] *Ibid.*, 234-235.
[32] Hilprecht, *Exploration in Bible Lands*, 308.
[33] *Ibid.*, 52.
[34] Hilprecht, *Recent Research in Bible Lands*, 52.

April 14 one of the Turkish sentries caught one stealing and shot him through the heart. This established a blood feud between the expedition and the family of the deceased, a practice not uncommon in the Near East. The family refused an offer of indemnity. It was decided that the party would have to leave secretly, and preparations were made to do so. As they were preparing to withdraw on the night of April 18, the workers set fire to the camp. About half of the horses perished in the flames, most of the firearms and $1,000 in gold fell into the hands of the brigands, but all the antiquities were saved. On the way to Baghdad Harper and Field handed in their resignations. Haynes remained in Baghdad as he had been appointed U.S. Consul to that city. Peters went back to Philadelphia, while Hilprecht remained in Constantinople to see about the U.S. getting a share of the antiquities brought back by the expedition.[35] Peters felt that the expedition was a failure; this is reflected in his statement, "Our first year in Nippur had ended in failure. I had failed to win the confidence of my comrades."[36]

Despite the fact that Peters felt the expedition had failed, there were others who did not. Pepper and E. W. Clark, the two most influential members of the Babylonian Exploration Fund, did not regard the situation in the same light as Peters. After all more than 2,000 cuneiform tablets and hundreds of other Assyriological objects had been recovered from Nippur.[37] These tablets would be deciphered later, giving a historical view of ancient Nippur.

Babylonian Expedition of 1890

In Constantinople Peters received a wire from the president of the Babylonian Exploration Fund asking him to resign. Peters felt that if he resigned this would mark the end of American exploration in the Near East; thus he refrained from doing so.[38] After arriving in New York on July 12, Peters went immediately to Philadelphia. There he found out that in Philadelphia the expedition was not considered a failure; in fact, the committee felt another party should be sent out very soon. This party was to be minus the scientific members, that is,

---

[35] Hilprecht, *Exploration in Bible Lands*, 316-318.
[36] Peters, *Nippur*, Vol. I, 288.
[37] Typewritten report by Peters on the first expedition, Archives, University Museum, University of Pennsylvania.
[38] Peters, *Nippur*, Vol. II, 4.

there were to be no Assyriologists nor architects, a fact much bemoaned by Hilprecht.[39] Peters, Haynes, and Noorian were the only members from the original party. Peters was to be director, assisted by Haynes; Noorian would have his old job of being interpreter and superintendent of the labor force.[40]

Peters arrived in Constantinople on August 21, 1889. Hamdy Bey was out of the city at the time but returned on the twenty-fifth and started the process of obtaining a new permit for the expedition. Finally, in October a new permit to excavate was granted by the Ottoman government to Peters, who then left for Baghdad on October 10.[41] He landed at Beirut on October 20, spent several days there, and went on to Damascus, arriving there November 7. Peters spent a week and a half in Damascus and then began a slow exploring journey on to Baghdad. He arrived in Baghdad on December 16, where he met Haynes and Noorian. The Ottoman commissioner assigned to the expedition was Mohammed Salih Effendi.[42]

The party left Baghdad on January 1, 1890, fearful of the problems awaiting them at Nippur. As it turned out, their fears were ungrounded. Back in May of 1889 a cholera epidemic had broken out all over Mesopotamia. The Arabs at Nippur thought that Allah had brought this down on them as punishment for having plundered and burned the camp of the earlier expedition.[43] Peters found out of this belief and decided to capitalize on their fear. The family of the dead man (the worker shot by one of the guards on the first expedition) stated that they would terminate the blood feud upon payment of ten Turkish liras ($ 44). Peters felt this would show a sign of weakness, and refused to do so. Shortly after their arrival at Nippur, Peters set up a fireworks display on a hilltop, then while Haynes entertained the natives with stories around the campfire, he and Noorian touched off the display. After this the natives were convinced that Peters and the other party members possessed magical powers[44] Members of the party hoped that this display of magic would keep the workers in line.

---

[39] Hilprecht, *Exploration in Bible Lands*, 320-321.
[40] Hilprecht, *Trans. Amer. Phil. Soc.*, XVIII, n.s., Pt. 2 (1896), 221-222.
[41] Peters, *Nippur*, Vol. II, 7.
[42] *Ibid.*, 49.
[43] Hilprecht, *Exploration in Bible Lands*, 324.
[44] Peters, *Nippur*, Vol II, 68-69.

Excavation began on January 14, 1890, with an Arab work force of about four hundred men.[45] Peters commenced by digging a series of trial trenches. He then assigned part of the labor force to uncovering the rooms in the southeast corner of a ziggurat they had discovered. Ziggurats were large terraced towers built by the Sumerians, and usually had shrines at the top for religious services. They were copied by the Akkadians and other Semites in Mesopotamia. The remainder of the work force then proceeded to excavate a large shrine or temple.[46] Peters was very satisfied with the operations but had fears about winding up the season, remembering what had happened previously. As a precautionary measure he sent a boatload of antiquities to Baghdad during the last week of April. The expedition came to an official end on May 3. On the evening of this day the workers were emboldened enough to plan an attack on the camp after dark. Peters discovered the plan in time to set off another fireworks display and stopped the attack. Just to be on the safe side, however, the party broke camp and quietly slipped away on this night of the 3rd, and reached Baghdad June 7. This expedition ended much more peacefully than had the first one.[47]

Peters reached Constantinople the last week of September. After settling affairs with the Ottoman government, he left the Imperial City on October 13, arriving in New York the first week of November.[48] This second expedition had uncovered about 8,000 cuneiform tablets from the Akkadian, Babylonian, and Kassite periods (ca. 2350-1150 B.C.), plus thousands of tools, weapons, vases, and miscellaneous objects.[49]

The Third Expedition, 1893-96

After returning home, Peters made every effort to have the Babylonian Exploration Fund send out a third expedition, citing as reason the finding of so many cuneiform tablets and other artifacts. He no longer wanted to devote his time to the excavations but

---

[45] Hilprecht, *Trans. Amer. Phil. Soc.*, XVIII, n.s., Pt. 2 (1896), 222.
[46] *Ibid.*
[47] Hilprecht, *Exploration in Bible Lands*, 345.
[48] Peters, *Nippur*, Vol. II, 364.
[49] Series of letters (typed) from Noorian to the Babylonian Exploration Fund describing the objects recovered, dated between January 6, 1890, and April 27, 1890, Archives, University Museum, University of Pennsylvania.

nominated Haynes as his successor.[50] At the urging of Hamdy Bey the Ottoman government had presented many more antiquities to the University of Pennsylvania than they had after the first expedition. This new and liberal attitude on the part of the government in Constantinople seemed to indicate that a third expedition could be very profitable, archeologically. In the spring of 1892 Provost Pepper held a meeting at his home. Pepper, E. W. Clark, Haynes, and Peters attended.[51] Not only did they plan a new expedition, but they decided that the results of the first two expeditions should be published as soon as possible.

Hilprecht was named editor-in-chief of the new series, to be called *The Babylonian Expedition of the University of Pennsylvania*. Series A would consist of the copied cuneiform texts. Art and archeology would comprise Series B. Transliterations and translations would make up Series C, while D would be concerned with researches and treatises. In connection with his new duties, Hilprecht went to Constantinople to look at the Nippur material in the summer of 1893. While there he organized the Babylonian section of the Imperial Museum. For this helpful work the Ottoman government showed its appreciation by giving more of the antiquities to the University of Pennsylvania.[52] It also smoothed the path for obtaining future excavation permits.

Those at the meeting decided that Haynes should conduct excavations, but to cut down on expenses he would work by himself. On August 28, 1892, Haynes left New York for Europe. After a few weeks of studying some of the cuneiform collections of Europe, he went on to the Near East, arriving at Alexandretta in January of 1893.[53] Haynes started immediately for the interior, and then travelled down the Euphrates to Nippur, arriving there on the 20th day of March.[54]

Haynes decided to construct a large house to live in, instead of using tents as the first two expeditions had. He built it of mud, without windows, and it served both as a dwelling and a storehouse.

---

[50] Peters, *Nippur*, Vol. II, 370.
[51] Hilprecht, *Exploration in Bible Lands*, 346-347.
[52] *Ibid.*, 347-348.
[53] *Ibid.*, 348.
[54] Unless otherwise noted events of the expedition were taken from letters of Haynes sent to Peters and Clark, Folder Box 237, 238, and 239, dated between June 3, 1893, and March 12, 1896; and Stack 229 which contains a typewritten report by Haynes, covering the third expedition, dated February 1908; Archives, University Museum, University of Pennsylvania.

This building was completed during the second week in April. On April 11, 1893, Haynes officially began excavation. Since he was alone, he had a much smaller labor force, keeping the number between fifty and sixty. Haynes set as his objective the systematic excavation of the area in the vicinity of the temple and the ziggurat down to the bedrock. By April of 1894 he had uncovered the ziggurat and excavated three sections of the temple down to the water level. On April 4, 1894, Haynes ceased operations temporarily and took the antiquities he had uncovered to Baghdad.

Haynes had been working alone in a different type of cultural environment for almost a year, and it began to tell on him We have only to read his letters and reports to realize that Haynes was in an anxious frame of mind. He felt that the workers were constantly plotting, not only to plunder the supplies, but to murder him. While in Baghdad Haynes met Joseph A. Meyer, a young architecture student from Massachusetts Institute of Technology, travelling in the Near East on a two-year grant. Haynes talked Meyer into going back to Nippur with him for one year to serve as architect. They arrived at Nippur on the 4th day of June.

At the site once again Haynes' spirits picked up considerably, and his reports became much more scientific in manner. The other contribution of Meyer was his architectural drawings of the temple and ziggurat that were sent back to Philadelphia along with the reports. Work continued unceasingly until late summer when Meyer fell sick of dysentery. Not only was Meyer lost, but Haynes spent a great deal of time nursing him. Toward the end of November his condition became so serious that he had to be taken by litter to Baghdad. There he remained critically ill at the home of the U.S. Consul until December 20th when he died.

Haynes was back at Nippur by the first of the year 1895 in rather dejected spirits. Once again his reports are full of fears of numerous dangers. In March he wrote the committee, asking them to relieve him. Shortly after this an Englishman visited the area and stayed awhile. This perked up the spirits of Haynes, so that he decided to remain at Nippur. Clark and Hilprecht felt that the expedition should have an architect, so they prevailed upon two young travelling Englishmen to go to Nippur and aid Haynes. They had helped Petrie in Egypt; thus, they had some experience in archeological excavation. Unfortunately, they did not arrive at Nippur until February of the next year, at which time Haynes was planning to depart. They wanted to stay and excavate, but Haynes induced them to leave with him; he felt they were too inexperienced. The third expedition officially ended on February 15, 1896.

Looking at the material side of the ledger there should be little doubt that the expedition was successful. Hundreds of vases, fragments of pottery, parts of statues, inscribed bricks, and hundreds of miscellaneous objects were uncovered. Add to this about 21,000 cuneiform tablets and most would agree that this third expedition could not be classed a failure.

The 1899-1900 Expedition

Three expeditions to Nippur had convinced the members of the Babylonian Exploration Fund that the site was very rich archeologically and had by no means been exhausted of its archeological treasures. There were many more artifacts to fill museums and tablets to tell the history of the city of Nippur. Up to this point the Fund had been working in affiliation with the University of Pennsylvania, and not controlled by it. In the 1890's, mainly through private subscription, the University had begun to build a museum. The University trustees appointed in 1891 a board of managers to administer the affairs of the new museum. This board was to consist of thirty-six members, twelve appointed by the University, and the other twenty-four by the University Archaeological Association, a group of private citizens.[55] In 1892 construction had begun on the museum, aided in 1895 by an appropriation of the Pennsylvania Legislature of $150,000, to be matched by private funds. Direct control of the expeditions was slowly passing under the tutelage of the University of Pennsylvania.

Although the Babylonian Exploration Fund ceased to exist in 1897, its members were all on the new board of managers for the museum and determined to continue their work. Early in 1898 the Museum board decided that a fourth expedition would be fruitful. They also decided that the new expedition would be carried out in more of a scientific manner than the previous ones. Hilprecht was appointed Scientific Director, Haynes was named Field Director, Mrs. Haynes was to be the secretary, and Clarence S. Fisher (without salary) of the University of Pennsylvania and a young Englishman by the name of H. Valentine Geere were to serve as architects. Hilprecht

---

[55] Madeira, *Men in Search of Man*, 22-23.

left for Constantinople in May to get things organized. All the details were worked out and agreed on by September 22, 1898. The expedition was to be for a period of two years, including travel time, at an expense of $30,000, and have an average work force of 180 Arabs.[56]

Haynes left New York on September 24, followed shortly by the others. Hilprecht had accomplished his mission in Constantinople; the sultan had granted the expedition a permit to excavate. He then returned to Philadelphia to organize the Babylonian portion of the University Museum before joining the others at Nippur later. Haynes, Fisher, and Geere arrived in Baghdad on the 18th day of December. Geere fell violently ill of dysentery, pneumonia, typhoid fever, and boils. Geere's recovery was so slow that Fisher remained with him in Baghdad while Haynes and his wife went on to Nippur, arriving there February 4, 1899.[57]

The Arabs welcomed Haynes happily upon his arrival. Three of them had appointed themselves guardians, watching over the property until Haynes returned. Haynes immediately set to work cleaning out a well he had dug on the third expedition.[58] With this task completed, he officially opened excavations on the 6th day of February with a work force of 150 Arabs. Later on in the spring Geere had recovered sufficiently to allow Fisher to go on to Nippur. No sooner had Fisher arrived at the excavation site than he and Haynes began to disagree over methods of excavation. Fisher resigned and returned to England. Some of the Museum board members went to England and talked Fisher into returning to Nippur. He arrived back at Nippur with Geere whom he had picked up in Baghdad on October 20. During the time Fisher had been away, Haynes had continued to excavate with a force that varied between 150 and 208 workmen.

In Philadelphia Hilprecht had finished organizing the Babylonian section of the museum by the middle of November and left the States before the end of the month. Due to storms in the Atlantic, and so many of the Near Eastern ports closed because of the plague, he did not arrive at Nippur untill March 1, 1900. After a discussion

---

[56] Hilprecht, *Exploration in Bible Lands*, 427-428.

[57] *Ibid.*, 429-432.

[58] Unless otherwise noted the events of this expedition are taken from reports, field notebooks, and letters from Haynes, Hilprecht, Fisher, and Geere to Clark and other University Museum officials, dated between February 6, 1899, and July 24, 1901, Archives, University Museum, University of Pennsylvania.

with Haynes, Hilprecht decided not only to look for tablets but to examine the architecture in detail. This, of course, made Geere and Fisher very happy. During April Hilprecht, Haynes, and Geere made a brief tour of the nearby sites of Abu Hatab and Fara. They noted that both sites would be ideal for future excavation. On May 11, 1900, the fourth Nippur expedition came to an end.

Results

The four expeditions to Nippur by the University of Pennsylvania marked the beginning of U.S. field archeology in Mesopotamia. With the possible exception of the last expedition these attempts could not be classified as scientific excavation. Peters and Haynes were digging at Nippur in order to obtain archeological treasures to fill a museum. They utterly disregarded any suggestions to establish sequences or cultural levels. Hilprecht felt that the scientific way should be employed, but his voice went unheeded The sponsors back home wanted quick results, and tangible evidence of how well their money had been spent. American archeology in Mesopotamia was still in the "looting" stage; the age of the professional archeologist had not yet arrived.

On the credit side, however, much good did come as a result of these expeditions. Not only was the University Museum of the University of Pennsylvania enriched with an archeological collection, but more than 30,000 cuneiform tablets were recovered. These tablets described the business, cultural, and intellectual history of the city of Nippur.

Two of the more important monuments uncovered at Nippur were the large Ekur temple and the ziggurat. The ziggurat was constructed in pre-Sargonid times (i.e. prior to 2334 B.C.), and Fisher's accurate drawings give the first detailed architectural study of one of these terraced towers. Excavation of the large temple reveals that it was dedicated to the god Enlil and was also pre-Sargonid in age. In Sumerian times the temple was not only the religious center but served as the administrative center, as well. It was this temple that contained a large library, holding many business, legal, and literary cuneiform documents.[59]

Besides the temple and ziggurat, other buildings at Nippur contributed to the knowledge of Sumerian architecture. These people gave the arch, vault, and dome to the architectural world.

---

[59] For the library controversy see below Chap. V.

CHAPTER FIVE

ASSYRIOLOGY COMES OF AGE

After 1880 Assyriology developed rapidly in the United States. Not only were Akkadian, Sumerian, Persian, and history and art courses of the area offered at the institutions of higher learning, but the University of Pennsylvania had sent out four expeditions to Mesopotamia. Literature kept pace with this expansion, and after 1880 the number of scholarly books and articles increased greatly. By 1900 the United States was ready to broaden its studies in the field of Assyriology, and it did just this during the next fourteen years. In this period from 1900 to 1914 Robert F. Harper of the University of Chicago became a prominent figure in Assyriology.

Robert F. Harper and the Assyrian Letters

Robert Francis Harper was born October 18, 1864, at New Concord, Ohio. He attended two Ohio schools, Denison College from 1876 to 1878, and Muskingum College between 1879 and 1880.[1] He earned his A.B. degree at the (Old) University of Chicago in 1883. At the age of sixteen young Harper had become interested in Hebrew due to the influence of his famous brother William Rainey Harper. From 1881 through 1883 he assisted his brother with the Hebrew Summer Schools. Then in the spring of 1884 Harper went to the University of Berlin where he studied Assyrian under Eberhard Schrader. In October of the same year he went to the University of Leipzig to study Ethiopic and Arabic. While there, however, he fell under the influence of Friedrich Delitzsch and began devoting most of his talent toward Assyriology. In 1886 he graduated with the Ph.D. degree.

Harper came to Yale in 1886 as an Instructor of Semitic Languages, teaching courses in Hebrew. Then in 1888-89 he took leave to accompany the University of Pennsylvania expedition to Nippur.[2] After returning to the United States in 1889, he resumed

---

[1] Biographical information on Harper taken from *W. W. in Amer.*, VIII, 1914-15, 1035; and "Robert Francis Harper, 1864-1914," *AJSL*, XXXI (1914-15), 89-92.

[2] See above Chap. IV.

his duties at Yale, where he remained until 1891. Harper spent a year at the British Museum in 1891-92. While there he began and completed the monumental task of copying the Assyrian and Babylonian letters found in the Kouyunjik Collections at the museum. This project was an asset to Assyriologists the world over, as Harper began to publish these letters in 1892. He finished the job just before his death in 1914, and it consisted of fourteen volumes, containing 1,471 hand-copied letters.[3] This work aided scholars who could not visit the British Museum. Later writers have praised the accuracy of these letters. In 1892 Harper returned to the United States, accepting the position of Associate Professor of Semitic Languages and Literature at the brand new University of Chicago.[4]

At the University of Chicago Harper continued his work on the letters from the British Museum, in addition to the heavy teaching load he was carrying. Funds for books and exploration were not easy to come by in those days, and led to an intense rivalry between Harper and James Henry Breasted (1865-1935), the budding Egyptologist at Chicago, for any funds that were available. From this rivalry a feud developed between Harper and Breasted, despite the fact that Breasted and Harper's brother William, the president of the university, remained the best of friends.[5] Still Chicago was rapidly advancing in the ranks of Egyptology and Assyriology, feud notwithstanding. In 1900 Robert Harper was promoted to the rank of Professor. Along with this promotion went the job of Curator of the Babylonian section of the new Haskell Oriental Museum. Mrs. Caroline E. Haskell had contributed $100,000 for the building of a museum. The cornerstone for the building had been laid on July 1, 1895, and the building was completed July 2, 1896.[6] By 1900 museum officials had created an Egyptian and a Babylonian section.

Prior to 1900 Harper published over twenty Assyriological articles, consisting mostly of descriptive accounts of phases of the University of Pennsylvania expeditions to Nippur. After 1900 he began to write longer works, more scholarly in nature. In 1901 Harper published *Assyrian and Babylonian Literature, Selected Translations*, which gave

---

[3] *Assyrian and Babylonian Letters Belonging to the Kouyunjik Collections of the British Museum* (14 vols.; Chicago: Univ. Chicago Press, 1892-1914).

[4] See above Chap. III.

[5] For more of this feud see Charles Breasted, *Pioneer to the Past* (New York: Chas. Scribner's Sons, 1943), 132.

[6] Thomas W. Goodspeed, *The Story of the University of Chicago 1890-1925* (Chicago: Univ. Chicago Press, 1925), 128.

the public a fairly good cross-section of Mesopotamian literature.[7] These were Harper's translations and were of a very scholarly nature. He published his version of the law code of Hammurabi in 1903-04.[8] In the latter part of 1904 the University of Chicago issued the second edition of this work.[9] This publication consisted of 102 plates of autographed texts, transliteration, translation, glossary, and index; one of the best renditions of the Hammurabi code to that date. Despite a heavy schedule of translating and publishing, teaching, and museum work, Harper found time to serve as director of the Oriental Exploration Fund to Babylonia from 1903-06, the expedition to Adab. He took time off at Chicago to serve as Director of American Schools for Oriental Study and Research in Palestine in 1908-09. Harper had other projects planned, but death cut short his career on August 5, 1914. Robert Francis Harper, with help from others, had put Chicago on the Assyriological map. The University of Chicago was also broadening its scope of studies by sending an expedition into the field.

The Expedition to Adab

Chicago's expedition went into the Near East in late 1903. This party excavated at the ancient Babylonian city of Adab, called Bismya by the natives of the area. The director of this expedition was Edgar James Banks (1866-1945). Banks, a native of Massachusetts, was born May 23, 1866.[10] He attended Amherst College the 1886-87 school year. Banks transferred to Harvard where he earned the A.B. in 1893, and the A.M. in 1895. While at Harvard he took all the Semitic language and history courses they had to offer. Like other American scholars, Banks went to Germany to further his education, and in 1897 received his Ph.D. from the University of Breslau.

Edgar Banks had held the desire to excavate in the Near East since early boyhood. He was forced to wait long years before this wish came true, but eventually his dreams materialized into fact. In order to get to the vicinity of Babylon, Banks wrote President McKinley,

---

[7] (New York: D. Appleton & Co., 1901).

[8] "Text of the Code of Hammurabi, King of Babylon," *AJSL*, XX (1903-04), 1-84.

[9] *The Code of Hammurabi, King of Babylon* (2nd ed.; Chicago: Univ. Chicago Press, 1904).

[10] Biographical information on Banks taken from an obituary notice in the *New York Times*, May 9, 1945, 23; and a personal interview with John A. Wilson of the University of Chicago, June 19, 1967.

applying for the post of American consul at Baghdad. Late in 1897, to his surprise and elation he received the appointment. It was the following year, however, before he reached the area, due to the slowness of the Ottoman government in granting final approval. In late summer of 1898 Banks reached Baghdad, more anxious to excavate than to perform his duties as U.S. consul. Much to his chagrin he learned that foreign government officials could not engage in excavation. Banks did manage to explore much of the area of southern Babylonia and bought a few Babylonian antiquities in Baghdad. During his travels he selected a site that he thought was the ancient city of Ur of the Sumerians. In the late spring of 1899 Banks resigned from his post and went to New York, hoping to raise funds to return and excavate at Mugheir, near the site of Ur.

In New York in the summer of 1899 Banks succeeded in arousing interest in his proposed expedition. A committee to plan the expedition to Ur was organized, including such personalities as William R. Harper, John P. Peters, and William H. Ward, to name only three. An application to excavate was sent to Constantinople in July. On December 3 Banks was appointed director of the expedition; $6,000 had been raised, and another $6,000 had been pledged. Banks left for London and Paris on the 24th to study the Assyrian and Babylonian collections at the British Museum and the Louvre. He arrived in Constantinople on January 15, 1900. Here he was to experience more of the slowness of the imperial government at acting on applications to excavate. Ten months later Banks received word that the application had been rejected; the reason given, the Arabs in the area of Mugheir were in revolt.[11]

Disheartened, but still determined, Banks remained in the Near East and applied for a permit to excavate at a new site. He chose as the new location the area of Birs Nimrud (Borsippa), and in the fall of 1901 applied for a permit to excavate there. He had only to wait two weeks for a refusal this time, as he was notified on October 31 that Robert Koldewey and the Germans had an option on this area.[12] Banks next applied for permission on November 1 to excavate at Tell Ibrahim but was turned down on this also; the reason given, there were numerous tombs of Abraham in the area that must not be defiled. In mid-1902 Banks received word that the activities of the

---

[11] Edgar J. Banks, *Bismya or the Lost City of Adab* (New York: G. P. Putnam's Sons, 1912), 2-14.
[12] *Ibid.*, 16.

New York committee had been temporarily suspended due to the death of one of the members. In order to meet living expenses, Banks took a job as Acting Professor of Ancient History at Roberts College, the American School, in Constantinople for the school year of 1902-03. In July 1903 he was notified that the committee had been disbanded.[13] Still hoping to salvage something, Banks remained in Constantinople, taking the job of secretary to the American minister to the Ottoman government; his appointment at Roberts College had been for only a year.

Meanwhile, President Harper of the University of Chicago had begun thinking in terms of sending an expedition to Mesopotamia, with the backing of the university. He was aware of excavations being conducted by the French, English, and Germans in Mesopotamia, and felt that if Chicago was going to obtain a relatively unexplored site, they had better act promptly. Harper presented this idea to John Davison Rockefeller, the school's great benefactor. Rockefeller liked the idea and donated $100,000 for this purpose. With these funds the Oriental Fund of the University of Chicago was created. As was seen earlier, Robert Francis Harper was made director of the Babylonian section of this fund. President Harper's next step was to go to Constantinople to discuss with Banks the possibility of excavating in Mesopotamia. He and Banks had worked for the same goal on the New York Committee. In September of 1903 an application was made to excavate at Bismya (Adab) by President Harper. There was trouble at the American Consulate in Beirut at about this time; an embassy official had been murdered, so an American fleet was dispatched to the area. The appearance of the fleet spurred the Ottoman government into acting quickly, and on October 3, 1903, the permit to excavate at Adab was granted.[14] *Realpolitiks* had accomplished what scholarly persistence had failed to do.

Haidar Bey, from the staff of the Imperial Museum, was appointed Ottoman commissioner for the expedition. On the morning of Saturday, October 23, Banks left for Beirut, remarking, "Nearly three years after I came to Constantinople, I left the city with the *irade* which I expected to obtain in two weeks."[15] Haidar and Banks reached Beirut on the 27th, and set out the following day overland by

---
[13] *Ibid.*, 17.
[14] *Ibid.*, 28.
[15] *Ibid.*, 33.

way of Damascus, arriving in Baghdad on November 30. The trip had been a weary one, as they had been forced to spend eight days in quarantine along the way, because of an outbreak of the plague. After making the necessary preparations, the party left Baghdad at 1:30 a.m. Saturday, December 12. The ruins at Adab were reached on the evening of the 18th.[16]

After the digging of two wells to assure a plentiful supply of water, Banks officially began excavation on Christmas Day with an Arab labor force of about 140 men. The crew immediately struck the remains of a tower and a large palace, which became the major projects at hand. While excavations were proceeding, Banks had some of the men build a large mud house to live in and in which to store antiquities. By the middle of January of 1904 they had found over 300 inscribed tablets which Banks identified as coming from the late Babylonian period (ca. 1600-910 B.C.). On the 26th the workers found a life-sized statue of a Babylonian king, which Banks claimed was the oldest statue in the world. In the weeks following they found more statues, some of them inscribed and some not.

Banks' wife decided to visit him and to bring an architect to aid the expedition. She telegraphed on March 13 saying that she and the architect, Jason Paige, were on their way to Baghdad. Five days later Banks met them at Kut-al-Amara and escorted them back to Adab. Paige built a photography lab, and from this time on, all of Banks' reports to Robert F. Harper were complete with architectural plans and photographs.[17] By the first of May the expedition laid bare more than thirty chambers in the palace and had uncovered more than 3,000 trade and political tablets, over 500 of which were in perfect condition.

Due to the unhealthy climate in the Tigris-Euphrates valley in the summertime, Banks brought the first season to an end on May 27, 1904, and spent the summer months in Baghdad. During this vacation he bought antiquities from the Arab dealers and visited ruins in the vicinity of the city. Early in September Mrs. Banks left for Europe, and on the 11th Banks set out for Adab. He reached camp on the 18th to find that two of his watchmen had broken into the building and made off with some of the supplies. Banks reopened

---

[16] Unless otherwise noted the developments of the expedition will be taken from E. J. Banks, *The Expediton of the Oriental Exploration Fund (Babylonian Section) of the University of Chicago, Reports 1-6* (Chicago: Univ. Chicago Press, 1904).

[17] Ibid., 13-44.

excavation on the following day. On September 27 an Ottoman military officer came to investigate the robbery, telling Banks that for the time being excavations would have to cease. Next day Banks left for Baghdad. Knowing the slowness of the Ottoman government he expected a long investigation, and hence seized the opportunity to take a leisurely sight-seeing journey back to the city, arriving there on Christmas Day. During the investigation the Ottoman government began to suspect that Banks was shipping antiquities out of the country without declaring them, but he denied these allegations. Shortly after Christmas he was given permission to continue the excavations, but by this time his health was failing, so he decided to abandon the expedition.

In the spring of 1905 Banks returned to the States, where he spent a year at Chicago cataloguing the materials he had brought back from Adab. In the summer of 1906 the expedition was officially abandoned by the University of Chicago because of ill feelings on the part of the Ottoman government.

The excavations at Adab revealed that the community had existed as early as 5000 B.C. or earlier. There was already a city on the site when the Sumerians assumed hegemony of the area in the fourth millenium B.C. We are at a loss when it comes to explaining who the builders were; it was the work of the Ubaids or some other pre-Sumerian ethnic group. At any rate the city was prosperous during the Sumerian period. Under the rule of Sargon of Akkad it seems the temples were sacked by the Akkadians. Adab was still inhabited during the Babylonian period, for Hammurabi boasts that he was the builder of the city. This we know is not true, but the great Babylonian king probably rebuilt large portions of the city. After the Assyrian conquest of Babylonia, Adab was gradually abandoned, and shortly after the Chaldean period had opened drifting sand covered the streets, it was on its way to becoming a forgotten city.

Banks went on to become a professor of Oriental languages and archeology at Toledo University in 1909, a position he held until 1921. He did not stay at Chicago because some of the faculty members felt that Banks had smuggled antiquities out of Mesopotamia. Like the University of Pennsylvania, the University of Chicago had now ventured into the field of Assyriological excavation. On the east coast another school was preparing to make its debut into this new and expanding area of American Assyriology.

Yale Joins the Ranks

At the turn of the century the administration at Yale felt the time had come to hire a faculty member with Assyriological training. Their choice was Charles Cutler Torrey (1863-1956), born December 20, 1863, at East Hardwick, Vermont. After receiving an A.B. degree from Bowdoin College in 1884, and graduating from Andover Theological Seminary in 1889, Torrey went to Germany for further training, winning his Ph.D. from the University of Strassburg in 1892.[18] Although Torrey studied and could read Akkadian, he was much more interested in Arabic. Torrey returned to the United States in 1892, taking the position of instructor and later professor of Semitic languages at Andover Theological Seminary. Then in 1900 Yale hired him as Professor of Semitic Languages in the Division of Language and Literature.[19] As Torrey had been appointed first director of the new American Schools of Archeology at Jerusalem, Yale gave him a year's leave of absence to fulfill these duties. Then in the fall of 1901 he returned to Yale and organized a two hour course called Elementary Assyrian.[20]

Cuneiform studies at Yale received a shot in the arm in 1910 when Albert Tobias Clay (1866-1925) was appointed Laffan Professor of Assyriology (a new chair) for the 1910-11 academic year.[21] Clay, a native of Hanover, Pennsylvania, was born December 4, 1866.[22] He took his A.B. degree at Franklin and Marshall College in 1889, then went on to graduate from Lutheran Theological Seminary, Mt. Airy, Pennsylvania in 1892. Next, Clay enrolled at the University of Pennsylvania, where he earned his Ph.D. in Assyriology under Hilprecht in 1894. After teaching several years at Lutheran Theological Seminary in Chicago, Clay returned to the University of Pennsylvania in 1899 as a Lecturer of Assyriology. In 1909 he was

---

[18] Biographical information on Torrey taken from Millar Burrows, "A Sketch of C. C. Torrey's Career," *BASOR*, No. 132 (1953), 6-8.

[19] *Report of the President of Yale University and of the Dean and Directors of its Several Departments for the Academic Year 1899-1900* (New Haven, Conn.: Yale Univ. Press, 1900), 28.

[20] *Catalogue of Yale University, 1901-02* (New Haven, Conn.: Yale Univ. Press, 1901), 91.

[21] *Yale Univ. President's Report for 1909-10*, 22.

[22] Biographical information on Clay obtained from "Proceedings for December, 1925," *Journal Soc. Biblical Literature*, XLV (1926), vii-viii; and a memoriam sketch by C. C. Torrey, *BASOR*, No. 19 (1925), 1-2.

promoted to Professor of Semitic Languages and Literature but left the next year to fill the position at Yale.

As Assyriology was not Torrey's first love, he left it up to Clay to develop the program, devoting himself, henceforth, to Arabic, Syriac, and Aramaic. By the 1911-12 school year Clay was offering nine courses in Assyriology at the graduate level.[23] He continued the elementary Akkadian course started by Torrey, and added seven courses dealing with the translation of business and legal documents and letters from the Akkadian and Sumerian cuneiform. To the above, Clay also added a course in Sumerian grammar. In 1912 Clay turned out his first Ph.D. in Assyriology; this was Clarence Elwood Keiser.[24] Yale was late getting started, but by 1914 she had made a great step forward in the field of Assyriology.

Peters-Hilprecht Controversy

Shortly after Yale had begun to make her bid for a place in the scholarly circles of Assyriology, the feud that had been smoldering between Hilprecht and Peters finally came into the open, referred to by many scholars as the *Peters-Hilprecht Controversy*. It was no secret to members of the first Nippur Expedition that there were ill feelings between H. V. Hilprecht and John P. Peters.[25] After the turn of the century the feud expanded, bringing others into the picture, as well. Peters accused Hilprecht of taking credit for discoveries made by others, while Hilprecht charged Peters with incompetency as an Assyriologist. Peters had a large following in the scholarly world, and as a result of various articles in newspapers questioning Hilprecht's abilities as a scholar, at least nine persons associated with the University Museum at the University of Pennsylvania resigned their positions on various boards and committees early in the year 1905.[26] On January 24, 1905, Hilprecht asked Provost Harrison of the University of Pennsylvania to make a full investigation of the matter in order to clear his name.

On March 27 the Board of Trustees of the university initiated the investigation and appointed a committee to act as a Court of

---

[23] *Bulletin of Yale University, Catalogue for 1911-12*, 374-375.
[24] Personal correspondence with Ferris J. Stephens, Yale University, June 20, 1967.
[25] See above Chap. IV.
[26] *Annual Report of the Provost, From September 1, 1904 to September 1, 1905* (Philadelphia: Univ. Penn. Press., 1906), 152-153.

Inquiry.[27] This committee was composed of Charles C. Harrison, Provost; Edgar F. Smith, Vice-Provost; and Joseph S. Harris, J. Levering Jones, Samuel F. Houston, and Robert G. Le Conte, members of the Board of Trustees.[28] On March 29 they sent out the following letter:

> Dear Sir (or Madam):
> The Trustees of the University of Pennsylvania have appointed a Committee, consisting of the Provost, Vice-Provost, and four Trustees, to hear statements which you may desire to make concerning the integrity of Dr. Herman V. Hilprecht, the Clark Research Professor of Assyriology.
> If you desire to make a statement, or any charges, please inform me of the fact, and I will send you word as to the time and place of the meeting.
>
>   Very respectfully yours,
> (Signed)   Charles C. Harrison, Provost [29]

Copies of this letter were sent to various Assyriologists and museum board members, such as Mrs. Cornelius Stevenson, Mrs. S. T. Bodine, Dr. Hermann Ranke, Dr. Morris Jastrow, Jr., Dr. William H. Furness III, Dr. A. T. Clay, Mr. Clarence S. Fisher, Mr. Calvin Wells, and Dr. Paul Haupt.[30]

On March 30 at 2:00 p.m. the committee held its second meeting. At this meeting Provost Harrison explained to the board why it was necessary to conduct the inquiry. He stated that an article by Dr. Peters in the *Philadelphia Press* of Sunday, March 19, has brought matters to a head. In this article Peters made charges that questioned the character and integrity of a professor (Hilprecht) at the University of Pennsylvania. On recommendation of the committee Provost Harrison sent out another letter on March 30, stating:

> Dear Sir (or Madam):
> I do not wish to intrude duly in the matter of the Peters-Hilprecht controversy, but, referring to my letter to you of yesterday, I have been to-day instructed to say that charges, in writing, will be received addressed to the Provost, at No. 400 Chestnut Street, until and including Monday, April 3, 1905.

---

[27] H. V. Hilprecht (comp.), *The So-Called Peters-Hilprecht Controversy* (Philadelphia: A. J. Holman, 1908), 3.
[28] *Ibid.*, 33.
[29] *Ibid.*, 7-8.
[30] *Ibid.*, 8.

Copies of these charges will be handed to Dr. H. V. Hilprecht.

When Dr. Hilprecht shall have informed the Provost that he is ready to make his reply, a session of the Committee will be called, and all those who have made charges in writing, will be invited to be present.

Very respectfully yours,
(Signed) Charles C. Harrison, Provost [31]

Copies of this letter went to the same persons as the previous letter.

During the first two weeks of April the committee received charges and statements for and against Hilprecht from those who wished to put them in writing. Then at 11:00 a.m., April 15, the Board of Inquiry held a meeting in Philadelphia in the Real Estate Trust Building. Those present at this meeting, besides the committee, were Hilprecht, Peters, John D. Prince, Robert Lau, and Hermann Ranke, all Assyriologists. Peters repeated the charges against Hilprecht that he had made in writing. He stated that he suspected Hilprecht of fraudulent scholarship.[32] After examination of statements and listening to oral testimony, the committee divided the charges against Hilprecht into three categories: (1) literary dishonesty, (2) improperly retaining property that belonged to the University of Pennsylvania, and (3) referring to the tablets found at Nippur as coming from a temple library.[33]

Charge one, literary dishonesty, stemmed mainly from Hilprecht's book, *Exploration in Bible Lands*, where his accusers stated that Hilprecht conveyed the impression that all the tablets brought back by the Nippur expeditions came from the fourth expedition, of which Hilprecht was the scientific director.[34] Jastrow told the committee that Delitzsch and other German scholars had questioned Hilprecht on this point.[35]

The second charge, improper possession of material belonging to the University of Pennsylvania, was more nebulous. Numerous antiquities, mainly tablets, were given to Hilprecht by the Ottoman government. He, of course, was honor bound to turn them over to the sponsoring organization, which he did. Hilprecht managed to show that the objects in his private collection were bought and paid for by him.[36]

---

[31] *Ibid.*, 8-10.
[32] *Ibid.*, 47-90.
[33] *Ibid.*, 267.
[34] *Ibid.*, 268.
[35] *Ibid.*, 114.
[36] *Ibid.*, 265-266.

Charge three, statement by Hilprecht that there was a temple library at Nippur, turned out to be a case of petty bickering among scholars. Most of the American Assyriologists, including Jastrow, felt that there was a temple library at Nippur.[37] Point in question seems to have been the definition of the term library.

Further meethings were held in which Hilprecht and his accusers continued to give testimony, and were cross-examined by members of the committee. The meetings took place on April 19, 22, 27, and 29th. In all, seven sessions were held to hear testimony, which was recorded by a stenographer, covering almost 600 pages.[38] Principal accusers of Hilprecht were John P. Peters and Morris Jastrow, Jr., Jastrow being a colleague of Hilprecht's at the University of Pennsylvania. On June 26, 1905, the Court of Inquiry made its report to the Trustees of the University of Pennsylvania, saying:

> And upon the charges against Dr. Hilprecht as a whole, your Committee find that they are unsustained and untrue.
>
> Your Committee in thus briefly summarizing the mass of testimony before them have found it necessary to confine themselves to the essential points at issue, and upon these they have reached and expressed very positive conclusions, and they ask the Board of Trustees to confirm their findings.
>
> Your Committee have thought it their duty to present this report at the earliest practicable moment, and they ask the prompt action of the Board, because Dr. Hilprecht, who is now abroad and working there for the University of Pennsylvania, has been for several months under charges which affect alike his integrity and the fair name of the University of Pennsylvania, and he is entitled to know at the earliest possible moment that the charges have been found baseless.[39]

Although one can see how the committee dismissed charges two and three as being unfounded, it is difficult to imagine their completely dismissing charge one, the charge of literary dishonesty. One has only to read *Exploration in Bible Lands* to get the impression that Hilprecht tends to take credit for all the finds of the four Nippur expeditions. He does not state this, but the idea is conveyed to the reader. Despite which side the reader might take if he cares to do further reading, the controversy did bring publicity to Assyriology. This publicity caused more copies of Peters' and

---

[37] *Ibid.*, 118-271.
[38] *Ibid.*, 267.
[39] *Ibid.*, 271.

Hilprecht's books to be sold, and as a result more laymen became aware of the field of Assyriology.

Institutions and Professional Societies

The Peters-Hilprecht Controversy was spectacular, but there was an undramatic, but very important, aspect of Assyriology that also continued its development. At the institutions of higher learning Assyriology was continuing to develop, or at least at most of them. David Lyon was still teaching Akkadian grammar and archeology of Mesopotamia at Harvard. Lyon as curator of the Harvard Semitic Museum was expending time and energy developing the museum, and making it known to the public. One could see earlier that the museum had its beginnings back in 1889, but it was not housed in its own building until 1903. In 1899 construction was started on a new museum building. Early in the year 1903 the structure was completed, and on February 5 the new museum building was formally dedicated.[40] The first floor contained a library of about 1,200 volumes, and three lecture rooms. A very large exhibit area, called the Babylonian-Assyrian Room, was located on the second floor. Antiquities from Palestine were found in the Palestinian Room, located on the third floor.[41] Harvard now had a museum to complement research and teaching in Assyriology.

Paul Haupt and Christopher Johnston were continuing to expand their Assyriological offerings at Johns Hopkins. By 1910 Haupt was teaching introductory Sumerian, plus another course entitled Assyrian and Sumerian Prose Composition.[42] Johnston, besides two Egyptology courses, taught History of the Ancient East, and Selected Assyrian Letters.[43] Another colleague had been added to the staff, Frank Ringgold Blake, who taught Assyrian for Beginners.[44] Blake had received his A.B. degree at Johns Hopkins in 1897, his Ph.D. under Haupt in 1902, and stayed on as a staff member.[45] Arno Poebel, the distinguished German Assyriologist, was a visiting professor at Johns Hopkins in 1910-11.[46]

---

[40] Harvard Univ., *Formal Opening of the Semitic Museum*, 1-2.
[41] E. E. Braithwaite, "The Semitic Museum of Harvard University," *Records of the Past*, IV (1905), 243-251.
[42] *JHUC*, No. 225 (1910), 133.
[43] *JHUC*, No. 225 (1910), 130-133.
[44] *Ibid.*, 132.
[45] *Ibid.*, No. 284 (1916), 24.
[46] *Ibid.*, No. 235 (1911), 142-143.

At the University of Pennsylvania the Peters-Hilprecht Controversy had seemingly taken its toll of Hilprecht. Albert Clay had left in 1910 to go to Yale, and the following year Hilprecht retired.[47] This left only Jastrow; thus the Assyriology courses were curtailed somewhat. Then in 1913 Jastrow began to get help from Edward Chiera (1885-1933). Chiera was born August 5, 1885, at Rome, Italy.[48] He earned a Bachelor of Divinity in 1911 and a Master of Theology in 1912 from Crozer Theological Seminary, Chester, Pennsylvania. Chiera went on to the University of Pennsylvania, earning the Ph.D. in 1913. Upon receiving this degree, he remained at Pennsylvania as an Instructor of Assyriology.

The University of Missouri made only one attempt to renew the program in Assyriology after the turn of the century. Gilbert Campbell Scoggin (1881-1947) was hired as Instructor of Sanskrit and Comparative Philology in 1908.[49] Scoggin was born April 27, 1881, at Glass, Tennessee. He earned his A.B. degree at Vanderbilt, and also his A.M., which he received in 1902. Scoggin then earned the Ph.D. from Harvard in 1906. After a year of study at Leipzig in 1907-08, he returned to accept the position at Missouri. During the 1908-09 school year he taught a graduate course in the Old Persian language.[50] After this however, he confined himself to Greek, Latin, and Sanskrit.

Princeton did not revive Assyriology in the period from 1900 to 1914, but Colgate University kept their program going. George Berry continued to expand Assyriological offerings at the school. By 1909 he had added four more courses, dealing with history, archeology, and religion of Mesopotamia.[51]

Hinckley Mitchell continued to teach a course in Akkadian in the early 1900's at Boston University. After he left in 1905, Albert C. Knudson of the School of Theology taught the Akkadian course.[52] This course was continued until 1913, and then dropped.[53] From time to time a history course that encompassed the area of Mesopotamia and Persia was taught by various members of the

---

[47] *Univ. Penn. Catalogue, 1911-12* (1911), 348-349.
[48] Biographical information on Chiera taken from a memoriam sketch by E. A. Speiser, *JAOS*, LIII (1933), 308-309.
[49] *Univ. Mo. Catalogue, 1908-09* (1909), 43.
[50] *Ibid.*, 146.
[51] *Colgate Univ. Catalogue, 1908-09* (1908), 34.
[52] *Boston Univ. Year Book, 1908-09* (1909), 69.
[53] *Ibid., 1913-14* (1913), 72.

History Department, but no more courses in cuneiform languages were offered.

At Bryn Mawr College, George Barton was keeping Assyriology alive. He offered two graduate level Semitic seminars, in which a student could study either Hebrew or Akkadian.[54]

Robert Francis Harper and Ira M. Price were continuing to enlarge and add Assyriological courses at the University of Chicago, despite Harper's other duties. Daniel Luckenbill, a product of the university, began to give them help after 1907.[55] According to the catalogue for 1911-12, Harper, Price, and Luckenbill had increased the offerings in Akkadian language and literature to eighteen courses.[56]

James A. Craig was still teaching the two Akkadian courses at the University of Michigan that had been developed by Belser.[57] Craig, however, left to go into business in 1912, and as the year 1914 approached Michigan was without an Assyriologist.

At Columbia, Abraham Jackson was still teaching language courses in Old Persian.[58] Richard Gottheil handled the Sumerian courses, while John Prince taught Akkadian, plus a course in the history of the ancient Near East.[59]

Prior to the turn of the century Nathaniel Schmidt had taught the history of Babylonia, Assyria, and Persia at Cornell. He began, however, to add language courses to the curriculum in 1904, when he initiated Elementary Assyrian.[60] Two years later he added Introductory Sumerian.[61]

John Prince left New York University in 1902 to go to Columbia. According to the NYU catalogues there have been no Assyriological courses since.

After the turn of the century James Stevenson at Vanderbilt University still offered the two Akkadian courses.[62] In 1902 a course in Old Persian was added, taught by Herbert Cushing Tolman (1865-1923).[63] He was born November 4, 1865, At South Scituate,

---

[54] *Bryn Mawr College Calendar, 1910-11* (1910), 132.
[55] More will be said of Luckenbill in Chapter VII.
[56] *University of Chicago Annual Register for 1911-12* (1912), 176.
[57] See above Chap. III.
[58] *Columbia Univ. Catalogue, 1901-02* (1902), 538.
[59] *Columbia Univ. Catalogue, 1910-11* (1910), 140.
[60] *Cornell Univ. Register, 1904-05* (1904), 84.
[61] *Ibid, 1906-07* (1906), 93.
[62] See above Chap. III.
[63] *Register of Vanderbilt Univ., 1902-03* (1903), 58-59.

Massachusetts. After receiving an A.B. degree from Yale in 1888, and a Ph.D. in 1890, Tolman went on to study at the University of Berlin in 1896, where he picked up his interest and training for Assyriology. He had been a Professor of Greek and Sanskrit at Vanderbilt since 1894.

The learned societies were also maintaining their interest in cuneiform studies during the period from 1900 to 1914. Examination of the *Proceedings* of the American Oriental Society indicates that at least forty-seven papers that dealt with ancient Mesopotamia and Persia were presented at the two yearly meetings.[64] Prior to the 20th century the American Philosophical Society had allowed their interest in the Near East to center mainly around Egyptology. After Morris Jastrow, Jr. (1897), Cyrus Adler (1900), and Paul Haupt (1902) joined the society, the interest in subjects of an Assyriological nature picked up considerably. In the fourteen-year period after the turn of the century at least eleven papers dealing with Assyriology were presented at the meetings of the society.[65] The Oriental Club of Philadelphia still devoted a major part of their discussion periods to cuneiform studies.[66]

In New York the New York Oriental Club, in operation since 1896, was still promoting Oriental research.[67] After 1900 the club began to devote a great deal of its energies toward promoting Assyriology. By 1914 the membership had increased to eighteen, including such Assyriologists as Richard Gottheil, William H. Ward, John D. Prince, and Francis Brown, to mention only four. Papers were not presented formally, but topics were discussed in an after-dinner informal atmosphere.

The Oriental Club of New Haven was founded in that city in 1913. One of the leading instigators in organizing this club was Albert T. Clay of Yale. Clay encouraged a group of eight Yale scholars to meet at his home on Saturday evening, March 15, 1913.[68] The object of the proposed club was to promote Oriental studies among scholars and laymen, alike. This group completed their plans and formally

---

[64] *JAOS*, XXI (1900-01) — XXIV (1915).

[65] *Proc. Amer. Phil. Soc.*, XXXIX (1900) — LIII (1914).

[66] R. G. Kent (ed.), *Thirty Years of Oriental Studies* (Philadelphia: Oriental Club of Phila., 1918), 11-14.

[67] Personal correspondence with Adolf L. Schrijver, Secretary, New York Oriental Club, June 4, 1968.

[68] C. Bradford Welles, *The Oriental Club of New Haven* (New Haven, Conn.: New Haven Oriental Cub, 1963), 1.

organized the club this same evening. E. Washburn Hopkins, professor of Sanskrit, was elected president for the first year, and Clay was voted secretary.[69] With Clay as a leader in the club, Assyriology ranked high on the program of most of the meetings. Other Assyriologists would be added to the membership later.

Literature

While these clubs were making cuneiform studies known to the general public, Assyriological literature was also playing an important role. Not only were publications increasing in quantity, but the quality was improving. Histories of Mesopotamia were becoming much more sophisticated, written more for the scholar than for the public. One such history is a two-volume work in 1900 by Robert William Rogers (1864-1930), *A History of Babylonia and Assyria*.[70] Rogers, a native of Philadelphia, earned A.B. degrees at the University of Pennsylvania in 1886, and at Johns Hopkins in 1887. Rogers then went on to get a Ph.D. at the University of Leipzig in 1895, after which he returned to the U.S. as a Professor of Hebrew at Drew University, a position he held until his retirement in 1929. In Volume I Rogers discusses travellers, explorers, history of excavation, decipherment of the cuneiform, geography, ethnology, and chronology of the area. The second volume deals with the history of the region. This was probably the best historical work on Mesopotamia to that date.

Another volume in the series of *The Babylonian Expedition of the University of Pennsylvania* was published in 1904.[71] As it turned out, only Series A and D were ever published, and these were not complete. Albert C. Clay published Volume X (they came out in no particular order), *Business Documents of Murashu Sons of Nippur, Dated in the Reign of Darius II*.[72] In this volume the tablets were transactions of a Nippur business firm covering the years 424-404 B.C. Other volumes in the series would come out later.

Henry C. Tolman, of Vanderbilt University, released a book in 1908, entitled *Ancient Persian Lexicon*, in which he gives transliterations and translations of the Persian inscriptions from

---

[69] *Ibid.*, 50.
[70] (New York: Eaton & Mains, 1900).
[71] See above Chap. IV.
[72] Vol. X of *The Babylonia Expedition of the Univ. Penn.*, H. V. Hilprecht, ed., Ser. A (Phila.: Univ. Penn. Press, 1904).

Behistun, Persepolis, Susa, and other localities.[73] From the vocabulary in these inscriptions he developed the lexicon. Tolman followed this work two years later with a supplement, containing autographed texts.[74]

In 1910 William H. Ward published a book, *The Seal Cylinders of Western Asia*.[75] This volume was the result of almost twenty years of research on the part of Ward. It contained discussions and 1,315 illustrations of seal cylinders from Asia Minor, Persia, Syria-Palestine, Mesopotamia, and even Egypt. These cylinders were from various private collections—the Louvre, Bibliotheque Nationale, Berlin Museum, British Museum, Harvard, and the University of Pennsylvania.

Morris Jastrow, Jr., who had published numerous articles on the religions of Mesopotamia, wrote two books on this subject. The first work appeared in 1911, *Aspects of Religious Belief and Practice in Babylonia and Assyria*, and was one of the best works of the time.[76] Three years later he compared Hebrew and Babylonian religions in a work entitled *Hebrew and Babylonian Traditions*, which grew out of his Haskell Lectures delivered at Oberlin College in 1913.[77]

This by no means even makes a dent in the number of books published between 1900 and 1914. It is only intended to give the reader a look at three or four of the outstanding works of the period.[78]

Several journals that carried Assyriological articles came into existence to join those already established. Two of these came to life in 1902, but both had ceased to exist by the end of 1914. One of these was *Records of the Past*, founded by the Records of the Past Exploration Society of Washington, D.C., devoted to the exploration in archeology all over the world. The last volume, XIII, appeared in 1914. The other journal was the *Semitic Study Series* that was published in Leiden by E. J. Brill, but the editors were Richard Gottheil of Columbia, and Morris Jastrow, Jr. of the University of Pennsylvania. This series ceased with Volume XIV in 1911.

---

[73] Vol. VI of *Vanderbilt Oriental Series* (New York: American Book Co., 1908).

[74] *Cuneiform Supplement to the Author's Ancient Persian Lexicon and Texts*, Vol. VII of *Vanderbilt Oriental Series* (New York: American Book Co., 1910).

[75] (Washington, D.C.: Carnegie Institution Publication No. 100, 1910).

[76] (New York: G. P. Putnam's Sons, 1911).

[77] (New York: Chas. Scribner's Sons, 1914).

[78] For a more complete list of books and articles for this period consult the bibliography.

In addition to these, several of the universities and museums began series in this period from 1900 to 1914. Some of these were *Columbia Univ. Oriental Studies* (1902), and *Columbia Univ. Contributions to Oriental History and Philology* (1908), *University of California Publications in Semitic Philology* (1907), *Museum Journal of the University of Pennsylvania Museum* (1910), *Harvard Semitic Series* (1912), and *Yale Oriental Series* (1912).

CHAPTER SIX

THE WAR YEARS

On June 28, 1914, Gavrilo Princip assassinated Archduke Francis Ferdinand of Austria-Hungary at the Bosnian provincial capital of Sarajevo. This murder set off a chain reaction that plunged the entire world into war. Five weeks after the crime at Sarajevo World War I had begun in earnest. Assyriology was now relegated to the background in the scholarly world. As most of the action took place in the Near East, archeological excavations came to an end. The Ottoman empire was on the side of the Central Powers. Although excavation ceased in the period from 1915 to 1920, research was still being carried on, books and articles were published, and scholars still taught Assyriology in the colleges and universities of the United States.

Literature

Several books that made sound contributions to Assyriology were published in 1915. One of these was a work by Albert T. Clay. *Miscellaneous Inscriptions in the Yale Babylonian Collection*, that spans a period of history between four and five thousand years.[1] In this book Clay has done an excellent job of copying the cuneiform texts. He included historical texts, votive and building inscriptions, a dynastic list, a syllabary, a mortuary inscription, a boundary stone, and a fragment of the Hammurabi code. This complemented the business documents that had been published previously.[2] At least two American Assyriologists felt that Clay's work added much to the field of Assyriology.[3]

A History of Babylonia and Assyria by Robert W. Rogers, first published in 1900, proved such a success, at least as far as the publishing house was concerned, that it was released in the 6th

---

[1] Vol. I of *Yale Oriental Series, Babylonia Texts* (New Haven, Conn.: Yale Univ. Press, 1915).
[2] See above Chap. V.
[3] Book reviews by D. D. Luckenbill, *AJSL*, XXXII (1916-17), 71-72; and R. W. Rogers, *Amer. Historical Review* (hereafter referred to as *AHR*), XXII (1917), 368-370.

edition in 1915.[4] Although Rogers made some use of new archeological evidence, the book did not differ a great deal from the first edition. Most American Assyriologists gave it lukewarm to favorable reviews.[5]

In this same year of 1915 Morris Jastrow, Jr. published a book entitled *The Civilization of Babylonia and Assyria*.[6] This work was not merely a list of the kings placed in a chronological framework, along with their achievements, but dealt with the development of societies, and the contributions of each group to the culture of Mesopotamia. Jastrow is one of the first to write a social and cultural history of the area. He includes such subjects as art, religion, law, commerce, history of excavation, and the decipherment of the cuneiform, as well as a basic outline of the political history. Most of the reviewers of this book have only praise for it.[7]

George Barton of Bryn Mawr College attempted in 1916 to relate recent archeological discoveries with the bible in a work called *Archaeology and the Bible*.[8] In this book Barton, after a glimpse at the history of exploration in the Near East, presents translations of ancient documents that confirm passages in the bible. Not only does the work contain documents of the Hebrews, but of the peoples of Mesopotamia as well, making it rich in Assyriological material. One reviewer states that the volume is so crammed full of material that it serves as a source book for the historian, rather than as a history.[9] The book sold so well, at least in religious circles, that a second edition was issued in 1917.

In 1916 one of the first historiographical studies appeared, when Albert T. Olmstead examined the sources available for Assyriology.[10] Olmstead's work, entitled *Assyrian Historiography*, was a critical study of the source material, and the dangers of taking the inscriptions of the Assyrian kings at face value.[11] At least one scholar felt that Olmstead was too critical of all earlier works based on the

---

[4] (New York: Abingdon Press, 1915).
[5] D. G. Lyon, *AHR*, XXI (1916), 563-565; and Leroy Waterman, *AJSL*, XXXIII (1916-17), 258-259.
[6] (Philadelphia: J. B. Lippincott, 1915).
[7] D. D. Luckenbill, *AJSL*, XXXIII (1916-17), 252-254; and D. G. Lyon, *AHR*, XXI (1916), 565-567.
[8] (Philadelphia: American Sunday School Union, 1916).
[9] Lewis B. Paton, *AHR*, XXII (1917), 370-371.
[10] More will be said of Olmstead in Chapter VII.
[11] Vol. III of *Univ. Missouri Studies* (Columbia: Univ. Mo. Press, 1916).

Assyrian inscriptions.[12] This work stands as one of the most important of the time, as it was not just another history, but a keen analytical analysis of the sources used for previous and future histories of Mesopotamia.

Edwin Lee Johnson, professor of languages at Vanderbilt University, made a major contribution to philology in 1917 with his book, *Historical Grammar of the Ancient Persian Language*.[13] Johnson felt that the recent work done by British Assyriologists Leonard King and Campbell Thompson, plus the American contributions of Herbert Tolman and Abraham Jackson, made a pressing need for a new grammar of the Old Persian language.[14] Two chapters are devoted to the decipherment of the cuneiform and the location and publication of all known inscriptions. The other seventeen chapters deal with grammar. This work stands as the best grammar for the period between 1915 and 1920.

Albert Clay made another major contribution to Assyriological literature of the period with a book in 1919, entitled *The Empire of the Amorites*.[15] Clay's thesis was that Amurru, the area included in modern-day Syria, was the cradle of Semitic civilization. He maintains that this civilization made a great impact upon Mesopotamia by modifying the Sumerain culture into the Akkadian one. Clay goes on to say that the culture of Israel was affected by this, rather than by the civilization of Babylonia. Today, although there was no empire as a political entity, most Assyriologists think that Clay's ideas were basically right.[16] Even though Clay's thesis was somewhat controversial at the time, many of his contemporaries felt that he had made a sound contribution to the field.[17]

A new journal that carried Assyriological articles was founded in 1917. This was the *Journal of the Society of Oriental Research*, edited by Samuel Alfred Browne Mercer. Mercer was the main instigator of this new journal that appeared semiannually until 1921, when it became a quarterly publication. He was professor of Semitic languages at Western Theological Seminary in Chicago. Mercer was

---

[12] Robert W. Rogers, Review of *Assyrian Historiography* by A. T. Olmstead, *AHR*, XXII (1917), 692-693.
[13] Vol. VIII of *Vanderbilt Oriental Series* (New York: American Book Co., 1917).
[14] *Ibid.*, V.
[15] (New Haven: Yale Univ. Press, 1919).
[16] Albrecht Goetze, "Professor Clay and the Amurrite Problem," *Yale Univ. Library Gazette*, XXXVI (1962), 133-137.
[17] R. W. Rogers, *AHR*, XXV (1920), 700-701.

avidly interested in Assyriology, which is revealed in many of his publications.[18]

The leading journal for Assyriological articles, at least as far as quantity of scholarly articles printed, was still the *American Journal of Semitic Languages and Literature*, but followed closely by the *Journal of the American Oriental Society*. In the period from 1915 to 1920 there are no less than forty articles in *AJSL*.[19] *JAOS* is close behind with a total of thirty-five.[20]

Few of the scholarly series begun by the universities contributed much to Assyriology during this period of wartime. One volume of the *Columbia University Oriental Studies* was issued in 1918.[21] Yale started another series, called *Yale Oriental Series, Babylonian Texts*, to go along with the *Researches* begun in 1912. One important work was issued in the series, *Vanderbilt Oriental Series*, but the entire series ended in 1918 with Vol. IX.

Institutions and Professional Societies

At the institutions of higher learning in the United States the teaching of courses dealing with Assyriology did not slacken. Perhaps, after America entered the war in 1917, there were fewer undergraduates to take the courses, but this condition did not prevail for any length of time. David Gordon Lyon continued the teaching of Akkadian grammar courses at Harvard, plus the art and archeology courses concerned with Mesopotamia. He did very little writing for publication between 1915 and 1920, mainly because of his teaching load and his duties as curator of the Harvard Semitic Museum.

Johns Hopkins continued their practice of keeping several faculty members on the staff who were competent in the sphere of Assyriology. It is true that Christopher Johnston had died in 1914, but Georgy Stewart Duncan had taken over his duties.[22] Duncan received his Ph.D. degree from Dickinson College in 1894.[23] According to the catalogue for 1915-16 Paul Haupt taught Bilingual

---

[18] *Religious and Moral Ideas in Babylonia and Assyria* (Milwaukee: Morehouse Publ. Co., 1919); see also the bibliography.
[19] *AJSL*, XXXI (1914-15) — XXXVI (1919-20).
[20] *JAOS*, XXXIV (1915) — XXXIX (1919).
[21] Samuel A. B. Mercer, *A Sumero-Babylonian Sign List*, Vol. XIV of *Columbia Univ. Oriental Studies* (New York: Columbia Univ. Press, 1918).
[22] *JHUC*, No. 284 (1916), 40.
[23] *Ibid*.

Hymns and Incantations and Assyrian and Sumerian Prose Composition, Blake offered Assyrian for Beginners, and Duncan taught the Code of Hammurabi and Babylonian and Sumerian Contracts.[24] William Foxwell Albright, who would later distinguish himself as one of the world's leading experts on Palestinian studies, earned his Ph.D. at Johns Hopkins in 1916. He stayed on for the 1916-17 academic year as an Instructor of Semitic Languages, and the 1917-18 year as a Fellow in this area. During his stay at Johns Hopkins, Albright taught a course in elementary Akkadian and one called Cuneiform Historical Texts.[25] As the year 1920 approached, Blake and Haupt together continued to offer at least four Assyriological courses each semester.[26]

With Hilprecht gone, the University of Pennsylvania had limited offerings in the area of cuneiform studies. Edward Chiera and Morris Jastrow, Jr. were handling all Assyriological offerings at Pennsylvania between 1915 and 1920. Jastrow retained his position as librarian, thus, was unable to devote a great deal of time to the field. In 1919 Chiera's title was changed from Instructor of Assyriology to Instructor of Semitic Languages; as a result he had to devote a portion of his energies to Hebrew and the other Semitic languages. Under these conditions it was rare when the school offered more than two courses in Assyriology per semester.[27]

A survey of the catalogues of the University of Missouri, Princeton, and Colgate reveals that no courses that could be categorized as Assyriological were offered between 1915 and 1920. At Bryn Mawr College, George Barton still offered his graduate seminar in which a student could study either Hebrew or Akkadian. On the other hand, Barton published quite a few articles and some books that made contributions to the field during this period. Besides his book *Archaeology and the Bible*, he published two other works. In one of these, *Sumerian Business and Administrative Documents from the Earliest Times to the Dynasty of Agade*, Barton copied 132 business tablets from the University of Pennsylvania collection from Nippur.[28] His other book, *Miscellaneous Babylonian Inscriptions*, was also

---

[24] Ibid., 203.
[25] Ibid., No. 304 (1918), 232.
[26] Ibid., No. 314 (1919), 211-212.
[27] Univ. Penn. Catalogue, *1917-18* (1917), 328-329.
[28] Vol. IX, Part 1 of *Univ. Penn. Museum, Publications of the Babylonian Section* (Philadelphia: Univ. Penn. Press, 1915).

concerned with tablets from the Pennsylvania collection.[29] Aside from these works, Barton also published at least seven articles in the leading Assyriological journals.[30]

Since 1900 the University of Chicago had the distinction of offering more courses in Assyriology than any other institution. After Harper's death in 1914 these offerings did not cease but were carried on by Ira Price and Daniel Luckenbill.[31] On the publication side of the picture Price did not contribute much during the five-year period, but Luckenbill came out with five Assyriological articles in this same period.[32]

The University of Michigan had been without an Assyriologist since Craig's departure in 1912. This began to change in the fall of 1915 when Leroy Waterman was made Professor of Semitic Languages and chairman of the Department of Oriental Languages and Literature.[33] Waterman was born July 4, 1875, at Pierpoint, Ohio. He had attended several educational institutions, as he received an A.B. degree in 1898 from Hilldale College in Michigan, a B.D. in 1900, studied at Oxford University from 1900 to 1902, at the University of Berlin between 1906 and 1907, and received his Ph.D. from the University of Chicago in 1912. Waterman was a student of Robert Francis Harper. Although he only organized one Akkadian language course, Waterman did introduce more history courses of the Ancient Near East.[34] Thanks to the efforts of Waterman, Assyriology was revived at Michigan for three decades.

At Columbia University Richard Gottheil had begun to restrict himself to the teaching of Arabic and Syriac. The Sumerian and Akkadian courses, however, were carried on by John Prince and Frederick Vanderburgh, a fellow faculty member at the school.[35]

Nathaniel Schmidt continued to offer Assyriological courses at Cornell Univerisity. During the war years Schmidt had a little trouble with some of the other faculty members. He was Swedish by birth and a pacifist. Schmidt felt that it was morally wrong to buy liberty bonds, and despite pressure refused to do so. There were efforts by some of the faculty and leading citizens of Ithaca to have him

---

[29] Part 1 of *Sumerian Religious Texts* (New Haven: Yale Univ. Press, 1918).
[30] See bibliography.
[31] *Univ. Chicago Annual Register, 1914-15* (1915), 176.
[32] See bibliography.
[33] *Univ. Michigan Catalogue, 1915-16* (1916), 152.
[34] *Ibid, 1916-17* (1917), 163-164.
[35] *Columbia Univ. Catalogue, 1917-18* (1917), 157.

removed from the university. All of this was to no avail, as Schmidt had established his reputation as a sound scholar.[36]

An examination of the catalogues for Vanderbilt University between 1915 and 1920 shows that the format for Assyriological courses remained as it had been earlier. James Stevenson continued to teach Akkadian, while Herbert Tolman taught the course in Old Persian. Stevenson died, however, on December 12, 1919, and this ended the teaching of Akkadian at Vanderbilt. In fact, his death marked an end to all Semitic languages at the institution, with the exception of Hebrew in the Divinity School.

Albert Clay was busily making Yale known in Assyriological circles, not only in the field of publication but in turning out top-notch scholars. During the war years no fewer than four students earned their Ph.D. degrees under the tutelage of Clay. They were Henry Frederick Lutz (1916), Ettaline Mears Grice (1917), Raymond Philip Dougherty (1918), and Arch Tremayne (1919). [37]

The learned societies, for the most part, kept their interest in Assyriology going strong in the years between 1915 and 1920. Upon examination of the *Proceedings* of the American Oriental Society, we find that there are at least twenty-eight papers of an Assyriological nature presented at the meetings.[38] At the society's meeting in Washington, D.C., April 24-26, 1916, the members who lived in the Midwest and West decided to form a branch of the society.[39] This group held their first meeting the following year at the Haskell Museum of the University of Chicago; thus, the Middle West Branch of the American Oriental Society was born.[40]

Many of the citizens in and around the city of Philadelphia still showed an avid interest in Assyriology. The American Philosophical Society, that devoted only a fraction of its energies to this field, had six Assyriological papers presented at their meetings in the five-year period.[41] On the other hand, the Oriental Club of Philadelphia devoted a great portion of their energies toward cuneiform studies. The club celebrated its 30th anniversary on April 30, 1918. Four papers that dealt with the topic of Assyriology and other Semitic

---

[36] Bishop, *History of Cornell*, 429.
[37] Personal correspondence with F. J. Stephens, Yale Univ., June 20, 1967.
[38] *JAOS*, XXXV (1915) — XXXIX (1919).
[39] *Ibid.*, XXXVI (1916), 423-425.
[40] *Ibid.*
[41] *Proc. Amer. Phil. Soc.*, LIV (1915) — LVIII (1919).

studies were presented at this meeting. Roland Grubb Kent (1877-1952) commemorated this anniversary by publishing these four papers as a small book.[42] Kent, a native of Wilmington, Delaware, was born February 24, 1877. He received his Ph.D. degree from the University of Pennsylvania in 1903 and stayed on as a teacher, first of Greek and Latin, and later comparative philology. In 1916 Kent was promoted to Professor of Comparative Philology and began to devote a great deal of time to the study of Old Persian.

Up the coast the Oriental Club of New York was keeping alive their interest in Assyriology in their informal meetings. Between 1915 and 1920 their membership increased from eighteen to thirty.[43] The New Haven Oriental Club was also pursuing their interest in cuneiform studies with such members on the rolls as Albert T. Clay and Charles C. Torrey.

Founding of the Oriental Institute

In 1919 an event occurred that seemed not too important at the time but later would have a powerful influence on the continued development of American Assyriology. This event was the founding of the Oriental Institute at the University of Chicago. The person responsible for the founding and development of this institution was James Henry Breasted (1865-1935), America's leading Egyptologist. Breasted was born August 27, 1865, at Rockford, Illinois, son of Charles and Harriet Breasted.[44] After receiving an A.B. degree from North Central College (Illinois) in 1888, and an A.M. from Yale in 1892, he went on to earn his Ph.D. from the University of Berlin in 1894. In the spring of 1895 Breasted became Instructor of Egyptology at the new University of Chicago, the first such chair in the United States.

Many scholars felt that the key to unlocking the secrets of the origin of mankind and the development of human culture lay in the mist-shrouded history of the long-dead civilizations of the ancient Near East. Breasted believed this very strongly, feeling that an institution was needed that would cut across many fields and disciplines of learning to probe this potential storehouse of

---

[42] *Thirty Years of Oriental Studies*, 1918.

[43] Personal correspondence with Adolf Schrijver, Sec.-Treas., June 4, 1968.

[44] Biographical information on Breasted obtained from Charles Breasted, *Pioneer to the Past*; and *Dict. Amer. Biog.*, XXI, Supplement 1, 110-113.

knowledge. This idea is revealed in his writings which were published later:

> It is a task which demands in the first place sufficient funds for the organization of a group of efficient and scientific field expeditions including men with practical archeological training who can be associated with the home staff of philologists and historians forming the University's Department of Oriental Languages. The field staffs and the University Department at home can then cooperate in a far-reaching two-fold process: first, the task of salvaging the vast body of evidence still surviving in the field; and second, the task of studying, interpreting, and correlating that evidence as it is received from the field by the scientific staff at home. Thus the otherwise more or less helpless University Department of Oriental Languages becomes part of an effective organization, in which it serves as the interpretive organ. We thus link together the far-flung salvaging operations in the field and the interpretative group at home in one great co-operative organization.[45]

He goes on further to state:

> How did man become what he is? That is really the question which the Oriental Institute has been organized to study. The Institute is therefore a research laboratory for the investigation of the early human career. It endeavors to trace the course of human development from the merely physical man disclosed by the paleontologists to the rise and advance of civilized societies, the product of a social and material evolution culminating in social idealism.
>
> A generation of archeological research has dispelled all doubts as to the scene of this evolution, which now recognized as having been the ancient Near East, the region folded like a horseshoe around the eastern end of the Mediterranean. The ancient lands of this region today constitute an almost inexhaustible storehouse filled with perishing and still unsalvaged evidences disclosing early human development. Heretofore no comprehensive and systematic effort has been made to save and study *as a whole* these enormous bodies of perishing evidence.[46]

Unfortunately, the realization of a need is not all that is required to begin a project, as many scholars have found out down through the ages. To build and develop this institution would require money. On February 16, 1919, Breasted wrote a letter to his friend and son of the benefactor of the University of Chicago, John D. Rockefeller, Jr., in which he outlined a plan and told of the need for funds to develop

---

[45] J. H. Breasted, *The Oriental Institute*, Vol. XII of *The University of Chicago Survey* (Chicago: Univ. Chicago Press, 1933), 2.
[46] *Ibid.*, 2-3.

this institution that would make a thorough investigation of the history, archeology, and geology of the Near East.[47] For two disappointing months Breasted had no word from young Rockefeller. Then when hope seemed to be gone, he received a letter dated May 2, 1919, in which Rockefeller agreed to contribute $10,000 annually for a period of five years toward financing the project. President Judson of the University and Martin Ryerson of the University's Board of Trustees pledged more support in the way of additional funds.[48] Thus, in the summer of 1919 the organization of the Oriental Institute, as it was named, was completed with Breasted as the director.

In August Breasted and five assistants set out on a reconnaissance mission to determine the most suitable archeological sites in the Near East and to purchase ancient documents and other antiquities. This was the first task of the new director of the Oriental Institute.[49] This trip lasted a year and took the party to Egypt, Palestine, Syria, Mesopotamia, Persia, and Asia Minor. The Oriental Institute had been born, but when would it begin to make its impact on Assyriology? For an answer to this question the reader is forced to move on to the next chapter and a new era in American Assyriology.

---

[47] C. Breasted, *Pioneer to the Past*, 238-239.
[48] *Ibid.*, 240-241.
[49] Breasted, *The Oriental Institute*, 35.

CHAPTER SEVEN

OUT OF CHICAGO

By 1920 the "Great War" was over; normalcy was returning to Europe and the rest of the world. Tumult and conflict had ended, American and European savants could once again turn their complete attention toward scholarly pursuits. Hostilities ended on November 11, 1918, but the peace treaties were hammered out with the incividual Central Powers, beginning with the Trianon Treaty (Hungary) on March 22, 1919, and concluding with the Treaty of Sevres (Ottoman Empire) on August 10, 1920. The period from 1920 to 1939 was marked by the expansion of the Oriental Institute of the University of Chicago into all areas of Oriental study. One of the scholars who aided in the expansion of Assyriology at the University of Chicago was Albert Olmstead.

The Breasted of Assyriology

Albert Ten Eyck Olmstead (1880-1945) was born March 23, 1880, at Troy, New York, son of Charles and Ella Olmstead.[1] While an undergraduate at Cornell University he became very interested in Assyrian history, thanks to the teaching of Nathaniel Schmidt. In 1901 at the suggestion of Schmidt Olmstead began to study all the known inscriptions of the Assyrian king Sargon II (722-705 B.C.). By this time he had gained a good reading knowledge of Akkadian. Olmstead received his A.B. degree in 1902 and stayed on at Cornell, working on the inscriptions of Sargon, which earned him an A.M. degree in 1903. Between May of 1904 and August of 1905 he was a Fellow at the American Schools for Oriental Studies at Jerusalem. While at the American Schools young Olmstead visited many of the sites described in the tablets of Sargon. Upon returning to the U.S. in 1905, he continued his graduate work by writing a detailed historical

---

[1] Biographical information on Olmstead taken from personal correspondence with Mrs. Albert T. Olmstead, April 19, 1967; personal interview with Mrs. Olmstead at Kansas City, Missouri, June 22, 1967; personal correspondence with George G. Cameron, Department of Near Eastern Languages, University of Michigan, May 1, 1967; and a biographical sketch by J. A. Wilson, "Albert Ten Eyck Olmstead, 1880-1945," *Journal Near Eastern Studies* (hereafter referred to as *JNES*), V (1946), 1-6.

study of the reign of Sargon, taken from these same inscriptions with which he had been working. This work entitled *Western Asia in the Days of Sargon of Assyria* was his doctoral dissertation at Cornell, earning him the Ph.D. in 1906. In 1908 this work was published as his first book.[2] Just as James Henry Breasted had published a history of Egypt from the inscriptions, Olmstead had traced the reign of one of the powerful Assyrian kings by this method.

After receiving his degree from Cornell, Olmstead spent a year in Greece as a Fellow at the American School of Classical Studies at Athens. The following year of 1907-8 he was director of the Cornell Expedition to Asia Minor. After Olmstead returned to the States he spent the school year of 1908-09 teaching Greek and Latin at Princeton Preparatory School.

In the fall of 1909 Olmstead began teaching at the University of Missouri as Instructor of Ancient History. Not only did he teach survey history courses of the ancient Near East but developed courses in Greek and Roman History, as well.[3] Continuing in the same vein as with his doctoral dissertation, Olmstead published an article in 1911, describing the political and diplomatic history of the reign of Sennacherib.[4] In this same year he was promoted to assistant professor, and then in 1914 he attained the rank of associate professor. Olmstead published his monograph on Assyrian historiography in 1916,[5] a work that many scholars felt was his most important contribution to the field of Assyriology.[6]

Assyrian Historiography firmly established Olmstead's reputation as an Assyriologist, and as a result the University of Illinois lured him away from Missouri in the fall of 1917 as Professor of Ancient History. At Illinois Olmstead did not develop any Akkadian language courses but concentrated on teaching the history of the ancient Near East, devoting a great deal of his time to the area of Babylonia and Assyria. While at the University of Illinois, he made his second great contribution to Assyriology, a book entitled *History of Assyria*, published in 1923.[7] Olmstead felt that for too long the historian had

---

[2] Vol. II of *Cornell Studies in History and Political Sciences* (New York: Henry Holt & Co., 1908).

[3] *Univ. Mo. Catalogue, 1910-11* (1911), 150-151.

[4] "Western Asia in the Reign of Sennacherib of Assyria (705-681)," *Amer. Historical Assn. Annual Report for 1909* (1911), 91-101.

[5] See above chap. VI.

[6] Personal correspondence with Cameron, May 1, 1967.

[7] (Chicago: Univ. Chicago Press, 1923).

placed the Assyrians in with the Babylonians in all historical studies; his feeling was that they deserved a place to themselves.[8] Why did the Assyrians deserve a niche to themselves; weren't they after all one of the civilizations of Mesopotamia? This is true, but northern Mesopotamia, or that land referred to as Assyria, was not politically united with the remainder of Mesopotamia until the Assyrian conquest of the 10th century B.C. Their culture was Sumero-Akkadian, but they quickly developed a different philosophic outlook. Babylonia was oriented toward trade and commerce, Assyria, like Sparta later, became an armed military camp, everything else was placed secondary to the interests of military preparedness. This difference in mentality, Olmstead felt, rated a full historical treatment; not a sidelight of Babylonian history. Olmstead wanted to pattern his book after Breasted's *History of Egypt*; in that he would let the tablets and inscriptions form the basis for the book, nothing would be taken from secondary sources.[9] This is good historical practice and is not unique to the present day. Breasted, however, was one of the first American scholars to write a history in this manner. Earlier histories had relied mainly on the works of classical scholars as they had not been able to check the inscriptions. In this respect the work is very similar to Breasted's great history.

Olmstead's book contains forty-nine chapters, two indices, 176 illustrations, and thirteen maps, for a total of 695 pages. Robert W. Rogers, reviewing the book in the *American Historical Review*, says, "It would be difficult to exaggerate the importance of this book."[10] His main criticism was the lack of footnotes. Despite this favorable review, and the others were very similar, Olmstead was deeply distressed at the reception accorded his work. He felt that documentation had been provided in his numerous articles already published, so why clutter up the book with footnotes.[11] Lack of footnotes cannot be condoned, as many scholars may not have easy access to Olmstead's earlier articles. As late as 1946 John A. Wilson, former director of the Oriental Institute, University of Chicago, had this to say of the book:

> After more than twenty years, the *History of Assyria* could, of course, be enlarged by recent discoveries, but needs no essential correction in its

---

[8] *Ibid.*, vii.
[9] *Ibid.*, xv.
[10] XXIX (1924), 529.
[11] Personal correspondence with Cameron, May 1, 1967.

presentation of the slow growth of a nation, the brilliant flowering of an empire, the first establishment of the principles of empire for future states to follow, and the basic elements of worth in the often maligned Assyrian.[12]

History of Assyria is crammed full of factual information, providing an excellent reference book for the Assyriologist. Olmstead's style, and the fact that he included every detail of information he was able to discover about the Assyrians, makes the book very difficult to read. The time spent in reading through the work, however, is certainly worth the effort, as today *History of Assyria* still stands as a monumental work. Olmstead has organized the book very well. It is, of course, a political and military history of Assyria, but this is only natural in the study of a nation whose chief deity was the god of war. Today this work could by improved upon as recent archeological work has brought to light more documents that tell the world of early Assyria, which could be incorporated. Also, much more is known of the religion and social history of the Assyrians. All in all, the book is a great improvement over Fraser's *Mesopotamia and Assyria*.[13] Had not *Assyrian Historiography* established Olmstead as one of the leading Assyriologists of the United States, then this book would have done so.

In 1929 Olmstead left Urbana, moving to the University of Chicago as a professor of Oriental History. At Chicago he did not teach any Akkadian language courses, but dealt with Mesopotamia and Persia through history courses, making use of Akkadian as a tool rather than as an objective.[14] His seminars were excellent Assyriological training grounds, and from them would emerge such students as George Cameron, Neilson Debevoise, Waldo Dubberstein, and Arthur Piepkorn.

For the first time in his career Olmstead found a place where he really belonged. He was a historian but had the Oriental Institute with its growing library and the philologists to teach the language courses needed to round out his history seminars. He also had Assyrian and Babylonian tablets to use in the continuation of his research, which allowed him to continue turning out scholarly articles in the leading journals. In 1936-37 he took a leave to serve as Annual Professor at the American Schools for Oriental Research at

---

[12] J. A. Wilson, *JNES*, V (1946), 4.
[13] See above Chap. II.
[14] Personal correspondence with Cameron, May 1, 1967.

Baghdad, where he had access to more of the Assyrian tablets. Olmstead brought the historian into a prominent position in the field of Assyriology. Wilson sums up Olmstead's abilities as a scholar very well by saying:

> Albert Ten Eyck Olmstead's scholarship formed a bridge between two traditions in ancient Oriental history. He was one of the last of the comprehensive ancient historians who addressed themselves to the full range of pre-Islamic history. He was one of the first of the professional ancient historians who subjected the pre-classical and classical cultures of the Orient to a methodological technique adopted from the researches in the natural sciences.[15]

Olmstead was the dominating figure of Assyriology at Chicago between 1929 and 1939, but not the only one; there were others. One of these was Daniel Luckenbill.

Luckenbill and the Assyrian Dictionary

The person who began the task of compiling a dictionary of the Akkadian language was Daniel David Luckenbill (1881-1927). He was born June 21, 1881, near Hamburg, Pennsylvania.[16] After receiving the A.B. degree from the University of Pennsylvania in 1903, Luckenbill went abroad to study, spending the year 1905 at the University of Berlin. In 1907 he earned the Ph.D. degree from the University of Chicago, working under Robert Francis Harper. The University retained Luckenbill as an Associate in Semitic Languages and Literature. In 1909 he was promoted to instructor, assistant professor in 1915, and attained the rank of associate professor in 1919. Not only did Luckenbill establish himself as a competent teacher of the Akkadian language but found the time to publish at least twelve scholarly articles, building himself a reputation as a competent Assyriologist.[17]

By 1920 there were thousands of cuneiform documents at the Universities of Chicago, Pennsylvania, Johns Hopkins, Yale, Harvard, and other schools and museums around the country. James H. Breasted, director of the Oriental Institute, could see the need for an

---

[15] Wilson, *JNES*, V (1946), 1.
[16] Biographical information for Luckenbill obtained from Leroy Waterman, "Daniel David Luckenbill, 1881-1927," *AJSL*, XLIV (1927-28), 1-11.
[17] See bibliography.

up-to-date dictionary of Akkadian, comparable to the Egyptian dictionary compiled by Erman and the Berlin School. Attempts had been made earlier to compile dictionaries, but within a few years they were badly out of date. Edwin Norris, as early as 1866, had published a small dictionary.[18] After this modest beginning he attempted to compile a larger dictionary, issuing the first volume in 1868, but never got beyond the third volume, published in 1872.[19] This work went through the letter N and took up 1,068 pages. Another Englishman, H. Fox Talbot, published a small but useful glossary in 1868[20]

In 1896 Friedrich Delitzsch published his dictionary known as *Assyriches Handwörterbuch*.[21] Even before Delitzsch had published his dictionary, the American William Muss-Arnolt (1860-1926?) had begun to issue one. It consisted of nineteen parts, the first published in 1895 and the last one in 1905, all by a Berlin publishing house.[22] Muss-Arnolt, a native of Cologne, Germany, was born May 7, 1860. He had come to the United States where he earned the Ph.D. in Semitic Languages at Johns Hopkins in 1888. Muss-Arnolt taught briefly in the 1890's and early 1900's at the Universities of Michigan and Chicago, before settling down to a career at the Boston Public Library, where he remained from 1906 to 1921. In 1905 an American publishing firm published the dictionary in two volumes.[23] There were other dictionaries published, but nothing that was of a satisfactory nature.

Breasted realized that his dictionary that he envisioned would have to be the work of hundreds of scholars, a project that would be international in scope, just as the Berlin *Egyptian Dictionary* had been. He obtained permission from the administration of the university, and on October 1, 1921, the Assyrian Dictionary Project got underway, complete with a staff of five. These five were Luckenbill, who was named Director of the project, the Secretary John Albert Maynard (1884-1963?), two graduate students, and a

---

[18] "Specimen of an Assyrian Dictionary," *Jour. Royal Asiatic Soc.*, n.s., II (1866), 225-256.
[19] *Assyrian Dictionary* (3 parts; London: Williams & Norgate, 1868-72).
[20] "Contributions towards a Glossary of the Assyrian Language," *Jour. Royal Asiatic Soc.*, n.s., III (1868), 1-64.
[21] (Leipzig: J. C. Hinrichs, and Baltimore: Johns Hopkins Univ. Press, 1896).
[22] *A Concise Dictionary of the Assyrian Language* (Berlin: Reuther & Reichard, 1895-1905).
[23] (2 vols.; New York: Lemcke & Büchner, 1905.)

stenographer.[24] Maynard was a product of the University of Chicago, having received his Ph.D. in Assyriology from the school in 1916.[25] He was hired in 1921 by the Oriental Institute for the specific purpose of aiding Luckenbill with the Assyrian Dictionary Project. Work began in the basement of Haskell Oriental Museum.

To aid the staff of five, there were three nonresident collaborators. These were Leroy Waterman of the University of Michigan, Samuel Mercer of Western Theological Seminary, and Theophile James Meek (1881-1966) of Meadville Theological Seminary (Pennsylvania).[26] Meek was also a product of the University of Chicago; he had received his Ph.D. from the school in 1915.[27] He was a professor at Meadville when he accepted the assignment, in 1922 he moved to Bryn Mawr, and in 1923 he joined the staff of the University of Toronto. Maynard left in 1923 to devote his time to teaching the history of religion at Western Theological Seminary, and was replaced by F. W. Geers. In this same year of 1923 two more prominent nonresident collaborators were added to the project—Ira Price, who was at the University of Chicago, and Raymond Philip Dougherty (1877-1933), Professor of Biblical Literature at Goucher College, Baltimore.[28]

The staff of the Assyrian Dictionary could draw upon the experiences of those who had helped produce the Egyptian Dictionary, and Breasted had been one of these. Unlike the Egyptian, which had to be hand-copied because of the hieroglyphics, the Akkadian was to be printed in the Latin alphabet; this had been decided upon from the beginning. It was the responsibility of the resident staff to select Akkadian cuneiform documents, using first those that had the most new words, eventually using all the texts that were available.[29] The documents were divided into paragraphs, each consisting of about forty words. These paragraphs were typed onto cards measuring about 4 1/4 x 6 3/4 inches (11 x 17 centimeters) after the cuneiform had been transliterated into the Latin characters.

---

[24] *Assyrian Dictionary*, A. Leo Oppenheim, editor-in-chief (Chicago: Oriental Institute, 1964), I, xii.

[25] His Ph.D. dissertation was *Studies in Religious Texts from Assur* (Chicago: Univ. Chicago Library, 1917).

[26] *Assyrian Dict.*, I, xii.

[27] His doctoral dissertation was *Old Babylonian Business and Legal Documents* (Chicago: Univ. Chicago Library, 1917).

[28] More will be said of Dougherty in Chapter IX.

[29] The mechanical process is taken from Breasted, *The Oriental Institute*, 378-400.

Special typewriters that had all the diacritical signs had to be purchased for this type of work. The transliterated paragraph was typed on the left half of the card; the right half was left blank. These cards were then sent to various collaborators, resident and nonresident, who made a literal translation of the paragraph. This translation was then checked by the most experienced scholars on the staff, and then typed on the right half of the card. In the upper right-hand corner of the card the source of the paragraph was cited. If the paragraph contained forty words, then forty copies of the card were made, using the hectograph system. On the first card the first word was underlined along with its translation on the right side, the second word on the second card, and so on down the line through the last word on the last card. The editors then inserted the underscored word in the upper left-hand corner of the card. After the entire document had been treated this way, the cards were then filed alphabetically, according to the cue word in the upper left-hand corner. In this manner, by going through all the documents, all uses of a particular word would be discovered. By June 28, 1923, Luckenbill reported that there were 270,000 cards in the dictionary file.[30]

Beginning in 1924, however, work on the project began to slow down. This was due mainly to the fact that Breasted began making frequent trips to the Near East, and in his absence Luckenbill was serving as acting director of the Oriental Institute. Thanks to his work with Assyrian Dictionary and also due to his scholarly publications, Luckenbill was promoted to the rank of full professor in the fall of 1923. Aside from his duties as director of the dictionary project and acting director of the institute at times, he managed to publish several scholarly articles and significant books.[31] Then on June 25, 1927, Luckenbill died very suddenly and unexpectedly. Chicago and the Assyrian Dictionary Project had lost a very capable and competent scholar.

In the fall of 1927 Edwin Chiera came to Chicago as Professor of Assyriology at the University and director of the Assyrian Dictionary

---

[30] *Assyrian Dict.*, I, xii.
[31] *The Annals of Sennacherib*, vol. II of *Oriental Institute Publications* (Chicago: Oriental Institute, 1924); *Ancient Records of Assyria and Babylonia, Oriental Institute Ancient Records* series (2 vol.; Chicago: Oriental Inst., 1926-27); for the articles see the bibliography.

Project. He had been an Assyriologist at the University of Pennsylvania since 1913.[32] Chiera inaugurated a new practice of using the mimeograph which worked much more efficiently than the hectograph. Three paragraphs could be placed on one stencil and as many copies as were needed could be made very quickly. By 1929 the project was in full swing once again. New additions to the resident staff were made under the direction of Chiera. One of the first was Thorkild Jacobsen who joined the project in 1929.[33] Professor Arno Poebel from the University of Rostock had come to the University and Oriental Institute in 1928 as a Professor of Sumerian, and in 1930 he joined the dictionary staff.[34] In this same year of 1930 Ignace Jay Gelb became an important member of the staff.[35] He was born October 14, 1907, in Tarnow, Poland. Young Gelb earned his Ph.D. degree at the University of Rome in 1929, after which he came to the University of Chicago where he was named a Fellow and Research Associate in the Oriental Institute.

Newer and much more spacious quarters were provided for the staff in 1931 in the new building that later came to be known as James H. Breasted Hall. After 1931 supervisory duties were divided between Poebel, who had the title of "Scientific Editor," and Chiera, who was called "Managing and Scientific Editor." Scholars from all over the world were invited to make contributions to the Dictionary Project. They were allowed two years to complete their assignment and paid an honorarium according to the difficulty of their task.[36] In 1932 twelve more members were added to the staff, including such names as Samuel Noah Kramer, George Cameron, and Arthur Piepkorn.

Chiera died on June 21, 1933, leaving Poebel to carry on the task of directing the project. At the death of Chiera the files contained about 1,500,000 cards.[37] His death caused an even further slowdown. By 1936 the "Great Depression" had slowed things to a snail's pace. Then in 1939 the outbreak of W. W. II forced the project to come to a complete halt until after the war.[38]

---

[32] See above Chap. V.
[33] More will be said of Jacobsen in Chapter VIII.
[34] Breasted, *Oriental Institute*, 390.
[35] *Assyrian Dict.*, I, xiii.
[36] *Ibid.*, xiv.
[37] Breasted, *Oriental Institute*, 392.
[38] *Assyrian Dict.*, I, xiv.

Oriental Institute Museum

Scholars at the University of Chicago recognized the need for an adequate museum, and the fact that such an institution would be an asset to college or university. The director of the Oriental Institute, James H. Breasted, was fully aware that a well organized museum not only attracted donors and propagated public interest but aided in teaching and scholarly research, as well. In 1920 the museum of the Oriental Institute was still housed in the cramped quarters of the building of the Haskell Oriental Museum.[39] After the Haskell Museum had opened in 1896, the Divinity School occupied a part of the building. Then, when the Oriental Institute was founded in 1919 and took over the collections of the Haskell Museum, both were forced to share the building, with very little space left for exhibition purposes. Finally, in 1925 the Divinity School moved into a new building, leaving the museum building to the Oriental Institute. The museum exhibits were completely reorganized, and all the Far Eastern collections were removed and sent to the Divinity School, the Oriental Institute recognized that they would have to limit themselves to Near Eastern antiquities.[40]

The collections of the Haskell Oriental Museum had been purchased in Europe and the Near East by Robert Francis Harper, had come from the Adab expedition by Banks, and had been purchased from other institutions and museums by Breasted and others. After World War I ended and the treaties had been signed, the museum expeditions sent out by the Oriental Institute began to send back large collections of antiquities from the Near East.[41] By 1926, due to the work of the field expeditions, the space in the museum building had become very insufficient.[42]

Late in the year 1926 Breasted began to appeal for help from the university administration to provide additional space. In December 1928 the International Board of Education voted funds to allow the Oriental Institute to construct a new building, to increase their operational budget, and to establish teaching endowments.[43] A site was chosen for the new building, and by February of 1930 the plans had been completed and accepted by the university. In April the

---

[39] For the opening of this museum see above Chap. V.
[40] Breasted, *Oriental Institute*, 105.
[41] See Chapter VIII.
[42] Breasted, *Oriental Institute*, 106.
[43] *Ibid.*, 108.

ground-breaking ceremonies took place, and one year later, April of 1931, the new building was ready for occupancy.[44]

This new building that would later come to be known as James H. Breasted Hall contained a basement and three floors. The basement was used for storage, preparation, and contained the photographic labs, workshops, and printing room. On the main floor there was a large lecture hall, plus the exhibition area of the museum. The administrative offices, faculty offices, classrooms, research labs, and the reading room of the library were housed on the second floor. Additional faculty and research space, library stacks, and the Assyrian Dictionary Project occupied the third floor.[45] By 1939 the Oriental Institute had a museum that the school and any other institution in the United States could well be proud of.

Publications of the Oriental Institute

When the Oriental Institute was founded in 1919 no budget of any type for publication purposes was included. With limited funds, however, the institute did begin to publish occasional works, starting in 1922.[46] Breasted had developed a capable and competent research and teaching staff, was in the process of getting a new physical plant, and was establishing a very good museum collection. Scholarly research is of no value, however, unless the results can be published. In 1926 Breasted began to develop a systematic program for the publication of the results of scientific research carried on by the Oriental Institute. The university had received funds in the fall of the year from the General Education Board to foster publication. Dr. George Allen, who had been secretary of the Oriental Institute since 1919, was appointed editorial secretary, assuming his new post on July 1, 1927. The International Education Board included in the appropriations to the Oriental Institute in 1928 more funds to aid in the program of publication.

With such Assyriologists on the staff of the Oriental Institute as Olmstead, Chiera, Geers, and Poebel, it was natural to expect a great number of the publications would deal with the area of Assyriology. Breasted and the editorial staff decided that the institute would issue

---

[44] Breasted, *Pioneer to the Past*, 397-398.
[45] Breasted, *Oriental Institute*, 108-128.
[46] Development of the publication program is taken from Breasted, *Oriental Institute*, 427-439.

five types of publications or series. The first series was to be called *Oriental Institute Communications* (abbreviated *OIC*). This series was to consist of preliminary reports, mainly from the field expeditions, written for the general reader in a non-technical language. In the period from 1922 [47] (first issue of *OIC*) through 1939, there were twenty-one volumes in this series, six of which were concerned with Assyriology. These six dealt with the Iraq expedition between 1930 and 1935, and an expedition to Iran.[48]

The second in the series was to be known as *Oriental Institute Publications (OIP)*. These publications were for the specialist rather than the general reader and were to be scientific presentation of source material. *OIP* would present detailed accounts and results of the field expeditions. Between 1924 and 1940 this series contained thirty-eight volumes, of which ten were of an Assyriological nature.

Studies in Ancient Oriental Civilization (SAOC) was to be the title of the third series. In this series scholars would discuss theories based upon philological evidence. Eighteen volumes of *SAOC* appeared between 1931 and 1940, two of which were Assyriological works.[49]

Another series in which discussion of theories was to be presented, but all evidence was to be based on cuneiform texts from Iraq, was to be entitled *Assyriological Studies (AS)*. Ten of these volumes were published between 1931 and 1940.

The last series that contained Assyriological material was the *Ancient Records (AR)*. By 1939 there were seven of these volumes that were English translations of original documents. Five of them were Breasted's *Ancient Records of Egypt* (1907, 3rd impression in 1927), and the other two were Luckenbill's *Ancient Records of Assyria and Babylonia*.

Publication was not hindered by the depression years but did slow down to an extent in 1939. On the eve of World War II the Oriental Institute had an impressive array of publications.

---

[47] Publications prior to 1927 were incorporated into the various series.

[48] Henri Frankfort, Thorkild Jacobsen, and Conrad Preusser, *Tell Asmar and Khafaje, OIC* No. 13, 1932; Frankfort, *Tell Asmar, Khafaje, and Khorsabad, OIC* No. 16, 1933; *Iraq Excavations of the Oriental Institute, 1932-33, OIC* No. 17, 1934; *Oriental Institute Discoveries in Iraq, 1933-34, OIC* No. 19, 1935; *Progress of the Work of the Oriental Institute in Iraq, 1934-35, OIC* No. 20, 1936; and E.F. Schmidt, *The Treasury of Persepolis, OIC* No. 21, 1939.

[49] H. Frankfort, *Archeology and the Sumerian Problem, SAOC* No. 4, 1932; and Ernst Herzfeld, *A New Inscription of Xerxes from Persepolis, SAOC* No. 5, 1932.

CHAPTER EIGHT

THE FIELD BECKONS

American archeological teams went to the field immediately after World War I. The span of time between 1920 and 1939 was a period when archeologists from the United States established a name for themselves. Prior to the war, five Assyriological excavating parties had gone out from the states—four were the Pennsylvania digs at Nippur, and one was the Chicago expedition to Adab. Although competent men had managed these expeditions, they were for the most part gifted amateurs, exhibiting none of the scientific skill of Sir Flinders Petrie in Egypt. Petrie had put archeology on a scientific footing by devising a systematic approach in which every fragment of artifact was noted, photographed in place, and neatly tagged. More attention was paid to what level the object occurred. As an object was removed it was very important to try to reconstruct possible events that happened at the time the artifact was buried. Archeology was divorcing itself from seeking only the spectacular. Between the two great wars archeology passed from the hands of capable amateurs to those of the professionals. A new era of archeology had dawned, and in this era U.S. teams would dominate the Assyriological area.

Penn and the British Museum

The British Museum had first excavated at the ancient city of Ur in 1854 under the direction of J. E. Taylor.[1] Two more expeditions had been sent there between 1918 and 1919 by the museum. R. C. Thompson had directed the 1918 excavations, and H. R. Hall had been the director the following year. In 1922 the British Museum and the University Museum of the University of Pennsylvania decided to combine forces and send a joint expedition to excavate at the site of Ur.[2] No longer did large amounts of governmental red tape have to be cut through; gone were the months and sometimes years of waiting for a permit to excavate; the Ottoman empire was a thing of

---

[1] See above Chap. I.
[2] Madeira, *Men in Search of Man*, 37.

the past; Mesopotamia, or Iraq as it would come to be known, was now a mandate of the British.

Charles Leonard Woolley (1880-1960), later to be knighted for his work, was chosen as director of the Joint Expedition to Ur. He had been hired as Assistant Keeper at the Ashmolean Museum of Oxford University in 1905, just a year after he had obtained an M.A. degree from the school.[3] Woolley had taken part in various expeditions to Nubia and Palestine between 1906 and 1914. After the war Woolley took part in the expedition to Carchemish in 1919, and between 1921 and 1922 he served on the Egyptian expedition to Tell el-Amarna. He was well versed in the scientific methods of Petrie.

An agreement was drawn up in the fall of 1922 by the Boards of Trustees of the two museums, whereby half of the antiquities uncovered would go to the new National Museum at Baghdad, and the other half would be divided between the University of Pennsylvania and the British Museum. The expedition left London on September 26, 1922.[4] After arriving at Ur on October 27, Woolley went to Baghdad to complete the final arrangements, returning to Ur on November 2. On the 15th day of November excavations of the Joint Expedition officially began. Woolley was assisted by the Englishmen F. G. Newton, A. W. Lawrence, and Sidney Smith. The major task of the expedition of the first season was to survey the topography to establish a pattern for future excavation. Secondary objectives were to clear the temple of E-nun-mah and the ziggurat. At the end of the first season, which ended in March of 1923, the history of the temple was worked out, and many antiquities were uncovered, including some of silver and gold.

In September of 1923 the second season at Ur began. Woolley placed C. J. Gadd in charge of digging while he took a crew and carried out excavations at Tell al-Ubaid, four miles to the northwest

---

[3] Biographical information on Woolley taken from a memoriam sketch in *Antiquaries Journal*, XL (1960), 127-130; and obituaries in the Editorial of *Antiquity*, XXXIV (1960), 81-82; and *New York Times*, 21 Feb., 1960, 92.

[4] Account of the Joint Expedition taken from typewritten reports and letters from Woolley to Dr. George Byron Gordon, Director of the University Museum, Folder entitled C. Leonard Woolley, Archives, University Museum, University of Pennsylvania; C. Leonard Woolley, "Excavations at Ur," *Antiquaries Journal*, III (1923), 311-333, IV (1924), 329-346, V (1925), 1-20, 347-402, VI (1926), 365-401, VII (1927), 385-423, VIII (1928), 1-29, 415-448, IX (1929), 305-343, X (1930), 315-343, XI (1931), 343-381, XII (1932), 355-392, XIII (1933), 359-383, XIV (1934), 355-378; and H. R. Hall, L. Legrain, and C. L. Woolley, *Ur Excavations* (Oxford Univ. Press, 1927-55, 6 vols.)

of Ur. He kept his base at Ur and drove there every day. By the end of the second season, in the spring of 1924, a major portion of the ziggurat had been exposed at Ur.

At the end of two seasons at Ur the British Museum and the University of Pennsylvania were well pleased with the results. So pleased, in fact, that they would support the Joint Expedition for ten more seasons, making a total of twelve years at the site. The last season was a very short one, beginning January 6, 1934, and coming to a close on February 25. Although the Joint Expedition had been directed by Woolley and the staff was mostly British, the United States benefited just as much. Not only did the University Museum at Pennsylvania obtain a large share of antiquities and more cuneiform tablets, but American archeologists joined the expedition from time to time, receiving valuable training that would serve them on later excavations.

One of the most significant results of the Joint Expedition was Woolley's reconstruction in detail of the history of the ancient city of Ur. This city of the ancient Sumerians was founded about 3100 B.C., or perhaps as early as 3500 B.C. In the third millenium B.C. Ur became one of the leading cultural centers of the land of Sumer. At this time Sumer was not a unified state but consisted of a series of city-states such as Ur. During the reign of Sargon I (2371-2316 B.C.), king of Akkad, all of Sumer was united with Akkad into a Semitic empire. This empire lasted only until about 2250 B.C. Sumer under the leadership of Ur then began to establish her dominance over the area. This Sumerian rule emanating from Ur ended about 2000 B.C. when the city was destroyed by the Elamites from the east, and the rest of the land of Sumer and Akkad was conquered by the Amorites, who came to be known as the Babylonians. Shortly after 2000 B.C. the Babylonians expelled the Elamites and rebuilt the city of Ur, but it remained in the shadow of the newer capital city of Babylon. During the Assyrian (910-612 B.C.) and Chaldean periods (612-539 B.C.) the city continued to flourish but by this time had lost all political significance and remained only a religious center. Then with the Persian conquest in 539 B.C. it lost its religious importance. By the middle of the 5th century B.C. Ur sank into stagnation and decay, just as Babylon would later.

This Joint Expedition was only one of six major archeological expeditions sponsored jointly or solely by American institutions to unravel the mysteries of ancient Mesopotamia and Persia. The

University of Pennsylvania would also have a hand in the expedition to Tepe Gawra.

Tepe Gawra

Tepe Gawra (great mound) lies in the northern part of Mesopotamia or Iraq about fifteen miles northeast of Mosul. Layard had mentioned the site but did not have the time to carry out more than a cursory examination of the mound.[5] Southern Iraq had undergone much exploration, but the northeastern sector, near the Persian border, had been subjected to very little exploration. Authorities of the American Schools of Oriental Research at Baghdad and Dropsie College of Philadelphia decided in the fall of 1926 to make a survey of northern Mesopotamia in order to find more excavation sites.[6] Field work was to be carried out for the most part by members of the staff of the American Schools, with Dropsie College helping with financial support.[7]

Ephraim Avigdor Speiser (1902-1965) was made director of this survey team. Speiser was born January 24, 1902, at Skalat, Galicia (then in Poland, but now in the USSR).[8] He came to the United States in 1920, where he earned an M.A. degree at the University of Pennsylvania in 1923, and the Ph.D. in 1924 at Dropsie College. Both degrees were in the field of Hebrew studies. Between 1924 and 1926 Speiser served as a Harrison Research Fellow in Semitics at the University of Pennsylvania. He went to Mesopotamia in 1926 as a Guggenheim Fellow (1926-28) and as Annual Professor at the American Schools of Oriental Research at Baghdad (1926-27).

The survey team led by Speiser set out in November of 1926 to

---

[5] *Ruins of Nineveh and Babylon*, 132.

[6] The development of the American Schools of Oriental Research at Baghdad is discussed in Chapter IX.

[7] Account of the Tepe Gawra expedition taken from Charles Bache, "First Report of the Joint Excavations at Tepe Gawra and Tell Billah, 1932-33," *BASOR*, No. 49 (1933), 8-14; "Tepe Gawra," *Amer. Jour. Archaeology*, XXXIX (1935), 185-188; "Report on the Joint Excavation of Tepe Gawra in Assyria," *BASOR*, No. 61 (1936), 5-10; and E. A. Speiser, "Preliminary Excavation at Tepe Gawra," *Annual Amer. Schools of Oriental Research* (hereafter referred to as *AASOR*), IX (1927-28), 17-94; "The Historical Significance of Tepe Gawra," *Annual Report of Smithsonian Institution for 1933* (1934), 415-427; *Excavations at Tepe Gawra* (Philadelphia: Univ. Penn. Press for Amer. Schls. Or. Res., 1935); "Closing the Gap at Tepe Gawra," *Ann. Rept. Smith. Inst. for 1939* (1940), 437-445.

[8] Biographical information on Speiser obtained from Moshe Greenberg, "In Memory of E. A. Speiser," *JAOS*, LXXXVIII (1968), 1-2.

explore the area of northern Mesopotamia. This survey covered the territory between the Sinjar Mountains near the Syrian border and the Awraman range near the Persian borderlands. The party reached the vicinity of Tepe Gawra on April 25, 1927. A brief examination revealed to Speiser that the site had not been inhabited for very long after the end of Sumerian and Akkadian times and was very rich in prehistoric material. After the survey had been completed in June, he sent in his report advising that Tepe Gawra was the most suitable and promising mound to excavate. Dropsie College and the American Schools appropriated $500 for Speiser to make a trial excavation at the mound, beginning in the fall of this same year. On October 9, 1927, with a crew of about sixty men he dug a trial trench at Tepe Gawra. In 1928 Speiser went back to the United States, accepting the position of Assistant Professor of Semitic Languages at the University of Pennsylvania, a rank he held until 1931 when he was promoted to full professor. He went again to Mesopotamia in the spring of 1930 when the University of Pennsylvania and the American Schools sent out a survey team to Tell Billah, in the vicinity of Tepe Gawra. During the few weeks they were at Tell Billah, Speiser made several trips to Tepe Gawra, just eight miles to the east, to further study the mound. He took Howard Leroy, one of the governors of Dropsie College, with him to Gawra, showing him the need for excavating this mound. Upon his return to Philadelphia, Leroy began to stimulate an interest in the excavation of Tepe Gawra. In the fall of 1930 the arrangements for an expedition were completed. It was to be a joint effort, with the University of Pennsylvania, Dropsie College, and the American Schools of Oriental Research at Baghdad participating.

On January 19, 1931, the first season of excavation began at Tepe Gawra with Speiser as director. This season lasted until the first of March. The second season began on October 12 and lasted until March 15, 1932. Speiser was assisted during the second season by the Englishman Cyrus H. Gordon and the American Charles Bache of the staff of the Baghdad School. All that Speiser expected and more came to light as the excavation continued; in fact, digging was carried on for four more seasons, making a total of six. Speiser was director of all but the third-season excavation, which was managed by Bache. The last season came to an end on March 25, 1937. Funds were getting much harder to come by, and Pennsylvania and the Baghdad School wanted to excavate at Tell Billah and Khafajeh. This area known as Diyala was given up by the Oriental Institute on January 1, 1937, and the Baghdad School and the University of Pennsylvania took over the concession.[9] Excavations were carried on by the Joint Expedition during December of 1937 at Khafajeh and Tell Billah, but the sites did not prove nearly so important as Tepe Gawra.[10] Only about half of the mound at Gawra was excavated, but the outbreak of World War II put a halt to any further attempts.

Just as at the other sites, antiquities were discovered which went to the National Museum at Baghdad, the Baghdad School, Dropsie college, and the University of Pennsylvania. More important, however, was the fact that much of the prehistory of Mesopotamia was developed from Tepe Gawra. As a metropolitan area it could not compare with Ur, Babylon, Nippur, Nineveh, and others, but its importance lay in its earlier age. Eight levels were excavated that went back to the middle of the fourth millenium B.C., but it was estimated that there were ten more levels, stretching time back into the early Neolithic. No other site at that time had afforded such a glimpse of prehistoric Mesopotamia. Shortly after 1500 B.C. the site ceased being inhabited.

The University of Pennsylvania had taken part in two joint expeditions. Other institutions would participate in this practice. One that would do this was the Field Museum of Chicago.

Chicago Field Museum and Oxford

In Chicago the officials at the Chicago Field Museum of Natural History (now the Chicago Museum of Natural History) began to see the need for an expedition to Mesopotamia to collect antiquities for their exhibits. After checking the excavation literature they discovered that the ancient city of Kish had not been explored to any extent. Kish was about 100 miles south of Baghdad and eight miles east of the site of Babylon. Jules Oppert had carried out minor excavations at the site in 1852 while working at Babylon, and then another Frenchman, Henri de Genouillac, had worked there briefly in 1912.[11] In the spring of 1922 Herbert Weld of Oxford University

---

[9] Speiser, "New Discoveries at Tepe Gawra and Khafaje," *Amer. Jour. Archaeology*, XLI (1937), 193.

[10] Work had been carried on briefly at Tell Billah from November 2, 1932, to April 4, 1933.

[11] Henry Field, *The Field Museum-Oxford Univerisity Expedition to Kish*,

also became interested in doing some excavations at Kish. When he found out that the Field Museum was interested in the site, he drew up a proposal for a joint expedition, which was agreeable to both the Field Museum and Oxford.[12]

Professor Stephen Langdon of Oxford University was chosen as Director of the Kish Expedition, and the American Ernest Mackay was selected as Field Director.[13] The first season was a short one, getting underway around the first of February and ending the first week of May 1923. Mackay excavated alone this first season, with just the help of an Arab work force. Much pottery was found, dating back to about 3000 B.C. The site seemed very old, not as old as Tepe Gawra, but seemingly older than Babylon or Ur. Both the Field Museum and Oxford were very happy with the results at Kish; thus, the excavations continued for ten seasons. In 1926 Mackay left the expedition and was replaced by the French archeologist Louis Charles Watelin. The tenth and final season came to an end in the spring of 1932.

From the antiquities uncovered, plus excavations of a very large cemetery, Langdon reconstructed the history of the area. Instead of being Akkadian as some had thought, Kish turned out to be one of the very early Sumerian cities. It was probably founded around 4000 B.C. or shortly thereafter and was inhabited until well into the Babylonian period (ca. 1500 B.C.). From studies made at Kish, Langdon formulated the theory that the Sumerians had moved into Mesopotamia from Elam, settling first in the vicinity of Kish, and then moving on down to the Persian Gulf.

While digging at Kish, Langdon made excavations at several other localities for the Joint Expedition. One of the more important of these sites was the city known as Jemdet Nasr, lying about eighteen miles northeast of Kish. This was also a Sumerian city, founded

---

Mesopotamia 1923-1929 (Chicago: Field Mus. Nat Hist., Anthropology Leaflet 28, 1929), 4.

[12] *Ibid.*

[13] Account of this expedition is taken from *Annual Report of the Director of the Field Museum*, Publication 217 (1924), 197-198, 227 (1925), 235, 297 (1926), 243, 425-426 (1927), 56-57, 248 (1928), 208-209, 252 (1929), 425-430, VIII (1930-31), 50-51, 318-320, Publ. 306 (1932), 67-69, 318 (1933), 319-320; Stephen Langdon & L. C. Watelin, *Excavations at Kish. The Herbert Weld (Oxford) and Field Museum of Natural History (Chicago) Expedition to Mesopotamia* (Paris: Geuthner, 1924-34); and Ernest Mackay, *Report of Excavations at Jemdet Natr, Iraq* (Chicago: Field Mus. Nat. Hist., 1931).

perhaps, a few years before Kish. Jemdet Nasr was destroyed by fire about 3500 B.C. and never occupied again.

In the 1920's and 1930's the system of pooling talent and money for these joint expeditions was proving very practical. Other schools and institutions took advantage of this system, including more ventures on the part of the Baghdad School.

Other Joint Expeditions

The American Schools of Oriental Research at Baghdad was very interested in uncovering the secrets of the past locked in the ruins of the ancient city of Nuzi, located near the modern site of Kirkuk, Iraq.[14] Edwin Chiera had been the first, as far as is known, to excavate at Nuzi. He had been Annual Professor at the Baghdad School for the academic year 1924-25. In the winter of 1924-25 Chiera had explored and dug a trial trench at the site of Nuzi. He was pleased with what he had discovered and made plans to excavate still further. Chiera was selected as director of the expedition for the year 1927. This season's expedition was a joint effort on the part of the American School of Oriental Research at Baghdad, Harvard Semitic Museum, and the Fogg Art Museum (Harvard). E. A. Speiser and Leroy Waterman served on this expedition, gaining valuable field experience. This second season began in the last week of October 1927 and came to a close in the middle of March 1928.

Campaign number three, which began at the end of October 1928 and lasted until mid-March of 1929, was a joint undertaking of Harvard (Semitic, Fogg, and Peabody Museums), the Baghdad School, and the Museum of the University of Pennsylvania. The leader for this season was Robert Henry Pfeiffer (1892-1958) of Harvard.[15] In the winter of 1929-30 and 1930-31 the fourth and fifth campaigns were carried out by Richard Starr of Harvard, and again were joint efforts on the part of the Baghdad School, Harvard, and the University of Pennsylvania.

From these campaigns, about 2,500 cuneiform tablets were recovered. Most of these were records of business transactions, giving

---

[14] Account of the Nuzi Expedition taken from E. Chiera, *Excavations at Nuzi*, Vol. I, Vol. V of *Harvard Semitic Series* (1929), v-viii; Ernest R. Lacheman, *Excavations at Nuzi*, Vols. V-VIII, Vols. XIV, XV, XVI, and XIX of *Harvard Sem. Ser.* (1950-62); T. J. Meek, *Excavations at Nuzi*, Vol. III, Vol. X of *H. Sem. Ser.* (1935), vii-xi; and Robert H. Pfeiffer, *Excavations at Nuzi*, Vol. II, Vol. IX of *H. Sem. Ser.* (1932), vi-xi.

[15] More will be said of Pfeiffer in Chapter IX.

a very good account of the business history of Nuzi. Gasur, as the city was probably called originally, was founded perhaps at the end of the fourth millenium or shortly after the beginning of the third millenium B.C. It was predominantly an Akkadian city, with many Sumerians residing there. Toward the middle of the second millenium B.C. the Hurrians of Asia Minor moved south and captured the city, changing the name to Nuzi. Then about 1500 B.C. the city was destroyed by fire, never to be occupied again.

Leroy Waterman of the University of Michigan was Annual Professor for 1927-28 at the American School of Oriental Research at Baghdad. While at the Baghdad School Waterman gained experience helping Chiera at Nuzi. Waterman became interested in the mound called Tell Umar near the ancient Parthian capital of Ctesiphon.[16] The first campaign began with Waterman as director on December 29, 1927, and ended on March 10, 1928. This season was sponsored by the American Schools of Oriental Research at Baghdad, with financial support from the Toledo Museum of Art of Ohio. Waterman directed all of these campaigns. In 1928 the University of Michigan with financial support from the Toledo Museum took over the excavation of Tell Umar. Waterman's second season ran from November 10, 1928, to February 28, 1929. Three more campaigns were undertaken, making a total of five. The last season ended April 1, 1932, a campaign in which the Cleveland Museum of Art added support to the University of Michigan and Toledo Museum.

Cuneiform documents and coins indicate that Tell Umar was probably a Sumerian city planted in Akkad in the third millenium B.C. It seemed to have been prosperous all through the Babylonian, Assyrian, Chaldean, Persian, and Hellenistic periods. About 142 B.C. the city was captured by the Parthians. Under Parthian rule it continued to prosper until 43 A.D. when the rulers destroyed the city because of a large revolt in the area. After 43 the city was abandoned and never rebuilt.

In 1930 Riza Shah passed a law opening Persia (officially became Iran in 1934) to archeological excavation. The Museum of the University of Pennsylvania and Pennsylvania Museum of Art of Philadelphia drew up an agreement to send a joint expedition to

---

[16] Account of the Tell Umar Expedition taken from L. Waterman, *Preliminary Report Upon Excavations at Tel Umar, Iraq* (Ann Arbor: Univ. Mich. Press, 1931); and *Second Preliminary Report Upon the Excavations at Tel Umar, Iraq* (Univ. Mich. Press, 1933).

Persia. Their objective was to excavate the site of Tepe Hissar near Damghan, lying east of Teheran. Erich Friedrich Schmidt (1897-1965?), a native of Baden-Baden, Germany, was named director of the Tepe Hissar expedition. Not long after he had come to the United States in 1923, Schmidt was named director of the American Museum of Natural History's archeological expedition to Arizona between 1924 and 1926. He had then served as director of the Asia Minor expedition sent out by the Oriental Institute of the University of Chicago, 1926-29. In 1929 he had received the Ph.D. from Columbia University. Schmidt came to the Tepe Hissar expedition well trained in field archeology.

Late in January of 1931 Schmidt and members of the expedition arrived in Baghdad, where they outfitted for the trip. It had been decided beforehand that the party would conduct a brief test excavation at Fara in Mesopotamia before moving on into Persia.[17] This excavation lasted from February 23, 1931, to April. Pottery and cuneiform tablets were found at Fara. Hilprecht had excavated here briefly in April of 1900, and Koldewey and the Germans from June 1902 to March 1903.

Testing completed at Fara, the party moved on into Persia, arriving at Damghan on June 22, 1931. On July 19 the excavations at Tepe Hissar officially got underway, lasting until December 20. The party wintered at Teheran. They returned to the site early in May of 1932 for the second season. Excavation came to an end with the start of the rainy season early in November. In February of 1933 the expedition started back to the United States.

At Tepe Hissar, Schmidt and colleagues arrived at the conclusion that a well developed culture had evolved in the area by about 4000 B.C. The city was probably occupied until the second millenium B.C. Then there were occupants again in Sasanid times (228-651). After the Islamic conquest the vicinity was deserted.

Not all institutions participated in joint expedition projects. One such was the Oriental Institute of the University of Chicago, undergoing a period of prosperity and expansion.

The Iraq Expedition of the Oriental Institute

After Breasted had begun to expand physical facilities at home, he turned his attention more fully toward the field. The Iraq Expedition

---
[17] Account of the expedition taken from Schmidt, *Excavations at Tepe Hissar Damghan* (Philadelphia: Univ. Penn. Press, 1937).

was actually divided in two parts. Work in the northern part of Mesopotamia, or Assyria proper, was known as the Assyrian section, while the southern and central sections was referred to as the Babylonian section.[18]

The Babylonian section of the Iraq Expedition confined its activities, for the most part, to the eastern side of the Tigris River. Breasted and his staff at the Institute felt that this sector had been neglected. Four major sites were selected to concentrate their energies upon. These were Tell Asmar, Khafajeh, Abu Khazaf, and Ischali; the last three known collectively as the Diyala region, lying along the Diyala River. Henri Frankfort (1897-1954) was appointed director of the Iraq Expedition (including both sections) in late 1929. Frankfort was born February 24, 1897, at Amsterdam, Holland. He received the Ph. D. from the University of Leiden in 1927. Frankfort arrived in Baghdad on December 23, 1929, to begin making preparations. He had an assistant to help him coordinate excavations in these different sectors, a young man by the name of Thorkild Jacobsen. Young Jacobsen was from Copenhagen, Denmark, born there June 7, 1904. After graduating with an A.M. degree from the University of Copenhagen in 1927, Jacobsen came to the United States where he earned his Ph.D. at the University of Chicago in 1929. The university then hired him as a field Assyriologist for the Iraq Expedition.

Excavation at Tell Asmar, the ancient city of Eshnunna, began on November 11, 1930. This locality lies about twenty-five miles to the east of Baghdad. In all, six seasons were devoted to excavating at Tell Asmar, the last season ending in the spring of 1936. Numerous inscribed bricks, statues, and cuneiform tablets were recovered from Tell Asmar in the six seasons. From the evidence uncovered it appeared that Eshnunna was a Sumerian city founded in the late fourth or early third millenium B.C. It had been part of the Akkadian empire of Sargon, and then under Sumerian rule out of Ur. After the Amorite conquest about 2000 B.C. Eshnunna became an independent kingdom, and it was not until near the middle of the reign of Hammurabi (1792-1750 B.C.) that the city was finally subjugated and brought into the Babylonian empire.

---

[18] Account of the Iraq Expedition taken from Frankfort, *OIC* No. 16; No. 17; No. 19; No. 20; "The Work of the Oriental Institute in Iraq," *Amer. Jour. Archaeology*, XXXVII (1933), 529-539; Frankfort, Jacobsen and Preusser, *OIC* No. 13; and Thorkild Jacobsen and Seton Lloyd, *Sennacherib's Aqueduct at Jerwan*, Vol. XXIV of *OIP* (Chicago: Oriental Institute, 1935).

The other major site that Frankfort concentrated on was the city of Khafajeh. Work began there on November 22, 1930, and continued for eight seasons, coming to a close on January 1, 1937, when the Oriental Institute gave up Khafajeh and the Diyala region to the Baghdad School and the University of Pennsylvania. This city was also a Sumerian city with a history very similar to that of Tell Asmar (Eshnunna). Khafajeh had been a part of the kingdom of Eshnunna, the period from 2000 to about 1777 B.C.

During the period of excavation at Tell Asmar and Khafajeh, digging was carried out at other sites. Some of these were Tepe Shenshi, spring of 1933; Jerwan, spring of 1933 and 1934; Ischali, winter of 1934-35, and 1935-36; and Tell Agrab, winter of 1935-36, and 1936-37. In the fall of 1937 Jacobsen returned to Chicago where he was appointed Instructor of Assyriology.

To the north the Assyrian section had actually gotten underway before the Babylonian section. Edwin Chiera had begun to excavate at the ancient Assyrian city of Dur-Sharrukin (modern name of Khorsabad) early in 1929. This city had been excavated to an extent by two French expeditions—Paul Botta, 1843-44, and Victor Place, 1852-55. Chiera only conducted minor exploratory excavation before he went back to Chicago to begin full-time duty on the Assyrian Dictionary Project.[19] This was enough to convince the staff of the Oriental Institute that Khorsabad was worthy of being excavated. In 1930 Frankfort took over direction of the excavation of the city, along with the rest of the Iraq Expedition. Five seasons were spent by the party excavating at Khorsabad, the last season ending in May of 1935.

This excavation of Khorsabad established the fact that the history of the city had been unique, the capital during the reign of only one king. Khorsabad lies very near ancient Nineveh and only about fifteen miles northeast of modern Mosul. When Sargon II, king of Assyria (722-705 B.C.), usurped the throne about 722 B.C. he desired to build a new capital. One day's march north of Nineveh, Sargon built this new city, which he named Dur-Sharrukin. He was assassinated in 705 B.C., and his son Sennacherib restored the capital to Nineveh. The city of Khorsabad remained the seat of a governor for about a century and then fell into ruin.

The Oriental Institute was not content to limit their Assyriological activities to Mesopotamia or Iraq. In 1930 their attention had been directed also to the east toward Persia or Iran.

---

[19] See above Chap. VII.

The Persian Expedition

Until 1930 the French had been the only foreigners allowed to come in and excavate in Iran. The Oriental Institute was given a concession to dig in Iran in 1930 by Shah Riza Pahlevi and the Iranian cabinet; the area was to be Persepolis and vicinity. Ernst Emil Herzfeld, who had been serving as archeological adviser to the Persian government, notified Breasted that a concession had been granted. Charles Breasted, executive secretary, of the Oriental Institute flew to Teheran to complete the arrangements.[20] Herzfeld accepted appointment as field director of the Persian Expedition for the Oriental Institute. He was born July 23, 1879, at Celle, Hanover, Germany. Herzfeld received the Ph.D. from the University of Berlin in 1907.[21] He had learned his field-work under Delitzsch excavating at Assur between 1903 and 1906. His main interest lay in archeological architecture. Since 1920 he had been a professor at the University of Berlin but had been in the field most of the time. In 1928 he excavated at Pasargadae, which lies just to the north of Persepolis.

Herzfeld began excavation at Persepolis in the spring of 1931. While excavating the ruins of the city, Herzfeld dug at a smaller mound in the vicinity that turned out to be a Neolithic village, dating back to about 4000 B.C. This made a great contribution to the knowledge of prehistoric Persia. At Persepolis the architecture was studied in detail, and new inscriptions were discovered. It was from this city that early knowledge of the cuneiform inscriptions was sent back to Europe.[22] The Persian Expedition came to an end in the spring of 1935. Herzfeld went first to England, then came to the United States in 1936, where he became a professor at the Institute for Advanced Studies at Princeton University, a post he held until 1946.

Herzfeld's work not only contributed to our knowledge of Persian architecture but gave more details on the history of the city. When

---

[20] Account of the Persian Expedition taken from Breasted, *Oriental Institute*, 89-91, 310-336; and Erich F. Schmidt, *OIC* No. 21; and *Persepolis* (Chicago: Univ. Chicago Press, 1953-56).

[21] Biographical information on Herzfeld extracted from obituaries, *New York Times*, 23 January 1948, 23, *Isis*, XLII (1951), 146; and George C. Miles (ed.), *Archaeologica Orientalia in Memoriam Ernst Herzfeld* (Locust Valley, N. Y.: J. J. Augustin, 1952).

[22] See above Chap. I.

Darius I became king of Persia in 522 B.C. the empire had three capitals. These were Ecbatana the old Median capital, Susa the headquarters of the old Elamite kingdom, and Babylon the queen city of the ancient Near East. In 513 B.C. Darius began building this new city which was completed by about 497 B.C.[23] Persepolis became the most important of all the Persian capitals; all kings were crowned there. It remained a very important city until it was destroyed by Alexander the Great in early 330 B.C.

By 1936 the Great Depression curtailed archeological activity in the Near East. Then in 1939 the outbreak of World War II put a complete halt to all archeological work. During the period from 1920 through 1939 American archeological teams not only filled museums with antiquities but unlocked more of the secrets of ancient Persia and Mesopotamia. During this same era European archeologists were also carrying out field work in these same countries.

European Expeditions

True, European archeological teams were not as numerous in Iran and Iraq between the wars as American groups, but they did make contributions to archeology. One of the major reasons that U.S. teams dominated the archeological scene was that the nations of Europe had suffered much from World War I and simply did not have the financial resources available to compete with the Americans.

The British reopened excavations at Nineveh in 1927. This was a joint undertaking on the part of the British Museum and Oxford University, with some financial support from the Antiquaries Society of London, and subscriptions from private citizens. R. Campbell Thompson directed these excavations that lasted from 1927 until 1932. He was assisted by R. W. Hutchinson, R. W. Hamilton, and M. E. L. Mallowan. In 1933 the British Museum and the British School of Archaeology in Iraq conducted a brief excavation at Tell Arpachiah. M. E. L. Mallowan led this expedition, lasting from February through April of 1933.

France continued her digging in Iraq in at least three localities. The excavations at Lagash were reopened early in 1929 and ran into 1930. Henri de Genouillac ran the expedition which was sponsored

---

[23] For a brief, but good treatment of the archeology of Persepolis see Donald N. Wilber, *Persepolis: The Archaeology of Parsa, Seat of the Persian Kings* (New York: Crowell, 1969).

by the Louvre. At Medain Roman Ghirshman carried out excavations at a cemetery for the Louvre. André Parrot dug at Larsa for two months in the spring of 1933. This was also sponsored by the Louvre.

The Germans excavated briefly at the sites of Dair and Sippar in 1927. Walther Andrae and Julius Jordan carried out the excavations for the Notgemeinschaft der Deutschen Wissenschaft during the month of January. Their most concentrated effort was at Erech (Warka, Uruk) where Julius Jordan excavated for eleven seasons for the same society that sponsored digs at the other two sites. These excavations began in November of 1928 and came to a halt in March of 1939

Giuseppe Furlani directed an expedition for the Italians at Kakzu in ancient Assyria. These excavations that lasted from February through April of 1933 were sponsored by the Missione Archeologica Italiana di Mesopotamia.

In Iran the only two nations to excavate besides the United States were France and Germany. Prior to 1930 the French had been the only foreigners allowed to excavate in that country. After the war France resumed her digging, but worked, for the most part, only in the vicinity of Susa, just as had been done prior to the war. Although they worked out a great deal of Elamite history, they contributed nothing to the knowledge of Achaemenid Persia. The Germans excavated briefly at Rishahr near Bushire, but for the most part Persian archeology was dominated by U.S. teams.

CHAPTER NINE

BLOOMING OF A SCIENCE

Just as the Oriental Institute of the University of Chicago was undergoing rapid expansion during the years from 1920 through 1939, and U. S. archeological teams were busily excavating in Persia and Mesopotamia, so were other facets of Assyriology in the process of blooming. At least one institution was founded that would propagate field work. Assyriological literature would be published in quantity and quality, the likes of which had not been seen before. Learned societies would devote more of their program time to Assyriology, and Assyriological articles would fill the pages of their journals. At the colleges and universities teachers would continue to expand their Assyriological offerings, carry out research, and publish the results of this scholarly research.

At the Institutions

David G. Lyon continued teaching Assyriological courses at Harvard University. His publications had dropped off, however, as he published only one significant article, this in 1928.[1] Lyon retired from teaching in 1922 but retained his position as curator of the Harvard Semitic Museum. At his retirement in 1922 Lyon offered an undergraduate course in the history of Babylonia and Assyria, and three graduate courses in the Akkadian language. These courses were kept alive by Robert Henry Pfeiffer, who became an instructor at Harvard in the fall of 1922.[2]

Pfeiffer was born February 14, 1892, at Bologna, Italy, son of George and Adelia Pfeiffer, who were U. S. citizens.[3] He attended the Theological School at Geneva, Switzerland, between 1911 and 1913 and received the Bachelor of Divinity from the University of Geneva in 1915. Working under Lyon at Harvard, Pfeiffer earned an A.M.

---

[1] "The Joint Expedition of Harvard University and the Baghdad School at Yargan Tepe Near Kirkuk," *BASOR*, No. 30 (1928), 1-6.
[2] *Harvard Univ. Catalog, 1922-23* (1922), 42.
[3] Biographical material on Pfeiffer taken from a memoriam sketch by W. F. Albright in *BASOR*, No. 150 (1958), 3-4.

degree in 1920, and the Ph.D. in 1922. He did not change the course offerings of Lyon but continued to offer them in essentially the same format. Pfeiffer was director of the excavations at Nuzi between 1928-29.[4] When he returned to Harvard he was appointed Lecturer of Assyriology for the 1929-30 school year. One year later Pfeiffer was promoted to Assistant Professor of Semitic Languages and Literature. In 1931 he also accepted the post of assistant curator of the Harvard Semitic Museum.

The "Father of American Assyriology" David Gordon Lyon passed away on December 4, 1935. America had lost one of the great pioneers and founding fathers of Assyriology. Pfeiffer reduced his teaching load by becoming Lecturer of Assyriology in 1936, as he became curator of the Semitic Museum. He continued to offer Assyriology at Harvard as the year 1940 dawned.

At Johns Hopkins Haupt and Blake were teaching the courses offered in Assyriology. Then on December 15, 1926, Paul Haupt died. This left only Blake to handle the courses.[5] Another of the pioneers of American Assyriology had passed from the scene. In the fall of 1929 W. F. Albright was made director of the Oriental Seminary, a post that had remained vacant since Haupt's death. The seminary was reorganized with Blake devoting himself to the instruction of Hebrew and Arabic, and Albright teaching Biblical archeology.[6] After 1930 Assyriological language courses were dropped at Johns Hopkins as part of the regular offerings.[7] From time to time Albright or a visiting professor would offer a course in Sumerian or Akkadian, but nothing that became part of the established curriculum.

Morris Jastrow, Jr. died on June 22, 1921, leaving the teaching load in Akkadian upon the shoulders of Edwin Chiera at the University of Pennsylvania. Jastrow's great rival and certainly one of the founding fathers of American Assyriology, Hermann V. Hilprecht, passed away in Philadelphia on March 19, 1925. Although both belittled the scholarly abilities of the other, each in his own way had contributed much to Assyriology at the University of Pennsylvania and the city of Philadelphia. In 1922 Chiera was promoted to Assistant professor and in 1926 attained the rank of

---

[4] See above Chap. VIII.
[5] *JHUC*, No. 378 (1927), 22.
[6] *Ibid.*, No. 419 (1930), 67.
[7] *Ibid.*, No. 431 (1931), 81.

Professor of Assyriology. One year later, however, he left Pennsylvania and went to the University of Chicago to become editor of the Assyrian Dictionary Project.[8] Leon Legrain, who had been Woolley's chief assistant at Ur for several seasons, came to the University Museum in 1920 to work on the decipherment of the Nippur tablets. He was a Roman Catholic priest, holding the Doctor of Divinity and Doctor of Science degrees. Legrain came from the Sorbonne to Philadelphia, intent on staying one year, but as it turned out he stayed twenty-eight.[9] He became curator of the Babylonian Section of the University Museum and Clark Research Professor of Assyriology. After Chiera's departure in 1927, Legrain continued the Assyriological offerings at the University of Pennsylvania, along with G. A. Barton, who came to the university as Professor of Semitic Languages from Bryn Mawr in 1922. Barton served ten years, retiring in 1932.

Princeton had not offered any type of course related to Assyriology since 1886. Cuneiform studies were revived at Princeton in the late 1930's by Philip Khuri Hitti, a native of Lebanon who had received his Ph.D. degree from Columbia in 1915. He came to Princeton in 1926. Although Hitti offered two graduate courses in Akkadian grammar in the fall of 1937, he would never really be considered an Assyriologist.[10] His claim to fame would come later as an Arab and modern Near Eastern historian.

George Barton continued to allow students to specialize in Akkadian or Hebrew language studies in his seminar at Bryn Mawr.[11] After Barton left for the University of Pennsylvania in 1922, Assyriology began to die out at the school. By 1926 Bryn Mawr no longer offered instruction in the Akkadian language.[12]

Research and excavation projects at the Oriental Institute have already been discussed in Chapters VII and VIII. At the teaching level the University of Chicago still had the largest number of Assyriological courses being taught by any U. S. institution. A. T. Olmstead taught Assyrian and Babylonian history; Arno Poebel handled the Sumerian courses; Luckenbill, Chiera, Price, and others taught Akkadian; and later George Cameron would teach Old Persian.

---

[8] See above Chap. VII.
[9] Madeira, *Men in Search of Man*, 37.
[10] *Princeton Univ. Catalog, 1937-38* (1937), 381.
[11] *Bryn Mawr Calendar, 1923-24* (1924), 13.
[12] *Ibid., 1927-28* (1927), 60.

At the University of Michigan Leroy Waterman continued to teach the Akkadian language course. Although not devoted just to Assyriology, Waterman taught history courses of the ancient Near East that included Assyriological material.

John Prince and Frederick Vanderburgh continued to offer Sumerian and Akkadian at Columbia University in the inter-war years. Prince went into the diplomatic service in 1921, leaving the courses to Vanderburgh. Even after he returned in 1933, Prince devoted himself to Slavic languages. Abraham Jackson continued to teach Old Persian until his retirement in 1935. Two years later Jackson died, and the United States lost one of its few Iranian language scholars.

Nathaniel Schmidt was the Assyriologist at Cornell University, where he taught history courses on Mesopotamia and Persia, and elementary language courses in Sumerian and Akkadian. According to the catalogues, after Schmidt's retirement in 1932, Cornell offered no more Assyriological studies.

The only Assyriological course being taught at Vanderbilt University in 1920 was Old Persian, handled by Herbert Tolman. This came to an end with the death of Tolman on November 24, 1923. After this, Assyriological studies were no longer a part of the Vanderbilt curriculum.

Albert Clay and his colleagues kept expanding the teaching, research, and publication phases of Assyriology at Yale after 1920. By the 1925-26 academic year Clay was teaching twelve courses in Sumerian and Akkadian with the help of graduate students.[13] He was also developing the Yale Babylonian Collection that had been growing since 1910. In 1922 Dr. James B. Nies donated his collection to Yale, bringing the number of antiquities to over 9,000.[14]

Unfortunately for Yale and the rest of the academic world, Clay passed away on September 14, 1925, shortly after the beginning of the school year. Raymond Philip Dougherty (1877-1933) was appointed William M. Laffan Professor of Assyriology and Curator of the Babylonian Collection in 1926 to fill the vacancy created by the death of Clay.[15] Dougherty was born August 5, 1877, at Lebanon,

---

[13] *Yale Univ. Catalog, 1925-26* (1925), 188-189.

[14] F. J. Stephens, "The Babylonian Collection," *Yale Univ. Library Gazette,* XIX (1945), 44-49.

[15] *Bull. Yale Univ., Reports to the President, 1926-27* (1927), 203.

Pennsylvania.[16] After earning the A.B. (1897) and A.M. (1903) from Lebanon Valley College, Pennsylvania, he went to Yale where he received the Ph.D. after studying under Clay in 1918. Dougherty was then employed as Professor of Biblical Literature at Goucher College from 1918 to 1926. He was Annual Professor at the American School of Oriental Research at Baghdad during the 1925-26 school year. While at Baghdad he had gained field experience in archeology.

Dougherty got help from another of Clay's former students. This was Ferris J. Stephens, who was appointed Assistant Professor of Assyriology in the fall of 1928.[17] Stephens was born December 26, 1893, in Fayette County, Indiana. After receiving the Ph.D. from Yale in 1925, he accepted the post of Professor of Old Testament and Ancient History at Culver-Stockton College, Canton, Missouri, a position he held until he went back to Yale.

On July 13, 1933, Dougherty passed away leaving Stephens to handle the twelve courses in Assyriology by himself. Yale recruited him some help, however, in the person of Albrecht Goetze for the school year of 1934-35.[18] Goetze, born January 11, 1897, at Leipzig, Germany, earned his Ph.D. at the University of Heidelberg in 1920, and remained in Germany until the Nazi forced him to leave in 1934. In 1934 Goetze was given the position of Visiting Professor. Two years later the appointment became a permanent one, as he was selected William M. Laffan Professor of Assyriology. Also, in this same year of 1936 the administrative organization was changed. All scholars of Semitic languages, Oriental religion, Oriental history, and Linguistics were grouped together into a new department, known as the Department of Oriental Studies. William F. Edgerton, an Egyptologist, was chosen as chairman, with Stephens and Goetze making up the Assyriological staff.[19]

One major university in the United States that would play a prominent role in Assyriology made its debut into Assyriological circles in the period between 1920 and 1940. This was the University of California at Berkeley. The person who inaugurated cuneiform studies at California was Henry Ludwig Frederick Lutz, who was born February 16, 1886, at New York City. After a strong background in

---

[16] Biographical information on Dougherty taken from "Necrology," *Amer. Jour. Archaeology*, XXXVII (1933), 467.

[17] *Bull. Yale Univ.*, Reports to the President, *1927-28* (1928), 224.

[18] George W. Pierson, *Yale: College and University 1878-1937* (New Haven, Conn: Yale Univ. Press, 1952, Vol. II, 677.

[19] *Ibid.*, 525.

theological training, Lutz enrolled at Yale, earning the Ph.D. Under Clay in 1916 and 1919 he was Research Fellow in Semitics at the University of Pennsylvania, then a research instructor at that school until 1921. Lutz was appointed Assistant Professor of Assyriology and Egyptology at the University of California beginning in the fall of 1921.[20]

This new and eager scholar was anxious to develop both Assyriology and Egyptology, and he was forced to divide his duties equally among the two disciplines. Despite this, however, according to the catalogues, Lutz had by 1923 initiated four courses in Akkadian and Sumerian, plus three more courses that dealt with the history, religion, and archeology of both Egypt and Mesopotamia.[21] His first promotion came in 1924, when he became associate professor, and he made professor in 1929. These same courses that Lutz developed early in the twenties remained in the curriculum without significant changes as the year 1939 came to a close. California had now entered the field.

Philology and archeology continued to be the areas that were emphasized in the sphere of Assyriology. American and foreign savants were concerned more with finding and translating the documents than they were with writing histories of Mesopotamia and Persia; this had been been the emphasis since the birth of the science, and the same could be said for Egyptology and the other fields of Oriental study. Histories came about as a result of translation and not as something that was planned for and achieved. Only rarely would a Breasted or Olmstead come along, men who were interested in using philology as a tool instead of an end result.

At the universities and colleges there was a period of Assyriological expansion, but they did not completely dominate the scene. The professional societies continued to make Assyriology known to the public, and to stimulate interest and new ideas among professors and laymen alike.

Learned Societies

The American Oriental Society was keeping very much alive its interest in the topic of Assyriology. Looking through the *Proceedings*

---

[20] *Annual Report of the President of the University 1921-22* (Berkeley: Univ. Calif. Bulletin XVI, No. 6, 1922), 59.
[21] *Univ. Calif. Register, 1921-22 with Announcements for 1922-23* (1922), Vol. I, 221-222.

of the society, which gives the papers that were presented at the annual meetings, one finds that cuneiform studies are represented at every meeting.[22] At these meetings of both the society and the Middle West branch at least eighty-two papers or communications of an Assyriological nature were presented. This is to be expected with such names on the rolls as Clay, Lyon, Olmstead, Gottheil, Haupt, and others—in fact, most of the Assyriologists of the United States. The meetings of the American Oriental Society were not dominated by the Assyriologists, however, but were divided equally among the areas of Assyriology, Egyptology, Palestinian studies, Indo-Iranian studies, and Far Eastern studies. On the other hand, the meetings of the Middle West branch of the Society were dominated by the Assyriologists; Olmstead was the driving force in this group.

After 1920 the American Philosophical Society included more papers devoted to Assyriology on the programs of their meetings. Barton, Chiera, Clay, Speiser, Haupt, and others contributed a steady stream of papers to the programs of the society meetings.[23]

The Oriental Club of Philadelphia celebrated its fiftieth anniversary in 1938 by holding their meeting with the annual meeting of the American Oriental Society in Philadelphia, April 19-21. This also happened to be the one hundred and fiftieth meeting of the American Oriental Society. Looking back over fifty years of existence, the club noted that there had been a total cumulative membership of one hundred and forty-four. Active membership was limited to fifty. The Oriental Club could note with satisfaction that they had promoted public interest in Assyriology in the city of Philadelphia and vicinity.[24]

In New York City the Oriental Club of New York was still pursuing the topic of Assyriology in the informal afterdinner discussions. They were not concerned a great deal with expanding their membership, as a look at the records shows thirty members in 1920, and in 1939 the rolls show only thirty-one members.[25] Club members, scholars, and educated laymen alike could discuss Assyriology among themselves or, for that matter, any other phase of Oriental studies.

---

[22] *JAOS*, XL (1920) — LIX (1939).
[23] *Proc. Amer. Phil. Soc.*, LIX (1920) — LXXVIII (1939).
[24] R. G. Kent and I. G. Matthews, "The Oriental Club of Philadelphia," *JAOS*, LVIII (1938), 2-4.
[25] Personal correspondence with Adolf Schrijver, Sec.-Treas., June 4, 1968.

The Oriental Club of New Haven continued to discuss topics having a bearing on Assyriology. With Clay as one of the prominent members, it seems only natural that most of their energies were devoted to discussions of cuneiform topics, particularly the religions of Mesopotamia and Persia. In 1922 the membership stood at twenty-two, and by 1939 had reached thirty-one. The New Haven Oriental Club was moving out of its phase of being a closed society. On March 12, 1938, the club celebrated its twenty-fifth anniversary. Some of the prominent- Assyriological names on the roster between 1920 and 1939 were A.T. Clay, C. C. Torrey, R. P. Dougherty, F. J. Stephens, and Albrecht Goetze.[26]

These clubs and learned societies filled a need to bridge the gap between the scholar and the public. Another method that kept the public informed of progress in the field of Assyriology was publications.

Publications

Literature kept pace with the expansion of the other facets of Assyriology. More books were published in the period from 1920 to 1940 than during any previous period mentioned. Edwin Chiera was a major contributor, writing, editing and publishing no less than seven significant books. In 1922 he published some of the cuneiform documents in the University Museum of the University of Pennsylvania in a work entitled *Old Babylonian Contracts.*[27] Emphasis during the twenties and thirties was placed on an economic interpretation, the main reason being that most of the tablets from Mesopotamia were business or legal documents. More is known of the economic history of Mesopotamia than any other area of the ancient world. Also, in this same year he published the autographed texts, transliteration, and translation of some of the temple tablets in the collection of Princeton University.[28] The number of tablets dealing with religion and mythology was second only to business and legal documents. This type of work was continued in 1929 when Chiera edited a work, *Sumerian Lexical Texts from the Temple School of Nippur*, in one of the series of the Oriental Institute.[29] He

---

[26] Welles, *Oriental Club*, 18-25.
[27] Vol. VIII of *Publ. Babylonian Section* (Phila.: Univ. Penn. Museum, 1922).
[28] *Selected Temple Accounts from Telloh, Yakha, and Drehem: Cuneiform Tablets in the Library of Princeton University* (Princeton, N. J.: Princeton Univ. Press, 1922).
[29] Vol. I of *Cuneiform Series*, OIP, XI, 1929.

followed this in 1934 with more of this type of study in works entitled *Sumerian Texts of Varied Contents*,[30] and *Sumerian Myths and Epics*.[31] Many of the tablets from the Nuzi expedition were published by Chiera in 1929.[32] He was making copies of cuneiform texts available to scholars all over the world. All of his work, however, was not of a descriptive nature. In 1938, five years after Chiera's death, George Cameron edited and published a work written by Chiera called *They wrote on Clay: The Babylonian Tablets Speak Today*.[33] The work gets away from economics and is more of a cultural approach. In this book Chiera tells of exploration in Mesopotamia and of the decipherment of the cuneiform. He then goes on to describe a little of the history of the area, as told by the tablets.

Albert T. Clay at Yale also edited and published some cuneiform tablets, documents that were concerned with the "Great Flood" of the Old Testament.[34] George Barton attacked Clay's theory that the Amorites had been the most influential of the Semites in the Near East. This had been advocated by Clay in a book released in 1919 called *Empire of the Amorites*.[35] Clay defended his thesis in a paper published in the *Journal of the American Oriental Society* in 1923.[36] The following year he had it published in book form.[37] This scholarly feud between Clay and Barton was still going on at Clay's death in 1925.

In 1923 the French scholar Louis J. Delaporte wrote a book on the history of Mesopotamia.[38] This work took into account the latest translations of cuneiform documents. An American publishing house contracted to publish an account in English. Gordon Childe translated the book, and it appeared in the United States in 1925.[39]

---

[30] Vol. IV of *Cuneiform Series*, *OIP*, XVI, 1934.

[31] *OIP*, XV, 1934.

[32] *Texts of Varied Contents*, Vol. I of *Excavations at Nuzi*, Vol. V of *Harvard Semetic Series* (Cambridge, Mass.: Harvard Univ. Press, 1929).

[33] (Chicago: Univ. Chicago Press, 1938).

[34] *A Hebrew Deluge Story in Cuneiform and other Epic Fragments in the Pierpoint Morgan Library*, Vol. V, Part 3 of *Yale Oriental Series, Researches* (New, Haven, Conn.: Yale Univ. Press, 1922).

[35] See above Chap. VI.

[36] A Rejoinder to Professor George A. Barton," *JAOS*, XLV (1923), 119-151.

[37] *The Antiquity of Amorite Civilization* (New Haven: Privately Printed, 1924).

[38] *Mesopotamie: les Civisisations Babylonienne et Assyrienne* (Paris: La Renaissance du Livre, 1923).

[39] *Mesopotamia: The Babylonian and Assyrian Cibilization*, trans. V. Gordon Childe (New York: Alfred A. Knopf, 1925).

Although the work encompasses a large geographical area, it was a superficial treatment, and could not compare with Olmstead's *History of Assyria*.[40]

A.V. Williams Jackson of Columbia released in 1928 a detailed monograph dealing with the religion of Persia. This book, entitled *Zoroastrian Studies*, was the most complete and exhaustive study of Persian dualism to that date.[41] The work is well documented and has an extensive bibliography.

Robert William Rogers, who had written a history of Babylonia and Assyria, turned his attention toward Persia[42] Rogers' book, *A History of Ancient Persia*, is a brief study of Persian history from the earliest times to the conquest of Alexander the Great, and was issued in 1929.[43] For the most part the work deals with the political growth of each of the Achaemenid kings, although in the first three chapters a little attention is devoted to the language and religion. One of the major shortcomings of the book is the complete lack of a bibliography.

In 1930 Ephraim A. Speiser published a work called *Mesopotamian Origins*.[44] Speiser discusses in this book the origins of the basic populations of Mesopotamia and the surrounding regions. He describes the influence of each of these groups upon the civilization of the Tigris-Euphrates valley. The book is an important contribution, well documented by footnotes, and contains a good bibliography. His other significant work of this period between 1920 and 1940 was *Excavations at Tepe Gawra* released in 1935.[45]

Between 1892 and 1914 Robert F. Harper had copied and published in fourteen volumes cuneiform texts of the kings of Assyria and Babylonia.[46] These were excellent copies, but were autographed texts only, and no translations. Leroy Waterman at the University of Michigan began in 1930 to publish translations of Harper's work. The first two parts were issued in 1930, containing transliterations and translations (on opposite pages) of all 1,471 of the letters.[47] These

---

[40] See above Chap. VII.
[41] (New York: Columbia Univ. Press, 1928).
[42] See above Chap. VI.
[43] (New York: Chas. Scribner's Sons, 1929).
[44] (Philadelphia: Univ. Penn. Press, 1930).
[45] See above Chap. VIII.
[46] See above Chap. V.
[47] *Translation and Transliteration*, Part I and II of *Royal Correspondence of the Assyrian Empire*, Vols. XVII and XVIII of *Univ. Mich. Humanistic Series* (Ann Arbor: Univ. Mich. Press, 1930).

volumes were entitled *Royal Correspondence of the Assyrian Empire* and were issued in the *University of Michigan Humanistic Series*. Part III was published in 1931, consisting of a commentary on each of the letters.[48] The last part was published in 1936, containing a supplement and indices.[49] In this last volume Waterman gives interpretations of some of the letters by other scholars and places the letters into their proper historical setting. This effort alone, the publication of these four volumes, made Waterman's reputation as a highly competent Assyriologist.

In 1935 Robert Pfeiffer of Harvard published a book, *State Letters of Assyria*, in which he transliterated and translated 355 official letters of the Assyrian empire.[50] These letters dated from the period between 722 and 625 B.C. Pfeiffer has done an admirable job on the translations, and the work is reviewed favorably by the leading Assyriologists of the day.

Theophile J. Meek continued this practice of making documents available to other scholars of cuneiform studies. In his work released in 1935, *Old Akkadian, Sumerian, and Cappadocian Texts from Nuzi*, he published the autographed texts and their transliteration.[51] Meek selected certain documents and offered translations of these.

Relatively few books, that is scholarly books, had been published dealing with the history of Persia. George Glenn Cameron attempted to rectify this situation in 1936. Cameron, a native of Washington, Pennsylvania, was born July 30, 1905. He attended the University of Chicago, earning an A.M. from the school in 1930. Cameron became quite interested in Persian studies and received the Ph.D. from Chicago in 1932.[52] After earning his degree Cameron was retained at Chicago as an Instructor of Oriental Languages teaching Old Persian. The following year of 1933 he was promoted to the rank of assistant professor. Cameron continued his study of early Persia by publishing *History of Early Iran* in 1936.[53] Prior to this most histories of Persia began with Cyrus the Great in the middle of the 6th century B.C. Cameron deals with the pre-history of Persia, making full use of the documents from Mesopotamia. He only devotes a few pages to the

---

[48] *Commentary*, Part III, Vol. XIX of *Univ. Mich. H. S.*, 1931.

[49] *Supplement and Indexes*, Part IV, Vol. XX of *UMHS*, 1936.

[50] (New Haven: Amer. Or. Soc., 1935).

[51] Vol. III of *Excavations at Nuzi*, Vol. X of *Harvard Semitic Series*, 1935.

[52] His Ph.D. dissertation was *A Pre-Achaemenid History of Persia: The Land and its People* (published later in 1936 by private printing).

[53] (Chicago: Univ. Chicago Press, 1936).

Achaemenid dynasty, a starting point for most histories. The book is well documented with footnotes. To this date *History of Early Iran* still stands as the most scholarly work on pre-Achaemenid Persia.[54]

Ferris J. Stephens at Yale published in 1937 *Votive and Historical Texts from Babylonia and Assyria*.[55] Many of these 149 texts were published for the first time. Probably the most important item about the publication was that two unknown kings, Nidnusha and Hashmargalshu, appear for the first time.

As would be expected articles are too numerous to mention. For the more important articles between 1920 and 1940 the reader is referred to the bibliography. Only one major periodical was founded in this period that carried Assyriological articles. This was the journal devoted to Persian art and archeology called *Iranian Institute of America Bulletin* published first in 1931. The organization was founded in New York in 1930 by scholars interested in Persia, and called the American Institute for Persian Art and Archaeology, changed its name to American Institute for Iranian Art and Archaeology in 1937. Two years later the name was changed again to Iranian Institute of America. Shortly after 1920 the *Annuals* and *Bulletins* of the American School of Oriental Research began to contain Assyriological articles as the branch in Baghdad had been opened.

Baghdad School

The American School of Oriental Research was founded in 1900 with a field office in Jerusalem. Objectives of the school were to carry out excavations in Palestine and surrounding areas, and to publish the results of these excavations.[56] At a meeting of the Archaeological Institute of America in December 1913 George A. Barton suggested that a school of archeology and research be established in Baghdad similar to the one in Jerusalem.[57] The Council of the Institute liked the idea and selected a committee to examine the feasibility of the plan. Barton, Albert Clay, and Morris Jastrow, Jr. were prominent Assyriologists chosen for this group, known as the Mesopotamian

---

[54] With the possible exception of the *Cambridge History of Iran* which began to be issued in late 1968.

[55] Vol. IX of *Yale Oriental Series, Babylonian Texts*, 1937.

[56] G. A. Barton, "Report of the Director of the School in Baghdad," *BASOR*, No. 16 (1924), 16-17.

[57] Barton, "The Baghdad School," *AASOR*, VI (1926), 10-12.

Committee. Later William H. Ward and John P. Peters were added. Before any progress was made, however, World War I began, and the project was shelved for the duration of the conflict.[58]

William H. Ward died in August 1916 and bequeathed his library to this school, if founded in Baghdad within ten years from the date of his death.[59] The Mesopotamian Committee of the Archaeological Institute sent Clay in 1920 on a scouting trip into Mesopotamia to see if it would be feasible to establish the school in Baghdad. Clay reported favorably and in 1921 the Committee was released from the supervision of the Archaeological Institute of America and merged with the American School of Oriental Research in Jerusalem. They incorporated, taking the name American Schools of Oriental research, with a branch at Jerusalem and one at Baghdad. George A. Barton was named director of the Baghdad branch, but his offices remained in New York City.[60]

Although provisions had been made to have a school at Baghdad, it was two years before it finally opened. Morris Jastrow, Jr. had died in 1921, and two years later his widow bequeathed a part of his library of about 500 volumes to the Baghdad school. With the Ward collection this made an adequate working library for the institute.[61] The Iraqi government provided land for the building, and on November 2, 1923, the school was formally opened. Albert T. Clay, first Annual Professor, presided over the ceremonies.[62]

The attitude of the Iraqi people was reflected in a speech given in New York by F. B. Riley. He had formerly been a member of the Ministry of Education in Iraq. Riley gave this speech before a board meeting of the Corporation of the American Schools on December 29, 1924. He spoke favorably of the school, concluding his speech by saying:

> It cannot be too much emphasized that work of this nature appeals to the people of Iraq, because it is felt to be disinterested. It has no suggestion of either political or economic exploitation; it is a work beneficial to all parties concerned, for the uncovering of buried cities which will reveal an early history common to all—be they Occidentals

---

[58] *Ibid.*
[59] *Ibid.*
[60] *Ibid.*
[61] Barton, "Report of the Chairman of the Committee on Mesopotamian Archaeology," *BASOR*, No. 8 (1922), 8-9.
[62] Barton, *BASOR*, No. 16 (1924), 16-17.

or Orientals. In such work, co-operation is both possible and desirable and, so far as they can, the Iraqis will be only too willing to co-operate.[63]

Barton who remained in New York was the director of the school between 1921 and 1934. At the school in Baghdad there was an Annual Professor selected each year to manage affairs in that city. The institute usually had a visiting lecturer, a research professor, and several research fellows, these latter filled from the ranks of graduate students. Clay as the first Annual Professor made a survey of some of the larger mounds of Mesopotamia. Edwin Chiera was Annual Professor for 1924-25 and made plans for the school to make an archeological map of Iraq, dividing the country into sections and doing section at a time.[64] As was seen in Chapter VII the Baghdad School engaged in several joint expeditions with certain institutions from the United States.

By 1927 the Baghdad School had made preliminary surveys, including basic mapping and collection of antiquities from about 153 sites, some of which were Adab, Fara, Lagash, Larsa, Erech, and Nippur.[65] In 1925 the school moved into the new Baghdad Museum, built by the Iraqi government. For these new quarters the school was indebted to Miss Gertrude Bell, the English writer and Honorary Director of Antiquities for the Iraqi government.[66]

On the eve of World War II the Baghdad School had proved to be a competent laboratory where professors and graduate students of Assyriology could learn field methods of archeology. Many of the prominent names in Assyriology, and those who would become prominent, obtained their field training here, such as Clay, Barton, Dougherty, Edwin Chiera, Leroy Waterman, Robert Pfeiffer, Henry Lutz, Theophile Meek, Samuel Kramer, and Albert Olmstead, to name only a few.[67] As a training ground for field archeology the Baghdad School was proving to be superb.

[63] F. B. Riley, "A Voice from Babylon," *BASOR*, No. 17 (1925), 10-11.
[64] Barton, *AASOR*, VI (1926), 10-12.
[65] R. P. Dougherty, "Searching for Ancient Remains in Lower Iraq," *AASOR*, VII (1927), 193.
[66] Barton, *AASOR*, VI (1926), 12.
[67] *AASOR*, IV (1924) — XIX (1940).

CHAPTER TEN

EPILOGUE

American Assyriology suffered its second major recession in 1939 as a result of the outbreak of World War II. Excavation in the Near East was forced to come to a complete halt. Between 1939 and 1946 field archeology was not carried on, but Assyriological activity did not completely die out, as it was maintained, mainly in the area of literature.

World War II and Assyriology

Samuel Noah Kramer began to make a name for himself in Sumerian Studies during the war years. Kramer was born September 28, 1897, in Russia, son of Benjamin and Yetta Kramer. He came to the United States in 1906. After earning a B.S. Degree at Temple University in 1921, and attending Dropsie College between 1926 and 1927, Kramer entered the University of Pennsylvania, receiving his Ph.D. in 1929. In 1930-31 he was an Honorary Fellow at the Baghdad School and participated in the Nuzi expedition.[1] From 1932 to 1935 Kramer served as Resarch Assistant at the Oriental Institute of the University of Chicago. He was promoted to Research Associate in 1936 and remained at that post until 1942.

While at the Oriental Institute, Kramer began to delve deeply into Sumerian mythology. This is revealed in 1940 when he published a book called *Lamentations over the Destruction of Ur.*[2] Kramer left Chicago in 1942 to go to the University of Pennsylvania Museum as a Research Assistant. The following year he was named Associate Curator of the Museum Tablet Collection. Kramer's next major publication was produced in 1944, a detailed study of the spiritual and literary achievements of the Sumerians in the third millenium B.C. This work was entitled *Sumerian Mythology*[3]

One important work on Iran appeared during this period. This book by Ernst Herzfeld, one of the former directors of the Persian

---

[1] See above Chap. VIII.
[2] *Assyriological Studies*, No. 12 (Oriental Inst., 1940).
[3] *Memoirs of the American Philosophical Soc.*, XXI, 1944.

expedition for the Oriental Institute, was entitled *Iran in the Ancient Near East*.[4] This book grew out of the Lowell Lectures delivered by Herzfeld in Boston in 1936. He revised and added new material to the lectures, and published them in book form. This work covers Persian history from prehistoric times to about the middle of the fourth century A.D. It is more of a cultural history than a political history.

Alexander Heidel discussed mythology of the Babylonians in 1942 in a work called *The Babylonian Genesis: The Story of the Creation*.[5] He had received his Ph.D. from the University of Chicago and was a member of the staff of the Assyrian Dictionary Project. Using material from the project, he wrote this book that dealt with the creation stories of the Babylonians and tried to relate it to the Old Testament.

An important work that helped establish a portion of Mesopotamian chronology was published in 1942. This book, *Babylonian Chronology 626 B.C.-A.D. 45*, was written by Richard Anthony Parker and Waldo Herman Dubberstein.[6] Parker was an Egyptologist who had done this type of work on the chronology of Egypt. He received his Ph.D. from the University of Chicago in 1938. Dubberstein was also at Chicago, one of Olmstead's students. This work was a major contribution to the field of Assyriology. It established the chronology from late Assyrian well into Parthian times.

Ignace Jay Gelb helped edit a work in 1943 called *Nuzi Personal Names*.[7] This was a study of the personal names from the tablets gathered by the Nuzi expedition. The following year Ferris J. Stephens of Yale continued the practice of providing scholars of the world with copies of the cuneiform texts to translate. His book was entitled *Old Assyrian Letters*, and consisted of discussion and copies of 270 autographed texts from five documents.[8]

These were not the only books published between 1939 and 1946 but were the more important. For a look at the articles published in this period the reader is referred to the bibliography. No new

---

[4] (New York: Oxford Univ. Press, 1941).
[5] (Chicago: Univ. Chicago Press, 1942).
[6] *SAOC*, No. 24 (Oriental Inst., 1942).
[7] *OIP*, Vol. LVIII (Oriental Inst., 1943).
[8] Vol. VI of *Babylonian Inscriptions in the Collection of James B. Nies, Yale University* (New Haven: Yale Univ. Press, 1944).

Assyriological journals were created during the war years, but the *American Journal of Semitic Languages and Literature* changed its name in 1942 to the *Journal of Near Eastern Studies*. It was still published, however, by the University of Chicago Press.

At the colleges and universities Assyriological courses were still offered, but on a much reduced basis. Most of the prospective students and many faculty members were serving in the armed services.

Since the War

World War II came to an end in 1945 with the surrender of Germany and Japan. In 1946 Assyriology and other scholarly disciplines began to expand once again. The literature since the war is very prolific, and just listing the books would take up endless pages. Certain books, however, made such major contributions to the field that they warrant at least a mention. Albert T. Olmstead passed away April 11, 1945; another giant of Assyriology had disappeared from the scene. Prior to his death Olmstead had been working on a history of Persia. Olmstead's daughter Cleta and his former student George Cameron edited and published the work in 1948. This book, *History of the Persian Empire*, is still today the best work on Achaemenid Persia. Unlike *History of Assyria* this work is well supplied with footnotes. Its one weakness is the lack of a bibliography.[9]

Roland Kent published a very good grammar of Old Persian in 1950. Kent's book, *Old Persian Grammar, Texts, Lexicon*, is not only one of the few Old Persian grammars, but it is a very good work, and a definite contribution to Assyriology.[10] The book was revised in 1953, but no major changes were made.

Samuel Kramer contributed three more important works concerned with Sumerian studies in this period. His first was *History Begins at Sumer* in 1958, consisting of twenty essays from Sumerian history.[11] In 1961 Kramer revised and published his original work of *Sumerian Mythology*.[12] He wrote another book in 1963 entitled *The Sumerians*.[13] This work is one of the most up-to-date and readable

---

[9] (Chicago: Univ. Chicago Press, 1948).
[10] Vol. XXXIII of *Amer. Oriental Series* (New Haven: Amer. Or. Soc., 1950).
[11] (London: Thames & Hudson, 1958).
[12] (New York: Harper, 1961).
[13] (Chicago: Univ. Chicago Press, 1963).

histories of the Sumerian civilization. It has a short, but very good select bibliography.

Two books have been published in the 1960's that are good general histories of Mesopotamia after the Sumerian period. One of these is by H. W. F. Saggs called *The Greatness That was Babylon*.[14] The other, *Ancient Mesopotamia*, was written by Adolf Leo Oppenheim.[15] This latter book is written for the scholar, rather than for the general public. Oppenheim discusses the social structure, philosophy, religion, literature, science, and technology of the Mesopotamians, not the traditional political history approach.

Since the war two journals that carry Assyriological articles have been created. *Journal of Cuneiform Studies* began in 1947 with a grant from the Baghdad branch of the American Schools of Oriental Research. It is a philological journal devoted to Sumerian, Akkadian, Hittite, Hurrian, Urartian, Elamite, Old Persian, Amorite, and Ugaritic material. *Archaeology* had its beginning in 1948, created by the Archeological Institute of America. It is intended to be more of a popular journal than the *American Journal of Archaeology*. *Archaeology* from time contains articles and book reviews concerned with Assyriology.

At the colleges and universities Assyriological courses expanded as students and faculty came home from the military services. Some of the schools that today offer advanced degree programs in Assyriological studies are Harvard, Yale, Princeton, Columbia, Johns Hopkins, California, Michigan, Pennsylvania, and Chicago.

It is with a great deal of sorrow that we note the death of Ferris J. Stephens of Yale University on October 31, 1969. Yale, the American Oriental Society, and the academic world have lost a true friend and a great scholar. We should also mention the passing away on September 19, 1971 of the great Palestinian archaeologist W. F. Albright, who did much for Assyriology.

Several major Assyriological field expeditions are being carried on at the present. The University Museum of the University of Pennsylvania has excavating parties in the field at Hasanlu and Tepe Malyun in Iran. Excavations are being carried on by the Oriental Institute of the University of Chicago at Nippur.

In 1946 work on the Assyrian Dictionary Project resumed once

---

[14] (New York: Hawthorn Books, 1962).
[15] (Chicago: Univ. Chicago Press, 1964).

again. Ignace J. Gelb was made editor-in-chief and began to make preparations to start publishing volumes as they were completed. In 1955 A. Leo Oppenheim took over as editor-in-charge. The first volume, Volume VI, the letter H, was issued in 1956. Since then ten more volumes have appeared. All the Assyriological world anxiously awaits the completion of this great project.

Today, Assyriology is a highly specialized and diverse field. No longer does one scholar attempt to cover the broad spectrum of the subject; in fact it is doubtful if one could. So many tablets have been uncovered since the early days of cuneiform studies that the vocabularies of the various cuneiform languages and dialects have grown very extant. It is a challenge now to learn one of these languages well. Literature is copius in the various branches of Assyriology, making it very difficult for a scholar just to keep up with the works in his area of specialization. All of this has led to fragmentation of the science. One limits himself to Persian studies, Sumerology, or one of the other sub-branches of the discipline. Assyriology has come a long way since Francis Brown started teaching Akkadian at Union Theological Seminary back in 1880.

APPENDIX I

CHRONOLOGY

1842 Founding of the American Oriental Society.
1843 James Fraser's *Historical and Descriptive Account of Persia* published in the United States.
1850 Layard's book *Nineveh and its Remains* published in the United States.
1863 Edward Taintor one of the first scholars in the U.S. to translate a cuneiform document.
1880 Francis Brown inaugurates the teaching of Akkadian at Union Theological Seminary.
1882 David Lyon begins teaching Akkadian at Harvard.
1883 Paul Haupt starts Assyriology at Johns Hopkins.
1884 The journal *Hebraica* is founded. Start of the Wolfe Expedition.
1885 James Blackwell offers Akkadian at the University of Missouri. John MacCurdy teaches an Assyriological course at Princeton.
1886 David Lyon publishes *An Assyrian Manual*. Hermann Hilprecht inaugurates Assyriology at the University of Pennsylvania.
1887 Hinckley Mitchell teaches Akkadian at Boston University. Founding of Babylonian Exploration Fund.
1888 Nathaniel Schmidt teaches history of Babylonia and Assyria at Colgate University. Oriental Club of Philadelphia founded. Pennsylvania sends out the First Nippur Expedition.
1889 *Beitrage zur Assyriologie* begins publication.
1890 Carl Belser begins the teaching of Akkadian at the University of Michigan. Second Nippur Expedition goes into the field.
1891 George Barton begins Assyriology at Bryn Mawr College.
1892 Robert Harper starts teaching Akkadian at the University of Chicago and to publish the *Assyrian Letters*. John Prince begins teaching Akkadian at New York University. Herbert Tolman publishes *A Grammar of the Old Persian Language*.
1893 Beginning of the Third Nippur Expedition.
1895 Richard Gottheil begins Assyriology at Columbia University. James Stevenson teaches Akkadian at Vanderbilt University.
1896 Abraham Jackson begins Persian studies at Columbia. Nathaniel Schmidt starts Assyriology at Cornell University. Founding of the New York Oriental Club. *Hebraica* changes title to *American Journal of Semitic Languages and Literature*. Opening of the Haskell Oriental Museum at the University of Chicago.
1898 Morris Jastrow, Jr. publishes *The Religion of Babylonia and Assyria*. Abraham Jackson publishes *Zoroaster the Prophet of Ancient Iran*.
1899 Fourth Nippur Expedition begins.
1900 Robert Rogers publishes *History of Babylonia and Assyria*.

1901 Charles Torrey introduces Akkadian at Yale.
1902 Herbert Tolman begins teaching Old Persian at Vanderbilt University.
1903 Robert Harper publishes *Law Code of Hammurabi*. University of Chicago sends out Adab Expedition. Harvard Semitic Museum opens.
1905 Hearings held to settle the Peters-Hilprecht Controversy.
1910 Albert Clay joins the faculty at Yale and takes over Assyriological courses.
1913 Oriental Club of New Haven founded.
1914 Outbreak of World War I.
1915 Morris Jastrow, Jr. publishes *The Civilization of Babylonia and Assyria*.
1916 Albert Olmstead publishes *Assyrian Historiography*.
1917 Edwin Johnson publishes *Historical Grammar of the Ancient Persian Language*.
1918 World War I comes to an end.
1919 Albert Clay publishes *The Empire of the Amorites*. Oriental Institute founded at Chicago.
1921 Beginning of the Assyrian Dictionary Project. Start of Assyriology at the University of California.
1922 Joint Expedition to Ur commences.
1923 Albert Olmstead publishes *History of Assyria*. Joint Expedition goes to Kish. Branch of American Schools of Oriental Research opened at Baghdad.
1924 Edwin Chiera conducts preliminary excavations at Nuzi.
1926 American Schools of Oriental Research sends out a survey team to explore for suitable excavation sites in Iraq.
1927 Edwin Chiera becomes director of the Assyrian Dictionary Project. Joint Expedition begins excavations at Nuzi. Leroy Waterman commences excavation at Tell Umar.
1928 Survey team for American Schools of Oriental Research digs as Tell Billah. Abraham Jackson publishes *Zoroastrian Studies*.
1929 Oriental Institute begins excavations at Khorsabad.
1930 Start of Babylonian section of Iraq Expedition of Oriental Institute. Leroy Waterman begins publishing *Royal Correspondence of the Assyrian Empire*.
1931 James Breasted Hall opened at Oriental Institute. Excavation commences at Tepe Gawrah. Tepe Hissar Expedition begins. Oriental Institute opens excavation at Persepolis.
1933 Arno Poebel becomes director of the Assyrian Dictionary Project.
1936 George Cameron publishes *History of Early Iran*.
1937 Excavation carried out at Tell Billah and Khafajeh.
1939 Outbreak of World War II.

APPENDIX II

MAJOR U.S. EXPEDITIONS TO IRAQ AND IRAN TO 1973

This list includes all major U.S. expeditions to Iraq and Iran through the year 1972. Survey parties or those concerned only with early prehistory are not included. Sites are listed in chronological order. The numbers that appear after literature indicate major works in the bibliographies that deal with the excavation site.

1. NIPPUR (Nuffar, Niffer)
    Four expeditions sent out by the University of Pennsylvania between 1889 and 1900.

    First — Feb. 6 to April 15, 1889.
    Director, John P. Peters; H. V. Hilprecht, Robert F. Harper, J. H. Haynes, R. H. Field, D. Noorian, and Bedry Bey.
    Over 2,000 cuneiform tablets and other antiquities.

    Second — Jan. 14 to May 3, 1890.
    Director, J. P. Peters; J. H. Haynes, D. Noorian, and M. Effendi.
    About 8,000 cuneiform tablets and other antiquities.

    Third — April 11, 1893 to April 4, 1894, and June 4, 1894 to Feb. 15, 1896.
    Director, J. H. Haynes; Joseph Meyer.
    21,000 cuneiform tablets.

    Fourth — Feb. 6, 1899 to May 11, 1900.
    Directors, H.V. Hilprecht and J. H. Haynes; C. S. Fisher, and H. V. Geere.
    Continued excavation of ziggurat and large temple.

    Oriental Institute of the University of Chicago, and the University Museum of the University of Pennsylvania. Nov. 15, 1948 to March 16, 1952 (3 seasons).
    Director, Donald E. McCown; J. Caldwell, C. S. Coon, V. Crawford, R. C. Haines, F. Hildebrand, T. Jacobsen, F. Safar, and F. R. Steele.
    Cuneiform tablets, pottery, figurines, and Temple of Enlil.

    Oriental Institute and American Schools of Oriental Research, Baghdad.
    November 1953 to the present (11 seasons).

V. Crawford, G. F. Doles, A. Goetze, R. C. Haines, D. P. Hansen, T. Jacobsen, and J. E. Knudstad.
Starting the 1973 season the director will be McGuire Gibson.
Cuneiform tablets, pottery, and the Temple of Inana.
Literature: 151, 152, 153, 172, 175, 177, 179, 180, 204, 206, 605, 655, 714, 715, 716, 717, 724, 725.

2. FARA (Shuruppak)
University of Pennsylvania.
April 1900.
Hilprecht, Haynes, and Geere from Nippur.
Pre-Sargonid brick and burial urns.
Literature: 178, 179, 180, 655.

3. ABU HATAB (Kissura)
University of Pennsylvania.
April 1900.
Hilprecht, Haynes, and Geere from Nippur.
Trial excavations.
Literature: 178, 179, 180, 655.

4. ADAB (Bismaya)
University of Chicago.
Dec. 25, 1903 to May 27, 1904, and Sept. 19 to Sept. 27, 1904.
Director (Field), Edgar J. Banks; V. S. Persons, and Haidar Bey.
Cuneiform tablets, statues, and Ishtar temple excavated.
Literature: 142, 143, 144, 173, 174, 655.

5. UR (Mukayyar)
British Museum and University of Pennsylvania.
Nov. 15, 1922 to Feb. 25, 1934 (12 seasons).
Director, C. L. Wooley; Leroy Legrain, C. J. Gadd, E. Burrows, C. J. Rose, M. E. L. Mallowan, and F. H. Newton.
Cuneiform tablets, ziggurat, temples, and Royal Cemetery.
Literature: 138, 149, 169, 228, 230-242, 655, 734, 735.

6. TELL AL UBAID (Tell al Obeid)
British Museum and University of Pennsylvania.
Fall and winter of 1922-23.
Woolley from Ur.
Three temples.
Literature: 229, 655, 735.

7. KISH (Al Uhaimir)
Oxford University and Field Museum of Natural History, Chicago.
Feb. 1923 to spring 1933 (10 seasons).
Director, Stephen Langdon; Ernst Mackay (Field director 1923-26), Eric Burrows (Field director 1926-33), David T. Rice, R. Watelin,

Herbert Weld, Louis C. Watelin, Henry Field, L. H. D. Buxton, W. H. Lane, Eric Schroeder, and T. K. Penniman.
Temples, cemeteries, ziggurats, and cuneiform tablets.
Literature: 159, 160, 182, 183, 184, 185, 193, 655.

8. DREHEM (Tell Duraihim)
   Oxford University and Field Museum.
   March 1924.
   Herbert Weld from Kish.
   Cuneiform tablets.
   Literature: 159, 655.

9. NUZI (Gasur, Yorgan Tepe)
   American Schools of Oriental Research, Baghdad and Iraqi Museum.
   Winter 1925.
   Edwin Chiera.
   Over 1,000 business documents.

   American Schools and Harvard University.
   Oct. 1927 to March 1928.
   Director, Edwin Chiera; E. A. Speiser, Leroy Waterman, Richard F. S. Starr, and Emanuel Wilensky.
   Private homes excavated, and about 1,000 cuneiform tablets.

   American Schools, Harvard, and University of Pennsylvania.
   October 1928 to March 1931 (3 seasons).
   Director, Robert Pfeiffer (1928-29), Richard Starr (1929-31); T. J. Meek, Charles Bache, H. F. Lutz, E. Wilensky, and Pinhas Delougaz.
   Temples, city walls, and cuneiform tablets.
   Literature: 145, 150, 192, 195, 207, 224, 655.

10. JEMDET NASR (Kidnun)
    Oxford and Field Museum.
    Dec. 1925 to March 1926.
    Ernst Mackay and Herbert Weld from Kish.
    Cuneiform tablets.
    March 1928.
    L. C. Watelin and H Weld from Kish.
    Temple and cemetery.
    Literature: 159, 194, 655.

11. TEPE GAWRAH
    American Schools of Oriental Research, Baghdad, University of Pennsylvania, and Dropsie College, Philadelphia.
    Oct. 9 to Oct. 27, 1927.
    E. A. Speiser.
    Preliminary exploration.
    Jan. 19, 1931 to May 7, 1938 (6 seasons).

Director, E. A. Speiser; Charles Bache, A. J. Tobler, Cyrus Gordon, and A. C. Piepkorn.
Numerous buildings and pottery.
Literature: 137, 139, 140, 146, 212-223, 655, 732.

12. TELL UMAR

American Schools of Oriental Research, Baghdad and Toledo Museum of Art.
Dec. 29, 1927 to March 10, 1928.
Director, Leroy Waterman; F. H. Sproule, and N. Manasseh.
Cuneiform tablets and other antiquities.
University of Michigan and Toledo Museum.
Nov. 10, 1928 to Feb. 1, 1930 (2 seasons).
Director, Leroy Waterman; C. S. Fisher, R. H. McDowell, and Charles Spicer.
Ziggurat, and Parthian and Seleucid coins and pottery.
Literature: 226, 227, 655.

13. KHORSABAD (Dur-Sharrukin)

Oriental Institute of the University of Chicago.
Feb. 1929.
Edwin Chiera.
Preliminary investigation.
Winter 1930 to May 1935 (5 seasons).
Director, Henri Frankfort (to April 1932), Gordon Loud (Nov. 1932 to May 1935); P. Delougaz, Seton Lloyd, and Thorkild Jacobsen.
Cuneiform tablets, palace of Sargon II, and winged bull.
Literature: 163, 164, 165, 166, 167, 186, 187, 655.

14. TELL BILLAH (Shibaniba, Baasheika)

American Schools of Oriental Research, Baghdad and University of Pennsylvania.
Oct. 1930 to April 1934 (4 seasons).
Director, E. A. Speiser, Charles Bache (after fall of 1932); S. N. Kramer, and C. S. Fisher.
Pottery and inscribed bricks.
Literature: 137, 138, 147, 655.

15. TELL ASMAR (Eshnunna)

Oriental Institute of the University of Chicago.
Nov. 11, 1930 to spring 1936 (6 seasons).
Director, H. Frankfort; Gordon Loud, P. Delougaz, S. Lloyd, and T. Jacobsen.
Temples, statues, and cuneiform tablets.
Literature: 163, 164, 165, 166, 167, 168, 608, 655, 706, 712.

16. KHAFAJEH

Oriental Institute.

Nov. 22, 1930 to Jan. 1, 1937 (8 seasons).
Director, H. Frankfort; P. Delougaz, S. Lloyd, T. Jacobsen, Conrad Preusser, and E. A. Speiser.
American Schools of Oriental Research, Baghdad and University of Pennsylvania.
Spring 1937.
Temple and Sumerian statues.
Literature: 163, 164, 165, 166, 167, 168, 222, 223, 608, 655, 706.

17. TEPE HISSAR
    University of Pennsylvania, Pennsylvania Museum of Art, Philadelphia, and American Institute for Persian Art and Archaeology, New York.
    July 19, 1931 to Nov. 3, 1932 (2 seasons).
    Director, Eric Schmidt; Ivan Gerasimoff, Boris Dubensky, and Kurt Leitner.
    Cemetery, pottery, and prehistoric artifacts. Literature: 209

18. PERSEPOLIS
    Oriental Institute of the University of Chicago.
    Spring 1931 to spring 1936 (6 seasons).
    Ernst Herzfeld.
    Buildings and other antiquities.
    Literature: 210, 711, 733, 845.

19. TURENG TEPE
    University Museum of the University of Pennsylvania for the William R. Nelson Trust of Kansas City.
    Summer 1931.
    Frederick R. Wulsin.
    Prehistoric artifacts.
    Literature: 711.

20. GIRUMU (Tell Barghuthiat)
    Oxford and Field Museum.
    Feb. 1933.
    I. C. Watelin and H. Weld from Kish.
    City walls.
    Literature: 160, 182, 655.

21. TEPE SHENSHI
    Oriental Institute of the University of Chicago.
    Spring 1933.
    P. Delougaz from Khafajeh and Tell Asmar.
    Pottery.
    Literature: 165, 655.

22. JERWAN
    Oriental Institute.

Spring 1933 and 1934.
T. Jacobsen from Khafajeh and Tell Asmar.
Sennacherib's aqueduct.
Literature: 165, 166, 167, 611, 655.

23. ISCHALI
Oriental Institute.
Winters of 1934-35 and 1935-36.
H. Frankfort from Khafajeh and Tell Asmar.
Cuneiform tablets and temple of Ishtar.
Literature: 167, 655.

24. RAYY (Rhages)
University Museum of the University of Pennsylvania, Boston Museum of Fine Art, and the Philadelphia Museum of Art.
1934 to 1939.
Erich F. Schmidt.
Pottery.

25. TELL AGRAB
Oriental Institute of the University of Chicago.
Winters of 1935-36 and 1936-37.
H. Frankfort from Khafajeh and Tell Asmar.
Sharu temple and pottery.
Literature: 167, 655.

26. NAQSH-I-RUSTEM
Oriental Institute, University Museum of the University of Pennsylvania, and the Boston Museum of Fine Arts.
1937 to 1939.
Eric F. Schmidt.
Pottery.
Literature: 711.

27. ISTAKHR
Oriental Institute, University Museum, and Boston Museum.
1937 to 1939.
E. F. Schmidt.
Pottery.
Literature: 711.

28. TAL-I-BAKUN
Oriental Institute, University Museum, and Boston Museum.
1937 to 1939.
E. F. Schmidt.
Pottery.
Literature: 711

29. JARMO
   Oriental Institute, and American Schools of Oriental Research, Baghdad (beginning in 1950).
   May 1948; Fall 1950 to summer 1951.
   Director, Robert J. Braidwood; R. M. Adams, Linda Braidwood, Charlotte Otten, and H. E. Wright, Jr.
   Fall 1954 to spring 1955.
   Director, R. J. Braidwood; Bruce Howe, H. E. Wright, Jr., F. R. Matson, and C. R. Reed.
   Pottery, houses, burials, and stone implements.
   Literature: 655.

30. KARIM SHAHIR
   Oriental Institute and American Schools of Oriental Research, Baghdad.
   March 14 to Sept. 5, 1951.
   Director, R. J. Braidwood; Bruce Howe, and H. E. Wright, Jr.
   Prehistoric artifacts.
   Literature: 655, 705.

31. TEPE HASANLU
   University Museum of the University of Pennsylvania, Iranian Archaeological Service, and the Metropolitan Museum of Art (since 1959).
   Summer 1956 to the present.
   Director, Robert H. Dyson, Jr.; Co-directors, Vaughan E. Crawford 1959-64) and Oscar W. Muscarella (1966-70); T. Cuyler Young, and Mary M. Voigt.
   Numerous expeditions have gone out from Hasanlu to Hajji Firuz, Dalma, Pisdeli Tepe, Ziwiye, Agrab, and Dinkha.
   Pottery, burials, city walls, and buildings.
   Literature: 707, 708, 709, 710, 711.

32. TEPE YAHYA
   Peabody Museum of Harvard University.
   Summers of 1967 through 1971.
   Director, C. Lamberg-Karlovsky; Philip L. Kohl.
   Bronze age artifacts, and pottery.
   Literature: 711, 718.

33. TEPE MALYUN
   University Museum of the University of Pennsylvania and American Institute of Iranian Studies.
   1971 to the present.
   William M. Sumner.
   Prehistoric artifacts.
   Literature: 711.

BIBLIOGRAPHY

This bibliography consists of two major parts. The first is a list of all major works in U.S. Assyriology up through 1939. The second part is a list of other works consulted in the preparation of this book.

LIST OF U. S. LITERATURE TO 1940

For ease of reference this list is divided into the following categories: (1) general; (2) history; (3) exploration, travel, and geography; (4) archeology; (5) philology and linguistic; (6) religion, culture, and mythology; (7) biography; (8) chronology; and (9) art and architecture.

GENERAL

1. Adler, Cyrus. "Review of 'Les Langues Perdues de la Perse et de l'Assyrie'," *Andover Review*, VIII (1887), 438-441.
2. ———."Progress of Oriental Sciental Science in America During 1888," *Annual Report of the Smithsonian Institution to July, 1888* (1890), 675-702.
3. Anonymous. "Announcement and Arrival in This Country of Some Nineveh Marbles at New York April 5, 1859," *Historical Magazine*, III (1859), 146.
4. Barton, George A. "The Names of Two Kings of Adab," *Journal of the American Oriental Society (JAOS)*, XXXIII (1913), 295-296.
5. ———. "Report of the Chairman of the Committee on Mesopotamian Archaeology," *Bulletin of the American Schools of Oriental Research (BASOR)*, No. 8 (1922), 8-9.
6. ———. "Report of the Director of the School in Baghdad," *BASOR*, No. 12 (1923), 23-24.
7. ———. "Report of the Director of the School in Baghdad," *BASOR*, No. 16 (1924), 16-17.
8. ———. "The Baghdad School," *Annual of the American Schools of Oriental Research (AASOR)*, VI (1926), 10-12.
9. Braithwaite, E. E. "The Semitic Museum of Harvard University," *Records of the Past*, IV (1905), 243-251.
10. Breasted, James H. *The Oriental Institute of the University of Chicago: A Beginning and a Program*, No. 1 of *Oriental Institute Communications (OIC)*. Chicago: Oriental Institute, 1922.
11. ———.*The Oriental Institute*, Vol. XII of *The University of Chicago Survey*. Chicago: Univ. Chicago Press, 1933.
12. Brown, Francis. "Recent Work in Assyriology," *American Journal of Philology*, II (1881), 225-230.
13. ———. *Assyriology: Its Use and Abuse in Old Testament Study*. New York: Chas. Scribner's Sons, 1885.
14. ———. "Semitic Study in the Theological Seminary," *Hebraica*, V (1888-89), 86-88.
15. Davis, John D., & Robert D. Wilson, "Assyriology," *Presbyterian and Reformed Review*, I (1890), 345-353.
16. Dougherty, Raymond P. "Miscellaneous Antiquities from Southern Babylonia," *AASOR*, VIII (1928), 43-54.

17. zu Eltz, Alexander. "Iranian Contributions to the Earliest Mesopotamian Civilization," *Bulletin of the American Institute for Iranian Art and Archaeology*, V (1938), 200-205.
18. Field, Henry. "Ancient Wheat and Barley from Kish, Mesopotamia," *American Anthropologist*, n.s., XXXIV (1932), 303-309.
19. Gadd, Cyril John. *History and Monuments of Ur*. New York: E. P. Dutton, 1929.
20. Frankfort, Henri. "Mesopotamia Sheds Light on Ancient India," *Illustrated London News*, 1 October 1932, 502-505.
21. Gray, Louis H. "Stylistic Parallels between Assyro-Babylonian and the Persian Inscriptions," *American Journal of Semitic Languages and Literature (AJSL)*, XVII (1900-01), 151-159.
22. Harper, Robert F. "*The Destruction of Antiquities in* the East," *Hebraica*, VI (1889-90), 225-226.
23. Harper, R. F., F. Brown & G. F. Moore. *Old Testament Studies in Memory of William Rainey Harper*. Chicago: Univ. Chicago Press, 1908.
24. Harper, William R. "Semitic Study in the University," *Hebraica*, V (1888-89), 83-85.
25. Haupt, Paul. "Contributions to the History of Assyriology, with Special Reference to the Works of Sir Henry Rawlinson," *Johns Hopkins University Circular (JHUC)*, VIII, No. 72 (1889), 57-62.
26. Harvard University. *Addresses Delivered at the Formal Opening of the Semitic Museum of Harvard University, February 5, 1903*. Cambridge, Mass.: Harvard Univ. Press, 1903.
27. Hilprecht, Hermann V. (comp.). *The So-Called Peters-Hilprecht Controversy*. Philadelphia: A. J. Holman, 1908.
28. *Hilprecht Anniversary Volume: Studies in Assyriology and Archaeology Dedicated to Hermann V. Hilprecht*. Chicago: The Open Court Publishing Company, 1909.
29. Jastrow, Morris, Jr. "The Present Status of Semitic Studies in this Country," *Hebraica*, V (1888-89), 77-79.
30. ———. "Did the Babylonian Temples Have Libraries?" *JAOS*, XXVII (1906), 147-182.
31. Kent, Roland G. (ed.). *Thirty Years of Oriental Studies*. Philadelphia: Oriental Club of Philadelphia, 1918.
32. Kent, R. G., & I. G. Matthews. "The Oriental Club of Philadelphia," *JAOS*, LVIII (1938), 2-4.
33. Langdon, Stephen. "The Toledo Collection of Cuneiform Tablets," *AJSL*, XXXIV (1917-18), 123-128.
34. Lane, W. H. *Babylonian Problems*. New York: E. P. Dutton, 1923.
35. Lyon, David G. "On some Recent Assyrian Publications," *JAOS*, XI (1885), ccii.
36. Mason, Otis T. "Progress and Result of Cuneiform Decipherment," *Baptist Quarterly*, VIII (1874), 191-208.
37. Maynard, John A. "A Survey of Assyriology During the Years 1915-1917," *Journal of the Society of Oriental Research (JSOR)*, II (1918), 28-46.
38. ———. "A Second Bibliographical Survey of Assyriology," *JSOR*, IV (1920), 16-28.
39. ———. "A Third Bibliographical Survey of Assyriology," *JSOR*, V (1921), 18-35.
40. ———. "A Fourth Bibliographical Survey of Assyriology," *JSOR*, VI (1922), 74-87.
41. ———. "A Fifth Survey of Assyriology," *JSOR*, VII (1923), 60-76.
42. ———. "A Sixth Survey of Assyriology," *JSOR*, VIII (1924), 135-166.
43. Muss-Arnolt, William. "Recent Contributions to Assyriology," *AJSL*, XXII (1905-06), 272-286.

44. Olmstead, Albert T. E. *Assyrian Historiography*, Vol. III of *Univ. Missouri Studies*. Columbia: Univ. Missouri Press, 1916.
45. Oriental Club of Philadelphia. *Oriental Studies*. Boston: Ginn & Co., 1894.
46. Pratt, Ida A. *Assyria and Babylon: A List of References in the New York Public Library*. New York: New York Public Library, 1918.
47. Riley, F. B. "A Voice from Babylon," *BASOR*, No. 17 (1925), 10-11.
48. Smith, S. A. "The Progress of Assyrian Study," *The Independent*, XL (1888), 721.
49. Ward, William H. "Assyrian Studies—Text-Books," *Bibliotheca Sacra*, XXVII (1870), 184-191.
50. ———."Retrospect and Prospect," *Hebraica*, V (1888-89), 80-82.

HISTORY

51. Albright, William F. "The Eighth Campaign of Sargon," *JAOS*, XXXVI (1917), 226-232.
52. Barton, G. A. "The Place of the Amorites in the Civilization of Western Asia," *JAOS*, XLV (1925), 1-38.
53. ———. "Whence Came the Sumerians?" *JAOS*, XLIX (1929), 263-268.
54. Boscawen, William St. Chad. *The First of Empires*. New York: Harper & Bros., 1903.
55. Brown, Francis. "Babylon and Egypt," *Presbyterian Review*, IX (1888), 476-481.
56. Cameron, George G. *A Pre-Achaemenid History of Persia: The Land and its People*. Chicago: Privately printed, 1936.
57. ———. *History of Early Iran*. Chicago: Univ. Chicago Press, 1936.
58. Clay, Albert T. *The Empire of the Amorites*. New Haven, Conn.: Yale Univ. Press, 1919.
59. ———. "The Antiquity of Babylonian Civilization," *JAOS*, XLI (1921), 241-263.
60. ———. "A Rejoinder to Professor George A. Barton," *JAOS*, XLV (1925), 119-151.
61. ———. *The Antiquity of Amorite Civilization*. New Haven, Conn: Privately printed, 1924.
62. Debevoise, Nelson C. *A Political History of Parthia*. Chicago: Univ. Chicago Press, 1938.
63. Dougherty, Raymond P. "Nabonidus in Arabia," *JAOS*, XLII (1922), 305-316.
64. ———. *Nabonidus and Belshazzar: A Study of the Closing Events of the Neo-Babylonian Empire*, Vol. XV of *Yale Oriental Series, Researches*. New Haven, Conn.: Yale Univ. Press, 1929.
65. Frankfort, Henri. "Sumerian, Semites, and the Origin of Copper-working," *Antiquaries Journal*, VIII (1928), 217-235.
66. Goodspeed, George Stephen, *A History of the Babylonians and Assyrians*. New York: Chas. Scribner's Sons, 1902.
67. Hall, H. R. "The Discoveries at Ur, and the Seniority of Sumerian Civilization," *Antiquity*, II (1928), 56-68.
68. Haupt, Paul. "Xenophon's Account of the Fall of Nineveh," *JAOS*, XXVIII (1907), 99-107.
69. Honor, Leo L. *Sennacherib's Invasion of Palestine*, No. 12 of *Contributions to Oriental History and Philology*. New York: Columbia Univ. Press, 1926.
70. Jacobsen, Thorkild. "The Assumed Conflict between Sumerians and Semites in Early Mesopotamian History," *JAOS*, LIX (1939), 485-495.
71. Jastrow, Morris, Jr. *The Civilization of Babylonia and Assyria*. Philadelphia: J. B. Lippincott Co., 1915.
72. Johns, Claude H. W. *Ancient Assyria*. New York: G. P. Putnam's Sons, 1912.
73. ———.*Ancient Babylonia*. New York: G. P. Putnam's Sons, 1913.
74. Johnston, Christopher. "The Fall of Nineveh," *JAOS*, XXII (1901), 20-22.

75. Kent, Roland G. "The Record of Darius' Palace at Susa," *JAOS*, LIII (1933), 1-23.
76. ———. "The Restoration of Order by Darius," *JAOS*, LVIII (1938), 112-121.
77. Kraeling, Emil G. "The Death of Sennacherib," *JAOS*, LIII (1933), 335-346.
78. Langdon, Stephen H. "Notes on the Annals of Asurbanipal," *JAOS*, XXIV (1903), 96-102.
79. ———. "Evidence for an Advance on Egypt by Sennacherib in the Campaign of 701-700 B.C.," *JAOS*, XXIV (1904), 265-274.
80. Luckenbill, Daniel D. "Akkadian Origins," *AJSL*, XL (1923-24), 1-13.
81. ———. *The Annals of Sennacherib*, Vol. II of *Oriental Institute Publications (OIP)*. Chicago: Oriental Institute, 1924.
82. ———. *Ancient Records of Assyria and Babylonia*. Chicago: Oriental Institute, 1926-27. 2 vols.
83. Lyon, David G. "When and Where was the Code of Hammurabi Promulgated?" *JAOS*, XXVII (1906), 123-134.
84. Olmstead, Albert T. *Western Asia in the Days of Sargon of Assyria, 722-705 B. C.*, Vol. II of *Cornell Studies in History and Political Science*. New York: Henry Holt and Co., 1908.
85. ———. "Western Asia in the Reign of Sennacherib of Assyria (705-681)," *Amer. Historical Assn., Annual Report for 1909* (1911), 91-101.
86. ———. "The Assyrian Chronicle," *JAOS*, XXXIV (1915), 344-368.
87. ———."The Political Development of Early Babylonia," *AJSL*, XXXIII (1916-17), 283-321.
88. ———."Tiglath-Pileser I and His Wars," *JAOS*, XXXVII (1917), 179-185.
89. ———. "The Calculated Frightfullness of Ashur Nasir Apal," *JAOS*, XXXVIII (1918), 209-263.
90. ———. "The Babylonian Empire," *AJSL*, XXXV (1918-19), 65-100.
91. ———. "Kashshites, Assyrians, and the Balance of Power," *AJSL*, XXXVI (1919-20), 120-153.
92. ———. "Babylonia as an Assyrian Dependency," *AJSL*, XXXVII (1920-21), 212-229.
93. ———. "Shalmaneser III and the Establishment of the Assyrian Power," *JAOS*, XLI (1921), 345-382.
94. ———. "The Fall and Rise of Babylon," *AJSL*, XXXVIII (1921-22), 73-96.
95. ———. *History of Assyria*. Chicago: Univ. Chicago Press, 1923.
96. Pfeiffer, Robert H. "Nuzi and the Hurrians," *Ann. Rept. of the Smithsonian Inst. for 1935* (1936), 535-558.
97. Prince, Ira M. "Some Light from Ur touching Lagash," *JAOS*, L (1930), 150-158.
98. ———. "Light out of Ur—The Devotion of Elamite Kings to Sumerian Deities," *JAOS*, LI (1931), 164-169.
99. Radau, Hugo. *Early Babylonian History Down to the End of the Fourth Dynasty of Ur*. New York: Oxford Univ. Press, 1900.
100. Ragozin, Zenoide A. *The Story of Assyria*. New York; G. P. Putnam's Sons, 1887.
101. ———. *The Story of Media, Babylon, and Persia*. New York: G. P. Putnam's Sons, 1888.
102. ———.*The Story of Chaldea*, 2nd. ed. New York: G. P. Putnam's Sons, 1898.
103. Rogers, Robert W. *A History of Babylonia and Assyria*, 6th ed. New York: Abingdon Press, 1915. 2 vols.
104. ———. "Fresh Light Upon the History of the Earliest Assyrian Period," Vol. I of *Ann. Rept. Amer, Hist. Assn. for 1914* (1916), 95-102.
105. ———. *A History of Ancient Persia*. New York: Chas. Scribner's Sons, 1929.

106. Speiser, E. A. "Southern Kurdistan in the Annals of Ashurnasirpal and Today," *AASOR*, VIII (1928), 1-42.
107. ———. *Mesopotamian Origins*. Philadelphia: Univ. Penn. Press, 1930.
108. ———. "The Bearing of the Excavations at Tepe Gawra and at Tell Billa upon the Ethnic Problems of Ancient Mesopotamia," *American Journal of Archaeology (AJA)*, XXXVI (1932), 29-35.
109. ———. "On Some Important Synchronisms in Prehistoric Mesopotamia," *AJA*, XXXVI (1932), 465-471.
110. ———. "Ethnic Movements in the Near East in the Second Millenium B. C.," *AASOR*, XIII (1933), 13-54.
111. Tiele, C. P. "Suzub the Babylonian and Suzub the Chaldaean, Kings of Babylon," *Hebraica*, II (1885-86), 218-220.
112. Walker, Dean A. "The Assyrian King Assurbanipal," *Old Testament Student*, VIII (1888-89), 57-62, 96-101.
113. Ward, William H. "The Babylonian Melchizedek," *The Independent*, LIV (1902), 3020-3023.
114. Winckler, Hugo. *The History of Babylonia and Assyria*, trans. J. A. Craig. New York: Chas. Scribner's Sons, 1907.

EXPLORATION, TRAVEL, AND GEOGRAPHY

115. Albright, William F. "Notes on the Topography of Ancient Mesopotamia," *JAOS*, XLVI (1926), 220-230.
116. Anonymous. "Layard's Discoveries," *The New Englander*, XI (n.s. V) (1853), 457-470.
117. Babelon, Ernest. "Recent Archaeological Discoveries in Persia," *AJA*, II (1886), 53-60.
118. Brown, Francis. "The Wolfe Exploring Expedition to Babylonia," *Presbyterian Review*, VII (1886), 155-159.
119. Clay, Albert T. "Topographical Map from Nippur," *Trans. Dept. Archaeology Free Museum of Science and Art, Univ. Penn.*, I (1905), 223-225.
120. Harper, Robert F. "A Visit to Zinjirli," *The Old and New Testament Student*, VIII (1888-89), 183-184.
121. ———. "A Visit to Carchemish," *The Old and New Testament Student*, IX (1889), 308-309.
122. ———. "Down the Euphrates Valley; I-III," *The Old and New Testament Student*, X (1890), 55-57, 118-119, 367-368.
123. Jackson, A. V. Williams. *Persia, Past and Present*. New York: Macmillan, 1906.
124. Kidder, Daniel P. *Nineveh and the River Tigris*. New York: Lane & Scott, 1851.
125. Peters, John P. "Miscellaneous Notes," *Hebraica*, I (1884-85), 115-119.
126. ———. "A Few Ancient Sites. I and II," *The Nation*, 23 May 1889, 423; 30 May 1889, 442-443.
127. ———. "From Niffer to Tello. I and II," *The Nation* 25 July 1889, 69-70; 1 August 1889, 90-92.
128. ———. "Zenobia, Palmyra, and the Arabs," *The Nation*, 3 April 1890, 276-277.
129. ———. "A Misrepresented Ruin," *The Nation*, 7 May 1891, 375-377.
130. Prince, Ira M. "Transportation by Water in Early Babylonia," *AJSL*, XL (1923-24), 111-116.
131. Toffteen, Olaf A. *Researches in Assyrian and Babylonian Geography*. Chicago: Univ. Chicago Press, 1908.
132. Ward, William H. "The Wolfe Expedition," *Journal of the Society of Biblical Literature and Exegesis*, V (1885), 56-60.
133. ———. "Sippara," *Hebraica*, II (1885-86), 79,86.

134. ———. *Report on the Wolfe Expedition to Babylonia, 1884-85.* Boston: Papers of the Archaeological Institute of America, Published for them by Cupples, Upham, and Co., 1886.
135. ———. "On the Proceedings of the Wolfe Expedition to Mesopotamia, During 1884 and 1885,0 *JAOS*, XII (1889), lxvi.

ARCHEOLOGY

136. Anonymous. "A Buried Temple and Palace," *American Antiquarian*, II (1879-80), 297-298.
137. Bache, Charles. "First Report on the Joint Excavations at Tepe Gawra and Tell Billah, 1932-3," *BASOR*, No. 49 (1933), 8-14.
138. ———. "Reports on the Joint Expedition at Tell Billah," *BASOR*, No. 50 (1933), 3-7.
139. ———. "Tepe Gawra," *AJA*, XXXIX (1935), 185-188.
140. ———. "Report on the Joint Excavation of Tepe Gawra in Assyria," *BASOR*, No. 61 (1936), 5-10.
141. ———. "The Joint Assyrian Expedition," *BASOR*, No. 62 (1936), 6-9.
142. Banks, Edgar J. *The Expedition of the Oriental Exploration Fund (Babylonian Section) of the University of Chicago.* Chicago: Univ. Chicago Press, 1904.
143. ———. "The Recent Excavations at Bismya," *The Independent*, LIX (1905), 1321-1324.
144. ———. *Bismya or the Lost City of Adab: A Story of Adventure, of Exploration, and of Excavation Among the Ruins of the Oldest of the Buried Cities of Babylonia.* New York: G. P. Putnam's Sons, 1912.
145. Barton, George A. "Our Excavations in Iraq," *BASOR*, No. 18 (1925), 1-5.
146. ———. "Dr. Speiser's Excavation of Teppe Gawra," *BASOR*, No. 29 (1928), 12-15.
147. ———. "Reports from our Expeditions in Iraq," *BASOR* No. 41 (1931), 1927.
148. ———. *Archaeology and the Bible*, 7th ed. Phila.: American Sunday School Union, 1937.
149. Burrows, Eric, J. Legrain et al. *Ur Excavations Texts.* Oxford Univ. Press, 1928-53. 5 vols.
150. Chiera, Edwin, & E. A. Speiser. "A New Factor in the History of the Ancient East," *AASOR*, VI (1926), 75-90.
151. Chiera, Edwin. *They Wrote on Clay: The Babylonian Tablets Speak Today.* Chicago: Univ. Chicago Press, 1938.
152. Clay, Albert T. "Excavations at Nippur," *Scientific American*, LXXXIV (1901), 133-134.
153. ———. "Explorations in Bible Lands," *The Independent*, LV (1903), 261-264.
154. Davis, Asahel. *Lectures on the Remarkable Discoveries Lately Made in the East: As Those of Nineveh, Persia, etc.* Buffalo, N. Y.: Phinney & Co., 1852.
155. Delougaz, Pinhas. *I. Plano-Convex Bricks and the Methods of Their Employment. II. The Treatment of Clay Tablets in the Field*, No. 7 of *Studies in Ancient Oriental Civilization. (SAOC).* Chicago: Oriental Institute, 1933.
156. Dougherty, Raymond P. "An Archaeological Survey in Southern Babylonia I," *BASOR*, No. 23 (1926), 15-28.
157. ———. "Searching for Ancient Remains in Lower Iraq," *AASOR*, VII (1927), 1-93.
158. ———. "An Archaeological Survey in Southern Babylonia II," *BASOR*, No. 25 (1927), 5-13.
159. Field, Henry. *The Field Museum-Oxford University Expedition to Kish, Mesopotamia 1923-1929*, Leaflet 28 of *Field Mus. Nat. Hist., Anthropology.* Chicago, 1929.
160. Field Museum. "Expedition at Kish," *Annual Report of the Director for*: 1923, Publ. 217 (1924), 197-198.

1924, Publ. 227 (1925), 297.
1925, Publ. 235 (1926), 425-426.
1926, Publ. 243 (1927), 56-57.
1927, Publ. 248 (1928), 208-209.
1928, Publ. 252 (1929), 425-430.
1929, VIII (1930), 50-51.
1930, VIII (1931), 318-320.
1931, Publ. 306 (1932), 67-69.
1932, Publ. 318 (1933), 319-320.
Field Musuem of Natural History (Chicago).

161. Frankfort, Henri. "New Light on the Ancient Sumerian Civilization," *Illustrated London News*, 8 October 1932, 526-529.

162. ———. "The City King Sargon Founded to Replace Nineveh," *Illustrated London News*, 15 October 1932, 571-573.

163. ———.*Tell Asmar, Khafaje, and Khorsabad: Second Preliminary Report of the Iraq Expedition*, No. 16 of *OIC*. Chicago: Oriental Institute, 1933.

164. ———. "The Work of the Oriental Institute in Iraq," *AJA*, XXXVII (1933), 529-539.

165. ———.*Iraq Excavations of the Oriental Institute, 1932/33: Third Preliminary Report of the Iraq Expedition*, No. 17 of *OIC*. Chicago: Oriental Institute, 1934

166. ———. *Oriental Institute Discoveries in Iraq, 1933/34: Fourth Preliminary Report of the Iraq Expedition*, No. 19 of *OIC*. Chicago: Oriental Institute, 1935.

167. ———. *Progress of the Work of the Oriental Institute in Iraq, 1934/35: Fifth Preliminary Report*, No. 20 of *OIC*. Chicago: Oriental Institute, 1936.

168. Frankfort, H., T. Jacobsen & C. Preusser. *Tell Asmar and Khafaje: The First Season's Work in Eshnuna, 1930/31*, No. 13 of *OIC*. Chicago: Oriental Institute, 1932.

169. Hall, H. R., & C. L. Woolley. *Ur Excavations*. Oxford Univ. Press, 1927-65. 7 vols.

170. Harper, Robert F. "Aus einem Briefe des Herrn Prof. R. F. Harper," *Zeitschrift Fur Assyriologie (ZFA)* IV (1889), 163-164.

171. ———. "The Expedition of the Babylonian Exploration Fund," *The Old and New Testament Student*, XIV (1892), 160-165, 213-217; XV (1892), 12-16.

172. ———. "The Expedition of the Babylonian Exploration Fund; Excavations at Niffer During the Season of 1889," *The Biblical World*, I (1893), 57-62.

173. ———. "Report from Bismya, I," *AJSL*, XX (1903-04), 207-208, 260-268.

174. ———. "Exploration and Discovery in Babylonia," *American Antiquarian and Oriental Journal*, XXVI (1904), 177-179.

175. Hilprecht, Hermann V. "Keilinschriftliche Funde in Niffer," *ZFA*, IV (1889), 164-168.

176. ———."Aus einem Briefe des Herrn Prof. H. V. Hilprecht," *ZFA*, IV (1889), 282-284.

177. ——— (ed.). *Recent Research in Bible Lands* Philadelphia: J. D. Wattles, 1896.

178. ———. "The University of Pennsylvania's Expedition in Babylonia," *The Independent*, LII (1900), 2717-2720.

179. ———(ed.). *Exploration in Bible Lands During the 19th Century*. Philadelphia: A. J. Holman, 1903.

180. ———. *The Excavations in Assyria and Babylonia*, Vol. I of *The Babylonian Expedition of the University of Pennsylvania (BEUP)*, H. V. Hilprecht, ed., Series D. Philadelphia: Univ. Penn. Press, 1904.

181. Lacheman, E. R. "New Nuzi Tablets and a New Method of Copying Cuneiform Tablets," *JAOS*, LV (1935), 429-431.
182. Langdon, Stephen, & L. C. Watelin. *Excavations at Kish. The Herbert Weld (Oxford) and Field Museum of Natural History (Chicago) Expedition to Mesopotamia*. Paris: Geuthner, 1924-34. 3 vols.
183. Langdon, Stephen. "The Field Museum-Oxford University Joint Expedition at Kish, 1926-7," *Art and Archaeology*, XXIV (1927), 103-111.
184. ———. "Excavating Kish: The Cradle of Civilization 1927-1928," *Art and Archaeology*, XXVI (1928), 155-168.
185. ———. "Excavations at Kish, 1928-29," *Journal of the Royal Asiatic Society (JRAS)* for 1930 (1930), 610-610.
186. Loud, Gordon. *Khorsabad. I. Excavations in the Palace and at the City Gate*, Vol. XXXVIII of *OIP*. Chicago: Oriental Institute, 1936.
187. Loud, Gordon, & C. B. Altman. *Khorsabad. II. The Citadel and the Town*, Vol XL of *OIP*. Chicago: Oriental Institute, 1938.
188. Luckenbill, Daniel D. "Excavations in Ashur," *Records of the Past*, V (1906), 86-89.
189. ———. "Documents from the Temple Archives of Nippur," *Records of the Past*, V (1906), 213-224.
190. ———. "The Black Stone of Esarhaddon," *AJSL*, XLI (1924-25), 165-173.
191. ———. *Cuneiform Series. II. Inscriptions from Adab*, Vol. XIV of *OIP*. Chicago: Oriental Institute, 1930.
192. Lyon, David G. (comp.). "The Joint Expedition of Harvard University and the Baghdad School at Yargan Tepa Near Kirkuk," *BASOR*, No. 30 (1928), 1-6.
193. Mackay, Ernest. *Report on the Excavations of the "A" Cemetery at Kish, Mesopotamia*. Chicago: Field Museum-Oxford Univ., 1925-29. 2 vols.
194. ———. "Report on Excavations at Jemdet Nasr, Iraq," *Field Mus. Nat. Hist., Anthropology Memoirs*, I (1931), 219-303.
195. Meek, T. J. "Some Gleanings from the Last Excavations at Nuzi," *AASOR*, XIII (1933), 1-12.
196. Olmstead, Albert T. "A Year of Research in the Near East," *BASOR*, No. 69 (1938), 21-25.
197. Peters, John P. "Miscellaneous Notes," *Hebraica*, I (1884-85), 184-186.
198. ———. "Letter on the Babylonian Expedition," *AJA* VII (1891), 472-475.
199. ———. "Notes on Murdter-Delitzsch' Geschichte," *ZFA*, VII (1891), 333-339.
200. ———. "Babylonian Expedition," *JAOS (Proc.)*, April 21-23, 1892 (1892), cxlvi-cliii.
201. ———. "Some Recent Results of the University of Pennsylvania Excavations at Nippur, Especially on the Temple Hill," *AJA*, X (1895), 13-46.
202. ———."University of Pennsylvania Excavations at Nippur," *AJA*, X (1895), 352-368.
203. ———. "University of Pennsylvania Expedition to Babylonia. III. The Court of Columns at Nippur," *AJA*, X (1895), 439-468.
204. ———. *Nippur; or, Exploration and Adventures on the Euphrates*. New York: G. P. Putnam's Sons, 1897. 2 vols.
205. ———. "Exploration of Nippur," *Records of the Past*, II (1903), 35-46.
206. ———. "The Nippur Library," *JAOS*, XXVI (1905), 145-164.
207. Pfeiffer, Robert H. "Yorgan Teppe, Preliminary Report of the Excavations During 1928-29," *BASOR*, No. 34 (1929), 2-7.
208. Pinches, T. G. "The Discoveries of the American Expedition to Babylonia," *The Academy*, XL (1891), 199.
209. Schmidt, Erich F. *Excavations at Tepe Hissar Damghan*. Philadelphia: Univ. Penn. Press, 1937.

210. ———. *The Treasury of Persepolis and Other Discoveries in the Homeland of the Achaemenians*, No. 21 of *OIC*. Chicago: Oriental Institute, 1939.
211. Smith, Azariah. "Ruins of Nineveh: Description of the Discoveries Made in 1843 and 1844," *American Journal of Science and Arts*, XLIX (1845), 113-128.
212. Speiser, E. A. "Preliminary Excavation at Tepe Gawra," *AASOR*, IX (1929), 17-94.
213. ———. "The Joint Excavations at Tepe Gawra," *AJA*, XXXVI (1932), 564-568.
214. ———. "First Steps in Mesopotamian Archaeology," *BASOR*, No. 52 (1933), 15-18.
215. ———. "The Historical Significance of Tepe Gawra," *Ann. Rept. Smithsonian Inst. For 1933* (1934), 415-427.
216. ———. "The Archaeological Promise of the Zagros," *Bull. Amer. Inst. for Persian Art and Archaeology*, III (1934), 3-4.
217. ———. *Excavations at Tepe Gawra*, Vol. I. Philadelphia: Univ. Penn. Press for Amer. Schls. Or. Research, 1935.
218. ———. "On Some Recent Finds From Tepe Gawra," *BASOR*, No. 62 (1936), 10-14.
219. ———. "First Report on the Current Assyrian Campaign," *BASOR*, No. 64 (1936), 4-9.
220. ———. "Progress of the Joint Assyrian Expedition," *BASOR*, No. 65 (1937), 2-8.
221. ———. "Three Reports on the Joint Assyrian Expedition," *BASOR*, No. 66 (1937), 2-19.
222. ———. "New Discoveries at Tepe Gawra and Khafaje," *AJA*, XLI (1937), 190-193.
223. ———. "Progress of the Joint Expedition to Mesopotamia," *BASOR*, No. 70 (1938), 3-10.
224. Starr, Richard F. S. *Nuzi; Report on the Excavations at Yorgan Tepa Near Kirkuk, Iraq*. Cambridge, Mass.: Harvard Univ. Press, 1939. 2 vols.
225. Ward, William H. "An Extraordinary Discovery," *The Independent*, LIV (1902), 2972-2973.
226. Waterman, Leroy *Preliminary Report Upon the Excavation at Tel Umar, Iraq*. Ann Arbor: Univ. Michigan Press, 1931.
227. ———. *Second Preliminary Report Upon the Excavation at Tel Umar, Iraq*. Ann Arbor: Univ. Michigan Press, 1933.
228. Woolley, C. Leonard. "Excavations at Ur of the Chaldees," *Antiquaries Journal*, III (1923), 311-333.
229. ———. "Excavations at Tell el Obeid," *Antiq. Jour.*, IV (1924), 329-346.
230. ——— "The Excavations at Ur, 1923-24," *Antiq. Jour.*, V (1925), 1-20.
231. ———. "The Excavations at Ur, 1924-1925," *Antiq. Jour.*, V (1925), 347-402.
232. ———. "The Excavations at Ur, 1925-26," *Antiq. Jour.*, VI (1926), 365-401.
233. ———. "Excavations at Ur, 1926-7," *Antiq. Jour.*, VII (1927), 385-423.
234. ———. "Excavations at Ur, 1926-7. Part II," *Antiq. Jour.*, VIII (1928), 1-29.
235. ———. "Excavations at Ur, 1927-8," *Antiq. Jour.*, VIII (1928), 415-448.
236. ———. "The Royal Tombs of Ur," *Antiquity*, II (1928), 7-17.
237. ———. "Excavations at Ur, 1928-9," *Antiq. Jour.*, IX (1929), 305-343.
238. ———. "Excavations at Ur, 1929-30," *Antiq. Jour.*, X (1930), 315-343.
239. ———. "Excavations at Ur, 1930-1," *Antiq. Jour.*, XI (1931), 343-381.
240. ———. "Excavations at Ur, 1931-2," *Antiq. Jour.*, XII (1932), 355-392.
241. ———. "Report on the Excavations at Ur, 1932-3," *Antiq. Jour.*, XIII (1933), 359-383.
242. ———. "The Excavations at Ur, 1933-4," *Antiq. Jour.*, XIV (1934), 355-378.

PHILOLOGY AND LINGUISTIC

243. Ahl, W. William. " 'Cyrus,' in the Light of Recent Research," *Trans. and Proc. Amer. Philological Assn.*, LXIII (1932), xli-xlii.
244. Arnold, William R. *Ancients Babylonian Records in the Columbia University Library*. New York: Columbia Univ. Press, 1896.
245. Albright, William F. "The Conclusion of Esarhaddon's Broken Prism," *JAOS*, XXXV (1917), 391-393.
246. Banks, Edgar J. "Eight Oracular Responses to Esarhaddon," *AJSL*, XIV (1897-98), 267-277.
247. Barton, George A. "Some Contracts of the Persian Period from the Kh Collection of the University of Pennsylvania," *AJSL*, XVI (1899-1900), 65-82.
248. ———. "The Haverford Library Collection of Cuneiform Tablets," *AJA*, VI (1902), 36-37.
249. ———. *Haverford Library Collection of Cuneiform Texts*. New Haven, Conn.: Yale Univ. Press, 1905-14. 3 vols.
250. ———. "On the Babylonian Origin of Plato's Nuptial Number," *JAOS*, XXIX (1909), 210-219.
251. ———. "On an Old Babylonian Letter Addressed 'To Lushtamar,' " *JAOS*, XXIX (1909), 220-223.
252. ———. "Hilprecht's Fragment of the Babylonian Deluge Story," *JAOS*, XXXI (1911), 30-48.
253. ———. "The Babylonian Calendar in the Reigns of Lugalanda and Urkagina," *JAOS*, XXXI (1911), 251-271.
254. ———. "Recent Researches in the Sumerian Calendar," *JAOS*, XXXIII (1913), 1-9.
255. ———. "Kugler's Criterion for Determining the Order of the Months in the Earliest Babylonian Calendar," *JAOS*, XXXIII (1913), 297-305.
256. ———. *Sumerian Business and Administrative Documents From the Earliest Times to the Dynasty of Agade*, Pt. 1 of Vol. IX of *Univ. Penn. Museum, Publ. Babylonian Section*. Philadelphia: Univ. Penn. Press, 1915.
257. ———. *Miscellaneous Babylonian Inscriptions*, Pt. 1 of *Sumerian Religious Texts*. New Haven, Conn.: Yale Univ. Press, 1918.
258. ———. "On the So-Called Sumero-Indian Seals," *AASOR*, VIII (1928), 79-95.
259. ———. *The Royal Inscriptions of Sumer and Akkad*. New Haven, Conn.: Yale Univ. Press for Aer. Oriental Soc., 1929.
260. ———. "A Comparative List of the Signs in the So-Called Indo-Sumerian Seal," *AASOR*, X (1930), 75-84.
261. ———. "A New Inscription of Entemena," *JAOS*, LI (1931), 262-265.
262. ———. "Some Observations as to the Origin of the Babylonian Syllabary," *JAOS*, LIV (1934), 75-79.
263. Baum, H. N., & F. B. Wright. "Laws of Hammurabi," *Records of the Past*, II (1903), 67-98.
264. Berry, Geo. R. "The Letters of the Rm2. Collection (ZA VIII, pp. 341-359)," *Hebraica*, XI (1894-95), 174-202.
265. Bradner, Lester, Jr. "A Classification of Sentences in the Sennacherib (Taylor) Inscription," *Hebraica*, VI (1889-90), 303-308.
266. ———. "The Order of the Sentence in the Assyrian Historical Inscriptions," *Hebraica*, VIII (1891-92), 1-14.
267. Breasted, James H. "The Assyrian Babylonian Dictionary," *AJSL*, XXXVIII (1921-22), 288-305.
268. Brown, Francis. "Assyriological Notes," *Hebraica*, I (1884-85), 182-183.
269. ———. "The Babylonian 'List of Kings' and 'Chronicle,' " *Presbyterian Review*, IX (1888), 293-299.

270. Chiera, Edwin. *Legal and Administrative Documents From Nippur, Chiefly from the Dynasties of Isin and Larsa*, No. 1 of Vol. VIII of *Univ. Penn. Museum, Publ. Babylonian Section*. Philadelphia: Univ. Penn. Press, 1914.
271. ——. *Lists of Personal Names from the Temple School of Nippur*, No. 1 of Vol. I of *Univ. Penn. Museum, Publ. Babylonian Section*. Philadelphia: Univ. Penn. Press, 1916.
272. ——. *Old Babylonian Contracts*, No. 2 of Vol. VIII of *Univ. Penn. Museum, Publ. Babylonian Section*. Philadelphia: Univ. Penn. Press, 1922.
273. ——. *Selected Temple Accounts from Telloh, Yokha, and Drehem: Cuneiform Tablets in the Library of Princeton University*. Princeton, N. J.: Princeton Univ. Press, 1922.
274. ——. *Inheritance Texts*. Paris: Geuthner, 1927.
275. ——. *Cuneiform Series. I. Sumerian Lexical Texts from the Temple School of Nippur*, Vol. XI of *OIP*. Chicago: Oriental Institute, 1929.
276. ——. *Texts of Varied Contents*, Vol. I of *Excavations at Nuzi*, Vol. V. of *Harvard Semitic Series*. Cambridge, Mass.: Harvard Univ. Press, 1929.
277. ——. *Sumerian Texts of Varied Contents*, Vol. IV of *Cuneiform Series*, Vol. XVI of *OIP*, Chicago: Oriental Institute, 1934.
278. Clay, Albert T. *Business Documents of Murashu Sons of Nippur, Dated in the Reign of Darius II*, Vol. X of *BEUP*, H. V. Hilprecht, ed., Series A. Philadelphia: Univ. Penn. Press, 1904.
279. ——. *Documents from the Temple Archives of Nippur, Dated in the Reigns of Cassite Rulers, With Complete Dates*, Vol XIV of *BEUP*, H. V. Hilprecht, ed., Series A. Philadelphia: Univ. Penn. Press, 1906.
280. ——. *Documents from the Temple Archives of Nippur, Dated in the Reigns of Cassite Rulers, With Incomplete Dates*, Vol. XV of *BEUP*, H. V. Hilprecht, ed., Series A. Philadelphia: Univ. Penn. Press, 1906.
281. ——. "The Origin and Real Name of NIN-IB," *JAOS*, XXVIII (1907), 135-144.
282. ——. *Legal and Commercial Transactions Dated in the Assyrian, Neo-Babylonian and Persian Periods*, Pt. I, *Chiefly from Nippur*, Vol. VIII of *BEUP*, H. V. Hilprecht, ed., Series A. Philadelphia: Univ. Penn. Press, 1908.
283. ——. *Personal Names from Cuneiform Inscriptions of the Cassite Period*, Vol. I of *Yale Oriental Series, Researches*. New Haven, Conn.: Yale Univ. Press, 1912.
284. ——. "Inscriptions of Nebuchadnezzar and Naram Sin," *Records of the Past*, XIII (1914), 73-75.
285. ——. *Miscellaneous Inscriptions in the Yale Babylonian Collection*, Vol. I of *Yale Oriental Series, Babylonian Texts*. New Haven, Conn.: Yale Univ. Press, 1915.
286. ——. "Name of the So-Called Deity Za-Mal-Mal," *JAOS*, XXXVII (1917), 328-329.
287. ——. *Neo-Babylonian Letters from Erech*, Vol. III of *Yale Oriental Series, Babylonian Texts*. New Haven, Conn.: Yale Univ. Press, 1919.
288. Clermont-Ganneau, M. "Mene, Tekel, Peres, and the Feast of Belshazzar," trans. R. W. Rogers, *Hebraica*, III (1886-87), 87-102.
289. Craig, James A. "Throne-Inscriptions of Salmanessar II," *Hebraica*, II (1885-86), 140-146.
290. ——. "The Monolith Inscription of Salmaneser II," *Hebraica*, III (1886-87), 201-232.
291. Craig, J. A., & R. F. Harper. "Inscription of Asurbanipal from a Barrel-Cylinder found at Aboo-Habba," *Hebraica*, II (1885-86), 87-89.
292. Craig, James A. *Astrological-Astronomical Texts Copied From the Original Tablets in the British Museum*. Leipzig: J. C. Hinrichs, 1899.

293. Dougherty, Raymond P. *Records From Erech, Time of Nabonidus*, Vol. VI of *Yale Oriental Series, Babylonian Texts*. New Haven: Conn.: Yale Univ. Press, 1920.
294. ——. *Archives From Erech*. New Haven, Conn.: Yale Univ. Press for Goucher College, 1923-33. 2 vols.
295. ——. "Writing Upon Parchment and Papyrus Among the Babylonians and Assyrians," *JAOS*, XLVIII (1928), 109-135.
296. Duncan, George S. "Babylonian Legal and Business Documents from the First Babylonian Dynasty, Transliterated, Translated, and Annotated," *AJSL*, XXX (1913-14), 166-195.
297. Gadbey, A. H. "Political, Religious, and Social Antiquities of the Sargonid Period," *AJSL*, XXI (1904-05), 65-82.
298. Geers, F. W. "A Babylonian Omen Text," *AJSL*, XLIII (1826-27), 22-41.
299. Goetze, Albrecht. "The t-Form of the Old Babylonian Verb," *JAOS*, LVI (1936), 297-334.
300. Gray, Louis H. "Indo-Iranian Studies," *American Journal of Philology*, XXI (1900), 1-22.
301. ——. "Notes on the Old Persian Inscriptions of Behistun," *JAOS*, XXIII (1902), 56-64.
302. Hackman, George G. (ed.). *Temple Documents of the Third Dynasty of Ur From Umma*, Vol. V of *Babylonian Inscriptions in the Collection of J. B. Nies*. New Haven, Conn.: Yale Univ. Press, 1937.
303. Harper, Robert F. "Some Corrections to the Texts of Cylinders A and B of the Esarhaddon Inscriptions as Published in IR., 45-47, and IIIR., 15, 16," *Hebraica*, III (1886-87), 177-185.
304. ——. "Some Unpublished Esarhaddon Inscriptions," *Hebraica*, IV (1887-88), 18-25.
305. ——. "Transliteration and Translation of Cylinder A of the Esarhaddon Inscriptions," *Hebraica*, IV (1887-88), 99-117.
306. ——. "Cylinder B of the Esarhaddon Inscriptions Transliterated and Translated," *Hebraica*, IV (1887-88), 146-157.
307. ——. "Babylonian Letter.—The Joseph Shemtob Collection of Babylonian Antiquities Recently Purchased for the University of Pennsylvania," *Hebraica*, V (1888-89), 74-76.
308. ——. "The Kh. Collection of Babylonian Antiquities Belonging to the University of Pennsylvania," *Hebraica*, VI (1889-90), 59-60.
309. ——. "Three Contract Tablets of Ashuritililani," *Hebraica*, VII (1890-91), 79.
310. ——. "A-bi-e-shu = Ebishum," *Hebraica*, VIII (1891-92), 103-104.
311. ——. *Assyrian and Babylonian Letters Belonging to the Kouyunjik Collections of the British Museum*. Chicago: Univ. Chicago Press, 1892-1914. 14 vols.
312. ——. "Assyriological Notes," *Hebraica*, X (1893-94), 196-201.
313. ——. *Assyrian and Babylonian Literature, Selected Translations*. New York: D. Appleton & Co., 1901.
314. ——. "Text of the Code of Hammurabi, King of Babylon (About 2250 B. C.)," *AJSL*, XX (1903-04), 1-84.
315. ——. *The Code of Hammurabi, King of Babylon*, 2d ed. Chicago: Univ. Chicago Press, 1904.
316. Harper, W. R., P. Haupt, & H. L. Strack. "The Study of Assyrian," *Hebraica*, I (1884-85), 130-132.
317. Haupt, Paul. "The Babylonian 'Woman's Language,'" *American Journal of Philology*, V (1884), 68-84.
318. ——. "Assyrian Phonology, With Special Reference to Hebrew," *Hebraica*, I (1884-85), 175-181.

319. ——. "Wateh-Ben-Hazael: Prince of the Kedarenes about 650 B.C.," *Hebraica*, I (1884-85), 217-231.
320. ——. "On the Etymology of Mutninu," *Hebraica*, II (1885-86), 4-6.
321. ——. "On the Etymology of Nekasim," *Hebraica*, III (1886-87), 107-110.
322. ——. "The Beginning of the Babylonian Nimrod Epic," *JAOS*, XXII (1901), 7-12.
323. ——. "The Introductory Lines of the Cuneiform Account of the Deluge," *JAOS*, XXV (1904), 68-75.
324. ——. "The Name Istar," *JAOS*, XXVIII (1907), 112-119.
325. ——. "Some Difficult Passages in the Cuneiform Account of the Deluge," *JAOS*, XXXII (1912), 1-20.
326. ——."The Five Assyrian Stems la'u," *JAOS*, XXXII (1912), 115-119.
327. Herzfeld, Ernst. *A New Inscription of Xerxes From Persepolis*, No. 5 of *SAOC*. Chicago: Oriental Institute, 1932.
328. Hilprecht, Hermann V. "Die Votiv-Inschrift eines nicht erkannten Kassitenkonigs," *ZFA*, VII (1892), 304-318.
329. ——. "Konig Ini-Sin von Ur," *ZFA*, VII (1892), 343-346.
330. ——. "Old Babylonian Inscriptions, Chiefly from Nippur," *Transactions of the American Philosophical Society*, XVII, n.s. (1893-96), Pt. 1, 5-54; Pt. 2, 221-282.
331. ——. "A Numerical Fragment from Nippur," in *Oriental Studies* by Oriental Club of Philadelphia. Boston: Ginn & Co., 1894.
332. ——. *Mathematical, Metrological and Chronological Texts From the Temple Library of Nippur*, Vol. XX of *BEUP*, H. V. Hilprecht, ed., Series A. Philadelphia: Univ. Penn. Press, 1906.
333. Hilprecht, H. V., & A. T. Clay. *Business Documents of Nippur, Dated in the Reign of Artaxerxes I*. Vol. IX of *BEUP*, H. V. Hilprecht, ed., Series A. Philadelphia: Univ. Penn. Press, 1898.
334. Hinke, William J. *A New Boundary Stone of Nebuchadnezzar I From Nippur*, Vol. IV of *BEUP*, H. V. Hilprecht, ed., Series D. Philadelphia: Univ. Penn. Press, 1907.
335. Hinke, W. J. "Selected Babylonian Kudurru Inscriptions,"*Semitic Study Series*, XIV (1911), 1-40.
336. Hussey, Mary I. "A Supplement to Brunnow's Classified List of Cuneiform Ideograms," *JAOS*, XXII (1901), 201-220.
337. ——. "Tablets from Drehem in the Public Library of Cleveland, Ohio," *JAOS*, XXXIII (1913), 167- 179.
338. ——. *Sumerian Tablets in the Harvard Semitic Museum*, Vols. III and IV of *Harvard Semitic Series*. Cambridge, Mass.: Harvard Univ. Press, 1912-15. 2 vols.
339. Jackson, A. V. Williams. "The Great Behistun Rock and Some Results of a Re-Examination of the Old Persian Inscriptions on It," *JAOS*, XXIV (1903), 77-95.
340. ——. "The Etymology of Some Words in the Old Persian Inscriptions," *JAOS*, XXXVIII (1918), 121-124.
341. Jacobsen, Thorkild. *Philological Notes on Eshnunna and Its Inscriptions*, No. 6 of *Assyriological Studies (AS)*. Chicago: Oriental Institute, 1934.
342. Jastrow, Morris, Jr. "Some Notes on the 'Monolith Inscriptions of Salmaneser II,'" *Hebraica*, IV (1887-88), 244-246.
343. ——. "Corrections to the Text of the Black Obelisk of Shalmaneser II," *Hebraica*, V (1888-89), 230-242.
344. ——. "On Assyrian and Samaritan," *JAOS*, XIII (1889), cxlvii-cl.

345. ———. "A Legal Document of Babylonia," in *Oriental Studies* by Oriental Club of Philadelphia. Boston: Ginn & Co., 1894.
346. ———. "The Inscription of Ramman-Nirari I," *AJSL*, XII (1895-96), 143-172.
347. ———. "A New Aspect of the Sumerian Question," *AJSL*, XXII (1905-06), 89-109.
348. ———. "The Sign and Name for Planet in Babylonian," *Proceedings of the American Philosophical Society*, XLVII (1908), 141-156.
349. ———. "Older and Later Elements in the Code of Hammurabi," *JAOS*, XXXVI (1917), 1-33.
350. ———. "Mesopotamia and Greece," *Trans. and Proc. American Philological Assn for 1919*, L (1920), xii-xiii.
351. ———. "E-NU-SUB = BIT SIPTI," *AJSL*, XXXVII (1920-21), 51-61.
352. ———. "An Assyrian Law Code," *JAOS*, XLI (1921), 1-59.
353. Johns, C. H. W. "Assyrian Deeds and Documents," *AJSL*, XLII (1925-26), 170-204, 228-235.
354. Johnson, Edwin L. *Historical Grammar of the Ancient Persian Language*, Vol. VIII of *Vanderbilt Oriental Series*. New York: American Book Co., 1917.
355. Johnston, Christopher. "Two Assyrian Letters," *JAOS*, XV (1893), 311-316.
356. ———. "The Sumero-Akkadian Question," *JAOS*, XV (1893), 317-322.
357. ———. "The Epistolary Literature of the Assyrians and Babylonians," *JAOS*, XVIII (1897), 125-175; XIX (1898), 42-96.
358. ———. "Explanation of an Assyrian Crux Interpretum," *American Journal of Philology*, XIX (1898), 384-388.
359. ———. "A Recent Interpretation of the Letter of an Assryian Princess," *JAOS*, XX (1899), 244-249.
360. ———. "Notes on Two Assyrian Works Hitherto Un-explained," *JAOS*, XXII (1901), 23-26.
361. Karpinski, Louis C. "New Light on Babylonian Mathematics," *AJSL*, LII (1935-36), 73-80.
362. Keiser, Clarence E. *Cuneiform Bullae of the Third Millenium B. C.* New Haven, Conn.: Yale Univ. Press, 1914.
363. ———. *Letters and Contracts from Erech Written in the Neo-Babylonian Period*, Vol. I of *Babylonian Inscriptions in the Collection of J. B. Nies*. New Haven, Conn.: Yale Univ. Press, 1917.
364. ———. *Patesis of the Ur Dynasty*, Vol. IV, Pt. 2 of *Yale Oriental Series, Researches*. New Haven, Conn.: Yale Univ. Press, 1919.
365. ———. *A System of Accentuation for Sumero-Akkadian Signs*, Vol. IX of *Yale Oriental Series, Researches*. New Haven, Conn.: Yale Univ. Press, 1919.
366. ———. *Selected Temple Documents of the Ur Dynasty*, Vol. IV of *Yale Oriental Series, Babylonian Texts*. New Haven, Conn.: Yale Univ. Press, 1919.
367. Kent, Charles F. "Annexion in Assyrian," *Hebraica*, VII (1890-91), 289-301.
368. Kent, Roland G. "Studies in Old Persian Inscriptions," *JAOS*, XXXV (1917), 321-352.
369. ———. "The Recently Published Old Persian Inscriptions," *JAOS*, LI (1931), 189-240.
370. ———. "More Old Persian Inscriptions," *JAOS*, LIV (1934), 34-52.
371. Kramer, Samuel N. "The Verb in the Kirkuk Tablets," *AASOR*, XI (1931), 63-119.
372. ———. *The Sumerian Prefix Forms be- and bi- in the Time of the Earlier Princes of Lagas*, No. 8 of *AS* Chicago: Oriental Institute, 1936.
373. Langdon, Stephen H. "List of Proper Names in the Annals of Asurbanipal," *AJSL*, XX (1903-04), 245-255.

374. ———. "An Assyrian Gramatical Treatise on an Omen Tablet; C. T. 20, pp. 34-42,0 *JAOS*, XXVII (1906), 83-103.
375. ———. "An Early Babylonian Tablet of Warnings for the King," *JAOS*, XXVIII (1907), 145-154.
376. ———. *Sumerian Grammatical Texts*, Vol XII, No. 1 of *Univ. Penn. Museum, Publ. Babylonian Section*. Philadelphia: Univ. Penn. Press, 1917.
377. ———. "Selection of Inscriptions Excavated at Kish," *AJSL*, XL (1923-24), 225-230.
378. Lau, Robert J. "Two Old-Babylonian Texts: Edited With a Note," *JAOS*, XVIII (1897), 363-365.
379. ———. *Old Babylonian Temple Records*, Vol. III of *Columbia Oriental Series*. New York: Columbia Univ. Press, 1906.
380. ———. "Supplement to the Old-Babylonian Vocabularies," *JAOS*, XXVII (1907), 297-300.
381. Lau, Robert J., & Stephen Langdon. "The Annals of Ashurbanipal," *Semitic Study Series*, II (1903), 1-63.
382. Lau, Robert J., & J. D. Prince. "The Abu Habba Cylinder of Nabunaid," *Semitic Study Series*, V (1905), 1-40.
383. Luckenbill, Daniel D. "Benhadad and Hadadezer," *AJSL*, XXVII (1910-11), 267-284.
384. ———. "Inscriptions of Early Assyrian Rulers," *AJSL*, XXVIII (1911-12), 153-203.
385. ———. "Notes on Some Texts from the Cassite Period," *AJSL*, XXXI (1914-15), 79-87.
386. ———. "Old Babylonian Letters from Bismya," *AJSL*, XXXII (1915-16), 270-292.
387. ———. "The Chicago Syllabary," *AJSL*, XXXIII (1916-17), 169-199.
388. ———. "The Name Hammurabi," *JAOS*, XXXVII (1917), 250-253.
389. ———. "Possible Babylonian Contributions to the So-called Phoenican Alphabet," *AJSL*, XXXVI (1919-20), 27-39.
390. Luckenbill, Daniel D. "The First Inscription of Shalmaneser V," *AJSL*, XLI (1924-25), 162-164.
391. ———. "Notes on the Assyrian Historical Texts," *AJSL*, XLIII (1926-27), 208-225.
392. Lutz, Henry F. *Early Babylonian Letters From Larsa*, Vol. II of *Yale Oriental Series, Babylonian Texts*. New Haven, Conn.: Yale Univ. Press, 1917.
393. ———. "A Cassite Liver-Omen Text," *JAOS*, XXXVIII (1918), 77-96.
394. ———. *Selected Sumerian and Babylonian Texts*, Vol. I, No. 2 of *Univ. Penn. Museum Publ. Babylonian Section*. Philadelphia: Univ. Penn. Press, 1919.
395. ———. "A Contribution to the Knowledge of Assyro-Babylonian Medicine," *AJSL*, XXXVI (1919-20), 67-83.
396. ———. "A Mathematical Cuneiform Tablet," *AJSL*, XXXVI (1919-20), 249-257.
397. ———. "Neo-Babylonian Administrative Documents from Erech," *University of California Publications in Semitic Philology*, IX (1927), 1-115.
398. ———. "Sumerian Temple Records of the Late Ur Dynasty," *Univ. Calif. Publ. Semitic Philology*, IX (1928), 117-268.
399. ———. "An Agreement Between a Babylonian Feudal Lord and His Retainer in the Reign of Darius II," *Univ. Calif. Publ. Semitic Philology*, IX (1928), 269-277.
400. ———. "Old Babylonian Letters," *Univ. Calif. Publ. Semitic Philology*, IX (1929), 279-365.
401. ———. "An Old-Babylonian Divination Text," *Univ. Calif. Publ. Semitic Philology*, IX (1929), 367-377.
402. ———. "A Fragment of the Anu-Enlil Series," *Univ. Calif. Publ. Semitic Philology*, IX (1931), 391-399.

403. ——. "A Legal Document from Nuzi," *Univ. Calif. Publ. Semitic Philology*, IX (1931), 405-412.
404. ——. "Legal and Economic Documents from Ashjaly," *Univ. Calif. Publ. Semitic Philology*, X (1931), 1-184.
405. ——. "Real Estate Transactions from Kish," *Univ. Calif. Publ. Semitic Philology*, X (1932), 187-216.
406. Lyon, David G. *An Assyrian Manual, for the Use of Beginners in the Study of the Assyrian Language*. Chicago: The American Publication Society of Hebrew, 1886.
407. ——. "The Structure of the Hammurabi Code," *JAOS*, XXV (1904), 248-265.
408. ——. "The Seal Impressions of an Early Babylonian Contract (Harvard Semitic Museum, No. 109)," *JAOS*, XXVII (1906), 135-141.
409. McCurdy, J. F. "Assyriological Notes," *American Journal of Philology*, II (1881), 461-464.
410. Margolis, Elias. *Sumerian Temple Documents*. New York: International Press, 1915.
411. Meek, Theophile J. "Old Babylonian Business and Legal Documents," *AJSL*, XXXIII (1916-17), 203-244.
412. ——. *Old Babylonian Business and Legal Documents*. Chicago: Univ. Chicago Library, 1917.
413. ——. "A Votive Inscription of Ashurbanipal," *JAOS*, XXXVIII (1918), 167-175.
414. ——. *Old Akkadian, Sumerian, and Cappadocian Texts From Nuzi*, Vol. III of *Excavations at Nuzi*, Vol. X of *Harvard Semitic Series*. Cambridge, Mass.: Harvard Univ. Press, 1935.
415. Meissner, Bruno. *Beitrage zum Assyrischen Worterbuch*. I. No. 1 of *AS*. Chicago: Oriental Institute, 1931.
416. ——. *Beitrage zum Assyrischen Worterbuch*. II. No. 4 of *AS*. Chicago: Oriental Institute, 1932.
417. Mercer, Samuel A. B. "The Oath in Cuneiform Inscriptions," *JAOS*, XXXIII (1913), 33-50.
418. ——. *A Sumero-Babylonian Sign List*, Vol. XIV of *Columbia Univ. Oriental Studies*. New York. Columbia Univ. Press, 1918.
419. ——. *Assyrian Grammar With Chrestomathy and Glossary*. London: Luzac & Co., 1921 (reprinted 1961 by F. Ungar of New York).
420. Merrill, Selah. "On the Assyrian Inscription at Andover, Mass.," *JAOS*, X (1880), lxxiii.
421. ——. "On the Use of Gold and Silver Among the Assyrians," *JAOS*, XI (1885), x-xi.
422. Miller, O. D. "The Antiquity of Sacred Writings in the Valley of the Euphrates," *American Antiquarian*, II (1879-80), 290-295.
423. Moldenke, Alfred B. *Babylonian Contract Tablets in the Metropolitan Museum of Art*. New York: Metropolitan Museum of Art, 1893.
424. ——. *Cuneiform Texts in the Metropolitan Museum of Art*. New York: Metropolitan Museum of Art, 1893.
425. ——. "A Cylinder of Nebuchadnezzar," *JAOS*, XVI (1896), 71-78.
426. Moore, Ellen W. *Neo-Babylonian Business and Administrative Documents*. Ann Arbor: Univ. Michigan Press, 1935.
427. ——. *Neo-Babylonian Documents in the University of Michigan Collection*. Ann Arbor: Univ. Michigan Press, 1939.
428. Muss-Arnolt, Wilhelm. "Notes on the Publications Contained in Vol. II of Eberhard Schrader's Keilinschriftliche Bibliothek. I. The Inscriptions of Sennacherib," *Hebraica*, VII (1890-91), 56-71.
429. ——. "Notes on the Publications Contained in Vol. II of Eberhard Schrader's

Keilinschriftliche Bibliothek. II. The Inscriptions of Esarhaddon," *Hebraica*, VII (1890-91), 81-103.

430. ———. "Assyrian Etymologies," *Hebraica*, VII (1890-91), 183-185; 253-256.

431. ———. "Comparative Study of the Translations of the Babylonian Creation Tablets with Special Reference to Jensen's Kosmologie and Barton's Tiamat," *Hebraica*, IX (1892-93), 6-23.

432. ———. *A Concise Dictionary of the Assyrian Language.* New York: Lemcke & Büchner, 1905. 2 vols.

433. Myhrman, David W. *Sumerian Administrative Documents From the Time of the Second Dynasty of Ur*, Pt. 1, *From the Nippur Collections in Philadelphia*, Vol. III of *BEUP*, H. V. Hilprecht, ed., Series A. Philadelphia: Univ. Penn. Press, 1910.

434. Nesbit, William M. *Sumerian Records From Drehem*, Vol. VIII of *Comlumbia Univ. Oriental Series*. New York: Columbia Univ. Pressl 1914.

435. O'Connor, J. F. X. "The Cylinder of Nebukadnezzar at New York," *Hebraica*, I (1884-85), 201-208.

436. ———. "Inscriptions of Nebuchadnezzar, Variants of an Unpublished Duplicate of the New York Cylinder," *Hebraica*, III (1886-87), 166-170.

437. Olmstead, Albert T. "The Text of Sargon's Annals," *AJSL*, XLVII (1930-31), 259-280.

438. Peters, John P. "Miscellaneous Notes," *Hebraica*, I (1884-85), 242-243.

439. Pfeiffer, Robert H. "Assyrian Epistolary Formulae," *JAOS*, XLIII (1923), 26-40.

440. ———. *The Archives of Shilwateshub Son of the King*, Vol. II of *Excavations at Nuzi*, Vol. IX of *Harvard Semitic Series*. Cambridge, Mass.: Harvard Univ. Press, 1932.

441. ———. *State Letters of Assyria*. New Haven, Conn.: American Oriental Society, 1935.

442. Pfeiffer, Robert H., & E. A. Speiser. "One Hundred Selected Nuzi Texts," *AASOR*, XVI (1936), 1-168.

443. Piepkorn, Arthur C. *Historical Prism Inscriptions of Ashurbanipal. I. Editions E, B1-5, D and K*, No. 5 of *AS*. Chicago: Oriental Institute, 1933.

444. Pinches, T. G. "An Assyrian Record of Receipt of Taxes", *Hebraica*, II (1885-86), 221-222.

445. ———. "The Law of Inheritance in Ancient Babylon," *Hebraica*, III (1886-87), 13-21.

446. ———. "An Early Babylonian Inscription from Niffer," *Hebraica*, VI (1889-90), 55-58.

447. ———. "Old Persian Names in Babylonian Contracts," *Hebraica*, VIII (1891-92), 134-135.

448. Poebel, Arno. *Babylonian Legal and Business Documents From the Time of the First Dynasty of Babylon*, Pt. 2, *Chiefly From Nippur*, Vol VI of *BEUP*, H. V. Hilprecht, ed., Series A. Philadelphia: Univ. Penn. Press, 1909.

449. ———. *Historical and Grammatical Texts*, Vol. V of *Univ. Penn.Museum, Publ. Babylonian Section*. Philadelphia: Univ. Penn. Press, 1914.

450. ———. *The Sumerian Prefix Forms e- and i- in the Time of the Earlier Princes of Lagas*, No. 2 of *AS*. Chicago: Oriental Institute, 1931.

451. Poebel, Arno. *Das Appositionell Bestimmte Pronomen der 1, Pers. Sing, in den Westsemitischen Inschriften und im Alten Testament*, No. 3 of *AS*. Chicago: Oriental Institute, 1932.

452. ———. *Studies in Akkadian Grammar*, No. 9 of *AS*. Chicago: Oriental Institute, 1936.

453. Price, Ira M. "Some Literary Remains of Rim-Sin (Arioch), King of Larsa, About

2285 B.C.," Vol. V of *Univ. Chicago Decennial Publications*. Chicago: Univ. Chicago Press, 1904.

454. ——. "The Laws of Deposit in Early Babylonia and the Old Testament," *JAOS*, XLVII (1927), 250-255.

455. Prince, John D. "The Syntax of the Assyrian Preposition *ana*," *JAOS*, XVIII (1897), 355-360.

456. ——. "Assyrian Prepositional Usage," *JAOS*, XX (1899), 1-11.

457. ——. "The First and Second Persons in Sumerian," *AJSL*, XIX (1902-03), 203-227.

458. ——. "The Vocabulary of Sumerian," *JAOS*, XXV (1904), 49-67.

459. ——. *Assyrian Primer: An Inductive Method of Learning the Cuneiform Characters*, No. 3 of *Columbia University Contributions to Oriental History and Philology*. New York: Col. Univ. Press, 1909.

460. ——. "Certain Grammatical Phenomena in Sumerian," *AJSL*, XXVII (1910-11), 328-330.

461. ——. "Striking Phenomena of Sumerian," *JAOS*, XXXIV (1915), 321-328.

462. ——. "Phonetic Relations in Sumerian," *JAOS*, XXXIX (1919), 265,279.

463. ——. "A Possible Sumerian Original of the Name Nimrod," *JAOS*, XL (1920), 201-203.

464. Radau, Hugo. *Letters to Cassite Kings From the Temple Archives of Nippur*, Pt. 1, Vol. XVII of *BEUP*, H. V. Hilprecht, ed., Series A. Philadelphia: Univ. Penn. Press. 1908.

465. Ranke, Hermann. *Early Babylonian Personal Names From the Published Tablets of the So-Called Hammurabi Dynasty*, Vol. III of *BEUP*, H. V. Hilprecht, ed., Series D. Philadelphia: Univ. Penn. Press, 1905.

466. ——. *Babylonian Legal and Business Documents From the Time of the First Dynasty of Babylon*, Pt. 1, *Chiefly From Sippar*, Vol. VI of *BEUP*, H. V. Hilprecht, ed., Series A. Philadelphia: Univ. Penn. Press, 1906.

467. Speiser, E. A. "New Kirkuk Documents Relating to Family Laws," *AASOR*, X (1930), 1-74.

468. ——. "An Assyrian Document of the Ninth Century B.C. from Tell Billah," *BASOR*, No. 54 (1934), 20-21.

469. ——. "Notes to Recently Published Nuzi Texts," *JAOS*, LV (1935), 431-443.

470. Stephens, Ferris J. *Votive and Historical Texts From Babylonia and Assyria*. New Haven, Conn.: Yale Univ. Press, 1937.

471. Stevenson, James H. *Assyrian and Babylonian Contracts With Aramaic Reference Notes*, Vol III of *Vanderbilt Oriental Series*. New York: American Book Co., 1902.

472. Strassmaier, J. N. "Inscription of Nebuchadnezzar, Son of Nin-eb-nadin-sum," *Hebraica*, IX (1892-93), 4-5.

473. Strong, S. Arthur. "On An Unpublished Cylinder of Esarhaddon," *Hebraica*, VIII (1891-92), 113-123.

474. ——. "A Letter to Assurbanipal," *Hebraica*, IX (1892-93), 1-3.

475. Tolman, Herbert C. *A Grammar of the Old Persian Language*. Boston: Ginn & Co., 1892.

476. ——. "The Cuneiform Inscriptions on the Monuments of the Achaemenides," *Trans. Wisconsin Academy of Sciences, Arts and Letters*, VIII (1892), 241-272.

477. ——. *A Guide to the Old Persian Inscriptions*, 2d ed. New York: American Book Co., 1893.

478. ——. *The Behistan Inscription of King Darius* Vol. I of *Vanderbilt Univ. Studies*. Nashville, Tenn.: Vanderbilt Univ. Press, 1908.

479. ———. *Ancient Persian Lexicon*, Vol. VI of *Vanderbilt Oriental Series*. New York: American Book Co., 1908.
480. ———. *Cuneiform Supplement to the Author's Ancient Persian Lexicon and Texts, With Brief Historical Synopsis of the Language*, Vol. VII of *Vanderbilt Oriental Series*. New York: American Book Co., 1910.
481. Ungnad, Arthur. "Selected Babylonian Business and Legal Documents of the Hammurabi Period," *Semitic Study Series*, IX (1907), 1-42.
482. ———. "Selected Business Documents of the Neo-Babylonian Period," *Semitic Study Series*, X (1908), 1-74.
483. Vanderburgh, F. A. "Three Babylonian Tablets, Prince Collection, Columbia University," *JAOS*, XXXIII (1913), 24-32.
484. Ward, William H. "On the Ninevetic Cuneiform Inscriptions in This Country," *JAOS*, X (1880), xxxv-xxxvi.
485. "Notes on Oriental Antiquities. VII. Two Stone Tablets with Hieroglyphic Babylonian Writing," *AJA*, IV (1888), 39-41.
486. Ware, James R., & R. G. Kent. "The Old Persian Cuneiform Inscriptions of Artaxerxes II and Artaxerxes III," *Trans, and Proc. Amer. Philological Assn.*, LV (1924), 52-61.
487. Waterman, Leroy. "Textual Notes of the Letters of the Sargon Period," *AJSL*, XXVIII (1911-12), 134-143.
488. ———. "Some Kouyunjik Letters and Related Texts," *AJSL*, XXIX (1912-13), 1-36.
489. ———. "Business Documents of the Hammurabi Period," *AJSL*, XXIX (1912-13), 145-204, 288-303; XXX (1913-14), 48-73.
490. ———. "Abbreviated Ideograms in the Assyrian Letter-Literature," *AJSL*, XLI (1924-25), 17-23.
491. ———. *Translation and Transliteration*, Pt. I of *Royal Correspondence of the Assyrian Empire*, Vol. XVII of *Univ. Michigan Humanistic Series*. Ann Arbor: Univ. Mich. Press, 1930.
492. ———. *Translation and Transliteration*, Pt. II of *Royal Correspondence of the Assyrian Empire*, Vol. XVIII of *Univ. Michigan Humanistic Series*. Ann Arbor: Univ. Mich. Press, 1930.
493. ———. *Commentary*, Pt. III of *Royal Correspondence of the Assyrian Empire*, Vol. XIX of *Univ. Michigan Humanistic Series*. Ann Arbor: Univ. Mich. Press, 1931.
494. ———. *Supplement and Indexes*, Pt. IV of *Royal Correspondence of the Assyrian Empire*, Vol. XX of *Univ. Michigan Humanistic Series*. Ann Arbor: Univ. Mich. Press, 1936.
495. Ylvisaker, S. C. "Dialectic Differences between Assyrian and Babylonian, and some Problems they Present," *JAOS*, XXXIII (1913), 397-401.

RELIGION, CULTURE, AND MYTHOLOGY

496. Barton, George A. "The Semitic Istar Cult," *Hebraica*, IX (1892-93), 131-165.
497. ———. "The Semitic Istic Istar Cult," *Hebraica*, X (1893-94), 1-74.
498. ———. "An Androgynous Babylonian Divinity," *JAOS*, XXI (1901), 185-187.
499. ———. *A Sketch of Semitic Origins: Social and Religious*. New York: Macmillan, 1902.
500. ———. "Religious Conceptions Underlying Sumerian Proper Names," *JAOS*, XXXIV (1915), 315-320.
501. ———. "Ancient Babylonian Expressions of the Religious Spirit," *JAOS*, XXXVII (1917), 23-42.
502. ———. "A Word With Reference to 'Emperor'-Worship in Babylonia," *JAOS*, XXXVII (1917), 162-163.

503. ———. "New Babylonian Material Concerning Creation and Paradise," *Amer. Journal Theology*, XXI (1917), 571-597.
504. ———. "A New Babylonian Account of the Creation of Man," *Proc. Amer. Philosophical Society*, LVI (1917), 275-280.
505. ———. "A New Babylonian Parallel to a Part of Genesis 3," *JAOS*, XXXIX (1919), 287.
506. ———. "An Important Social Law of the Ancient Babylonians—A Text Hitherto Misunderstood," *AJSL*, (1920-21), 62-71.
507. ———. "The Problem of the Origin and Early History of the Deity Nin-ib (Nin-urta, Nin-urash)," *JAOS*, XLVI (1926), 231-236.
508. Brewster, David. "Nineveh Lens and Glass," *The American Polytechnic Journal*, II (1853), 157.
509. Brooks, Beatrice A. *A Contribution o the Study of the Moral Practices of Certain Social Groups in Ancient Mesopotamia*. Leipzig: W. Drugulin, 1921.
510. ———. "The Babylonian Practice of Marking Slaves," *JAOS*, XLII (1922), 80-90.
511. Brown, Francis. "The Sabbath in the Cuneiform Records," *Presbyterian Review*, III (1882), 688-700.
512. ———. "The Religious Poetry of Babylonia," *Presbyterian Review*, IX (1888), 69-86.
513. Carnoy, Albert J. "Iranian Views of Origins in Connection with Similar Babylonian Beliefs," *JAOS*, XXXVI (1917), 300-320.
514. ———. "The Iranian Gods of Healing," *JAOS*, XXXVIII (1918), 294-307.
515. Chiera, Edwin. "A New Creation Story," *JAOS*, XLI (1921), 459-460.
516. ———. *Sumerian Religious Texts*. Upland, Pa.: Crozer Theological Seminary, 1924.
517. ———. *Sumerian Epics and Myths*, Vol. XV of *OIP*. Chicago: Oriental Institute, 1934.
518. Clay, Albert T. "The Liver in Babylonian Divination," *Records of the Past*, VI (1907), 307-316.
519. ———. *A Hebrew Deluge Story in Cuneiform and Other Epic Fragments in the Pierpoint Morgan Library*, Pt. 3, Vol. V of *Yale Oriental Series, Researches*. New Haven, Conn.: Yale Univ. Press, 1922.
520. Cook, Stanley A. *The Laws of Moses and the Code of Hammurabi*. New York: Macmillan, 1904.
521. Craig, James A. "Prayer of the Assyrian King Assurbanipal (Cir. 650 B.C.)," *Hebraica*, X (1893-94), 75-87.
522. ———. "An Assryian Incantation to the God Sin (Cir. 650 B.C.)," *Hebraica*, XI (1894-95), 101-109.
523. ———. *Assyrian and Babylonian Religious Texts*. Leipzig: J. C. Hinrichs, 1895-97. 2 vols.
524. Davis, John D. "The Babylonian Flood-Legend and the Hebrew Record of the Deluge," *Presbyterian Review*, X (1889), 415-431.
525. Dougherty, Raymond P. *The Shirkutu of Babylonian Deities*, Vol. II of *Yale Oriental Series, Researches*. New Haven, Conn.: Yale Univ. Press, 1923.
526. Hilprecht, Hermann V. *The Oldest Version of the Babylonian Deluge Story and the Temple Library of Nippur*, Fasc. 1 of *Fragments of Epical Literature From the Temple Library of Nippur*, Vol. V of *BEUP*, H. V. Hilprecht, ed., Series D. Philadelphia: Univ. Penn. Press, 1910.
527. Jackson, A. V. Williams. "The Religion of the Achaemenian Kings," *JAOS*, XXI (1901), 160-184.
528. ——— *Zoroastrian Studies*. New York: Columbia Univ. Press, 1928.
529. Jastrow, Morris, Jr. *The Religion of Babylonia and Assyria*, Vol. II of *Handbooks of the History of Religions*. Boston: Ginn & Co., 1898.

530. ———. "Nabopolassar and the Temple to the Sun-God at Sippar," *AJSL*, XV (1898-99), 65-86.
531. ———. "Adam and Eve Among the Babylonians," *AJSL*, XV (1898-99), 193-214.
532. ———. "The God Assur," *JAOS*, XXIV (1904), 282-311.
533. ———. "Another Fragment of the Etana Myth," *JAOS*, XXX (1909), 101-131.
534. ———. *Aspects of Religious Belief and Practice in Babylonia and Assyria*. New York: G. P. Putnam's Sons, 1911.
535. ———. *Hebrew and Babylonian Traditions*. New York: Chas. Scribner's Sons, 1914.
536. ———. "Sumerian Myths of Beginnings," *AJSL*, XXXIII (1916-17), 91-144.
537. ———. The Sumerian View of Beginnings," *JAOS*, XXXVI (1917), 122-135.
538. ———."Sumerian and Akkadian Views of Beginnings," *JAOS*, XXXVI (1917), 274-299.
539. Johns, Claude H. W. *Babylonian and Assyrian Laws, Contracts and Letters*. New York: Chas. Scribner's Sons, 1904.
540. Johnston, Christopher. "Assyrian and Babylonian Beast Fables," *AJSL*, XXVIII (1911-12), 81-100.
541. Kramer, Samuel N. *Gilgamesh and the Huluppu—Tree: A Reconstructed Sumerian Text*, No. 10 of *AS*. Chicago: Oriental Institute, 1938.
542. Langdon, Stephen H. *Sumerian Epics of Paradise, The Food and the Fall of Man*, Pt. 1, Vol. X of *Univ. Penn. Museum, Publ. Babylonian Section*. Phila.: Univ. Penn. Press, 1915.
543. ———. *Sumerian Liturgical Texts*, Pt. 2, Vol. X of *Univ. Penn. Museum, Publ. Babylonian Section*. Philadelphia: Univ. Penn. Press, 1917.
544. ———. *Sumerian Liturgies and Psalms*, Pt. 4, Vol. X of *Univ. Penn. Museum, Publ. Babylonian Section*. Philadelphia: Univ. Penn. Press, 1919.
545. ———. *Semitic Mythology*. Boston: Archaeological Institute of America, 1931.
546. Leonard, William E. *Gilgamesh: Epic of Old Babylonia*. New York: Viking Press, 1934.
547. Long, Albert L. "A Small Collection of Babylonian Weights," *AJA*, V (1889), 44-46.
548. Luckenbill, Daniel D. "A Neo-Babylonian Catalogue of Hymns," *AJSL*, XXVI (1909-10), 27-32.
549. ———. "The Temple Women of the Code of Hammurabi," *AJSL*, XXXIV (1917-18), 1-12.
550. Lutz, Henry F. "The Verdict of a Trial Judge in a Case of Assault and Battery," *Univ. Calif. Publ. Semitic Philology*, IX (1930), 379-381.
551. ———. "A Slave Sale Document of the Time of Neriglissar," *Univ. Calif. Publ. Semitic Philology*, IX (1931), 413-418.
552. Lyon, David G. "Was There at the Head of the Babylonian Pantheon a Deity Bearing the Name of *El?*" *JAOS*, XI (1885), clxiv-clxviii.
553. Maynard, John A. *Studies in Religious Texts From Assur*. Chicago: Univ. Chicago Library, 1917.
554. ———. "Studies of Religious Texts from Assur," *AJSL*, XXXIV (1917-18), 21-59.
555. Mendelsohn, Isaac. *Legal Aspects of Slavery in Babylonia, Assyria and Palestine*. Williamsport, Pa.: Bayard Press, 1932.
556. ———. "Gilds in Babylonia and Assyria," *JAOS*, LX (1940), 68-72.
557. Mercer, Samuel A.B. " 'Emperor'-Worship in Babylonia, *JAOS*, XXXVII (1917), 360-380.
558. ———. " '-Worship in Babylonia-A Reply," *JAOS*, XXXVII (1917), 331.
559. ———. *Religious and Moral Ideas in Babylonia and Assyria*. Milwaukee: Morehouse Publ. Co., 1919.
560. ———. "Divine Service in Ur," *JSOR*, V (1921), 1-17.

561. Myhrman, David W. *Babylonian Hymns and Prayers*, Pt. 1, Vol. I of *Univ. Penn. Museum, Publ. Babylonian Section*, Philadelphia: Univ. Penn. Press, 1911.
562. Offord, Joseph. "Hymns to Tammuz: A New Recovery of Babylonian Literature," *Amer. Antiquarian and Oriental Journal*, XXVI (1904), 337-341.
563. Olmstead, Albert T. "Ahura Mazda in Ayyrian," in *Oriental Studies in Honour of Cursetji Erachji Pavry*, Jal Dastur Cursetji Pavry, ed. Oxford Univ. Press, 1933.
564. ——. "Babylonian Astronomy-Historical Sketch," *AJSL*, LV (1938), 113-129.
565. Peters, John P. "Notes and Suggestions on the Early Sumerian Religion and its Expression," *JAOS*, XLI (1921), 131-149.
566. Pinches, T. G. "'Sonhood,' or Adoption Among the Early Babylonians," *Hebraica*, VII (1890-91), 198-189.
567. Price, Ira M. "The Relation of Certain Gods to Equity and Justice in Early Babylonia," *JAOS*, LII (1932), 174-178.
568. Prince, John D. "A Hymn to Tammuz," *JAOS*, XXX (1909), 94-100.
569. ——. "A Hymn to the Goddess Kir-gi-lu," *JAOS*, XXX (1910) 335-335.
570. Radau, Hugo. *NIN-IB, The Determiner of Fates, According to the Great Sumerian Epic, "Lugale ug melambi nergal,"* Fasc. 2 of *Fragments of Epical Literature From the Temple Library of Nippur*, Vol. V of *BEUP*, H. V. Hilprecht, ed., Series D. Philadelphia: Univ. Penn. Press, 1910.
571. ——. *Sumerian Hymns and Prayers to NIN-IB From the Temple Library of Nippur*, Pt. 1, Vol. XXIX of *BEUP* H. V. Hilprecht, ed., Series A. Philadelphia: Univ. Penn. Press, 1911.
572. Rogers, Robert W. *The Religion of Babylonia and Assyria, Especially in its Relations to Israel*. New York: Eaton & Mains, 1908.
573. —— (trans. & ed.). *Cuneiform Parallels to the Old Testament*. New York: Eaton & Mains, 1912.
574. Torrey, Charles C. "The Art of the Hairdresser in Ancient Babylonia," *AJA*, XXI (1916), 85-86.
575. Vanderburgh, Frederick A. *Sumerian Hymns*, No. 1 of *Columbia Univ. Contributions to Oriental History and Philology*. New York: Columbia Univ. Press, 1908.
576. ——. "Babylonian Legends," *JAOS*, XXXII (1912), 21-32.
577. Ward, William H. "Notes on Oriental Antiquities. III. A God of Agriculture," *AJA*, II (1886), 261-266.
578. ——. "Notes: I. Assyro-Babylonian Forgery. II. The Sun-God on Babylonian Cylinders," *AJA*, III (1887), 383-386.
579. ——. "Oriental Antiquities. VIII. 'Human Sacrifices' on Babylonian Cylinders," *AJA*, V (1889), 34-43.
580. Warren, William F. "Babylonian and Pre-Babylonian Cosmology," *JAOS*, XXII (1901), 138-144.

BIOGRAPHY

581. Abbott, Jacob. *Cyrus the Great*. New York: Harper & Bros., 1850 (3d ed. in 1900).
582. ——. *History of Xerxes the Great*. New York: Harper & Bros., 1850 (3d ed. in 1900).
583. ——. *Darius the Great*. New York: The St. Hubert Guild, 1850 (2d ed. in 1906 by Harper).
584. Anspacher, Abraham S. *Tiglath Pileser III*, No. 5 of *Columbia Univ. Contributions to Oriental History and Philology*. New York: Columbia Univ. Press, 1912.

585. Jackson, A. V. Williams. *Zoroaster the Prophet of Ancient Iran.* New York: Macmillan, 1898.
586. Johnston, Christopher. "Samas-sum-ukin the Eldest Son of Esarhaddon," *JAOS*, XXV (1904), 79-83.
587. Peters, John P. "Nebuchadnezzar I," *Hebraica*, II (1885-86), 171-173.
588. Rogers, Robert W. "Leonard William King, Assyriologist, 1869-1919," *AJSL*, XXXVI (1919-20), 89-94.

CHRONOLOGY

589. Albright, William F. "The Babylonian Antediluvium Kings," *JAOS*, XLIII (1923), 323-329.
590. Frankfort, Henri. *Archaeology and the Sumerian Problem*, No. 4 of *SAOC*. Chicago: Oiental Institute, 1932.
591. Jackson, A. V. Williams. "On the Date of Zoroaster," *JAOS*, XVII (1896), 1-22.
592. Jacobsen, Thorkild. *The Sumerian King List*, No. 11 of *AS*. Chicago: Oriental Institute, 1939.
593. Olmstead, Albert T. "Darius and His Behistun Inscription," *AJSL*, LV (1938), 392-416.
594. Orr, James. "Assyrian and Hebrew Chronology," *Presbyterian Review*, X (1889), 41-64.
595. Peters, John P. "The Dates of Sargon of Akkad," *Hebraica*, II (1885-86), 173-174.

ART AND ARCHITECTURE

596. Anonymous. "Babylonian Seals," *Amer. Antiquarian and Oriental Journal*, IX (1887), 255-256.
597. Banks, Edgar J. "The Oldest Statue in the World," *AJSL*, XXI (1904-05), 57-59.
598. ———. "The Statue of the Sumerian King David," *Scientific American*, 19 August 1905, 1370.
599. ———. "The Bismya Temple," *AJSL*, XXII (1905-06), 29-34.
600. ———. "The Bismya Temple," *Records of the Past*, V (1906), 227-236.
601. Barton, George A. "The Identification of a Portrait Statue of a Semitic Babylonian King," *AJA*, XXII (1918), 66.
602. Boscanten. W. S. C. "Babylonian and Assyrian Art," *Amer. Antiquarian and Oriental Journal*, V (1883), 322-330.
603. Fisher, Clarence S. "The Architecture of Nippur," *Records of the Past*, II (1903), 99-118.
604. ———. "The Mycenaean Palace at Nippur," *AJA*, VIII (1904), 403-432.
605. ———. *Excavations at Nippur: Plans, Details, and Photography, etc.* Philadelphia: Univ. Penn. Dept. Archaeology and Palaeontology, 1905.
606. ———. "The Archaic Arch at Nippur," *Trans. Dept. Archaeology Free Museum Science & Art, Univ. Penn.*, I (1917), 227-235.
607. Frankfort, Henri. "Some Notes on Pottery from Ur," *Antiquaries Journal*, IX (1929), 344-348.
608. ———. *Sculpture of the Third Millenium B. C. From Tell Asmar and Khafajah*, Vol. XLIV of *OIP*. Chicago: Oriental Institute, 1939.
609. Grimm, Carl J. "The Polychrome Lions Recently Found in Babylon," *JAOS*, XXII (1901), 27-34.
610. Hussey, Mary I. "Babylonian and Assyrian Chairs," *Art and Archaeology*, XXI (1926), 129-132.
611. Jacobsen, Thorkild, & S. Lloyd. *Sennacherib's Aqueduct at Jerwan*, Vol. XXIV of *OIP*. Chicago: Oriental Institute, 1935.

612. Jastrow, Morris, Jr. "The Palace and Temple of Nebuchadnezzar," *Harper's Monthly Magazine*, CIV (1902), 809-814.
613. Luckenbill, Daniel D. "The Temples of Babylonia and Assyria," *AJSL*, XXIV (1907-08), 291-322.
614. Lutz, Henry F. "Two Assyrian Apotropaic Figurines Complementing Kar. 298, Rev. 4-7," *Univ. Calif. Publ. Semitic Philology*, IX (1930), 383-384.
615. ———. "The Warka Cylinder of Ashurbanipal," *Univ. Calif. Publ. Semitic Philology*, IX (1931), 385-390.
616. ———. "A Larsa Plaque," *Univ. Calif. Publ. Semitic Philology*, IX (1931), 401-403.
617. Lyon, David G. "Notes on the Hammurabi Monument," *JAOS*, XXV (1904), 266-278.
618. Mackay, Ernst. "Notes on a Bas-Relief found at Ur," *Antiquaries Journal*, IX (1929), 26-29.
619. Marquand, Allan. "The Palace at Nippur not Mycenaean but Hellenistic," *AJA*, IX (1905), 7-10.
620. Merrill, Selah. "Assyrian and Babylonian Monuments," *Bibliotheca Sacra*, XXXII (1875), 320-349.
621. ———. "On the Assyrian and Babylonian Monuments in America," *JAOS*, X (1880), xcix-c.
622. Muller, E. B. "The Prehistoric Temple of Stratum IX at Tepe Gawra," *BASOR*, No. 54 (1934), 13-18.
623. Peters, John P. "The Palace at Nippur Babylonian Not Parthian," *AJA*, IX (1905), 450-452.
624. Prince, John D., & Robert Lau. "The Pierpoint Morgan Babylonian Axe-Head," *JAOS*, XXVI (1905), 93-97.
625. Salisbury, E. W. "Remarks on Two Assyrian Cylinders Received from Mosul," *JAOS*, V (1856), 191-194.
626. Speiser, E. A. "Mesopotamian Miscellanes," *BASOR*, No. 68 (1937), 7-13.
627. Van Buren, Elizabeth D. *Clay Figurines of Babylonia and Assyria*, Vol. XVI of Yale Oriental Series, Researches. New Haven, Conn.: Yale Univ. Press, 1930.
628. Ward, William H. "On Certain Points Connected with Chaldean Seals," *JAOS*, XI (1885), xxxix-xli.
629. ———. "Notes on Oriental Antiquities. I. Two Babylonian Seal-Cylinders," *AJA*, II (1886), 46-48.
630. ———. "Notes on Oriental Antiquities. IV. The Rising Sun on Babylonian Cylinder," *AJA*, III (1887), 50-56.
631. ———. "Notes on Oriental Antiquities. IV. An Eye of Naby. V. A Babylonian Bronze Pendant. VI. The Stone Tablets of Abu-Habba," *AJA*, III (1887), 338-343.
632. ———. "Notes on Oriental Antiquities. IX. A Babylonian Cylindrical Basrelief from Urumia in Persia. X. Tiamat and Other Evil Spirits, As figured on Oriental Seals," *AJA*, VI (1890), 286-298.
633. ———. "The Representation of Babylonian Gods in Art," *AJA*, XIV (1910), 83-85.

BIBLIOGRAPHY

LIST OF OTHER WORKS CONSULTED

This list is divided into primary and secondary source material. The secondary sources are subdivided into the same nine categories as the previous list.

PRIMARY

Manuscript Collections

634. Brown, Francis. Personal Papers. Archives, Library, Union Theological Seminary, New York, N. Y. One large box consisting of eleven notebooks, personal and professional letters dated between 1893 and 1906, reports, and a typewritten report on the introduction of Akkadian at Union.
635. Harper, William Rainey. President's File. Archives, Library, University of Chicago, Chicago, Illinois. Letter in R. F. Harper Folder dated June 12, 1892, telling of the appointment of R. F. to the faculty of the university.
636. Harper, W. R. Personal Papers. Archives, Library, University of Chicago. Box 1, Folders 9, 10, 17, 19 and 22 consist of letters dated between April 1889 and March 1892 describing Chicago's attempts to build up an Assyriological library and collection. Box 2, Folder 18 tells of the development of the Haskell Museum in a letter dated September 28, 1895.
637. Lyon, David Gordon. Personal Diaries. Archives, Library, Harvard University, Cambridge, Mass. Thirty-nine diaries beginning October 8, 1870 and ending December 31, 1934 (with some minor gaps).
638. University of Pennsylvania. Records of the Nippur Expeditions. Archives, University Museum, University of Pennsylvania, Philadelphia. Approximately twenty-five File Folder boxes of letters and reports of the four expeditions to Nippur dated between 1889 and 1903. Also, includes twelve volumes of typewritten reports from Peters, Haynes, and Hilprecht covering the four expeditions, dated between 1889 and 1900. There are also numerous drawings, sketches, and photographs from Fisher and others describing architecture at Nippur.

Personal Correspondence

639. Cameron, George G. Department of Near Eastern Languages and Literature, University of Michigan, Ann Arbor. Letter, May 1, 1967 to author, dealing with the professional career of A. T. Olmstead.
640. Olmstead, Mrs. Albert T. 101 Sheridan Avenue, Tacoma Park, Maryland. Letter, April 19, 1967 to author, dealing with life and career of A. T. Olmstead.
641. Schrijver, Adolf I. Secretary, New York Oriental Club, New York. Letter, June 4, 1968 to author regarding records of New York Oriental Club.
642. Stephens, Ferris J. Yale University, New Haven, Conn. Letter, June 20, 1967 to author concerning the career of Albert T. Clay.

Oral Interview

643. Wilson, John A. Personal Interview, Oriental Institute, University of Chicago, Chicago, Illinois, 19 June 1967, with author regarding the career of Edgar J. Banks.

SECONDARY

General

644. Adams, Robert M. "Settlements in Ancient Akkad," *Archaeology*, X (1957), 270-273.
645. Adler, Cyrus, & Aaron Ember (eds.). *Oriental Studies Published in Commemoration of the 40th Anniversary of Paul Haupt*. Baltimore: Johns Hopkins Press, 1943.
646. Budge, E. A. Wallis. *The Rise and Progress of Assyriology*. London: Martin Hopkinson & Co., 1925.
647. Diodorus Siculus. *Diodori Siculi Bibliothecae Historicae*, ed. by Ludwig Dindorf. Paris: A. Firmin-Didot, 1855. 2 vols.
648. Finklestein, J. J. "Mesopotamian Historiography," *Proc. Amer. Philosophical Soc.*, CVII (1963), 461-472.
649. Hogg, Hope W. *Survey of Recent Publications on Assyriology*. Edinburgh: O. Schulze, 1910.
650. Kildahl, Phillip A. "British and American Reactions to Layard's Discoveries in Assyria (1845-1860)," Unpublished Ph.D. dissertation, University of Minnesota, 1959.
651. Menant, Joachim. *Les Langues de la Perse et de l'Assyrie. Assyrie*. Paris: Ernest Leroux, 1886.
652. ———. "Forgeries of Babylonian and Assyrian Antiquities," *AJA*, III (1887), 14-31.
653. Miles, George C. (ed.). *Archaeologica Orientalia in Memoriam Ernst Herzfeld*. Locust Valley, N. Y.: J. J. Augustin, 1952.
654. Oppenheim, A. L. "Assyriology—Why and How?" *Current Anthropology*, I (1960), 409-420.
655. Pallis, Svend Aage. *The Antiquity of Iraq: A Handbook of Assyriology*. Copenhagen: Ejnar Munksgaard, 1956.
656. Pavry, Jal Dastur Cursetji (ed.). *Oriental Studies in Honour of Cursetji Erachji Pavry*. Oxford Univ. Press, 1933.
657. Sayce, A. H. "Assyriology in the North," *The Academy*, XXXVI, No. 905 (1889), 156-157.
658. Stephens, Ferris J. "The Babylonian Collection," *Yale Univ. Library Gazette*, XIX (1945), 44-49.
659. ———. "History of the Babylonian Collection," *Yale Univ. Library Gazette*, XXXVI (1962), 126-132.
660. Ward, William H. *The Seal Cylinders of Western Asia*. Washington, D. C.: Carnegie Institution Publ. No. 100, 1910.

History

661. Budge, E. A. Wallis. *Babylonian Life and History*, 2d ed. London: The Religious Tract Society, 1925.
662. Delaporte, Louis J. *Mesopotamia: The Babylonian and Assyrian Civilization*, tran. V. G. Childe. New York: Alfred A. Knopf, 1925.
663. Fraser, James B. *Historical and Descriptive Account of Persia, From the Earliest Ages to the Present. Time*. New York: Harper, 1834.
664. ———. *Mesopotamia and Assyria, From the Earliest Ages to the Present Time; With Illustrations of Their Natural History*. New York: Harper, 1845.
665. Goetze, Albercht. "Professor Clay and the Amurrite Problem," *Yale Univ. Library Gazette*, XXXVI (1962), 133-137.
666. Herzfeld, Ernst E. *Iran in the Ancient East*. Oxford Univ. Press, 1941.

667. Huart, Clement. *Ancient Persian and Iranian Civilization*, trans. M. R. Dobie. New York: Alfred A. Knopf, 1927.
668. King, Leonard W. *A History of Sumer and Akkad*. London: Chatto & Windus, 1910.
669. ——. *A History of Babylon*. London: Chatto & Windus, 1915.
670. Kramer, Samuel N. *History Begins at Sumer*. London: Thames & Hudson, 1958.
671. ——. *The Sumerians*. Chicago: Univ. Chicago Press, 1963.
672. Olmstead, Albert T. *History of the Persian Empire*. Chicago: Univ. Chicago Press, 1948.
673. Oppenheim, A.L. *Ancient Mesopotamia*. Chicago: Univ. Chicago Press, 1964.
674. Pinches, T. G. *The Old Testament in the Light of Historical Records and Legends of Assyria and Babylonia*. New York: E. & J. B. Young & Co., 1902.
675. Saggs, H. W. F. *The Greatness That Was Babylon*. New York: Hawthorn Books, 1962.
676. Sayce, A. H. "The Latest Cuneiform Discovery," *American Antiquarian*, II (1879-80), 287-289.
677. Speiser, E. A. "Some Factors in the Collapse of Akkad," *JAOS*, LXXII (1952), 97-101.
678. ——. "Akkadian Documents from Ras Shamra," *JAOS*, LXXV (1955), 154-165.
679. Woolley, C. Leonard. *The Sumerians*. Oxford Univ. Press, 1928.

Exploration, Travel, and Geography

680. Barbaro, Giosafat, & Ambrogio Contarini. *Travels to Tana and Persia*, trans. W. T. Thomas & S. A. Roy. London: Hakluyt Society, 1873.
681. British Naval Intelligence. *Iraq and the Persian Gulf*. Oxford: Naval Intelligence Division, 1944.
682. Buckingham, J. S. *Travels in Mesopotamia*. London: H. Colburn, 1827.
683. Cartwright, John. *The Preacher's Travels*. London: W. Burre, 1611.
684. Chardin, Jean. *Sir John Chardin's Travels in Persia*. London: The Argonaut Press, 1927 (reprint of the 1720 edition).
685. Delitzsch, Friedrich. "Discoveries in Mesopotamia," *Smith. Inst. Annual Rept. for the Year Ending June 30, 1900* (1901), 535-549.
686. Finkelstein, J. J. " 'Mesopotamia,' " *Journal of Near Eastern Studies (JNES)*, XXI (1962), 73-92.
687. Figueroa, Garcia de Silva. *L'Ambassade de D. Garcias de Silva Figueroa en Perse*, trans. M. de Wicqfort. Paris: Jean du Puis, 1667.
688. Fletcher, J. P. *Notes From Nineveh*. Philadelphia: Lea & Blanchard, 1850.
689. de Gouvea, Antoine. *Relacam em que se trata das Guerras*. Lisbon: Pedro Craesbeek, 1611.
690. Ives, Edward. *A Voyage From England to India*. London: E. & C. Dilly, 1773.
691. Jones, Felix. "Topography of Nineveh, ... ," *Journal of the Royal Asiatic Society (JRAS)*, XV (1855), 297-397.
692. Kaempfer, Engelbert. *Amoenitates Exoticae*. Lemgo: H. W. Meyer, 1712.
693. Kinneir, J. McDonald. *Journey Through Asia Minor*. London: J. Murray, 1818.
694. Lloyd, Seton. *Ruined Cities of Iraq*, 3d ed. Oxford Univ. Press, 1945.
695. Loftus, William K. *Travels and Researches in Chaldaea and Susiana*. New York: R. Carter & Bros., 1857.
696. Morelli, Jacopo. *Dissertazione Intorno ad Alcuni Viaggiatori Eruditi Venezioni* . . . . . Venice: Stamperia di A. Zatta, 1803.
697. Niebuhr, Carsten, *Travels Through Arabia and Other Countries in the East*, trans. Robert Heron. Edinburgh: R. Morrison & Son, 1892. 2 vols.

698. Newman, John P. *The Thrones and Palaces of Babylon and Nineveh.* New York: Harper, 1876.
699. Pallis, Svend Aage. "Early Exploration in Mesopotamia," *Det Kongelige Danske Videnskabernes Selskab*, XXXIII (1954), 1-58.
700. Pinches, T. G. "Assur and Nineveh," *Records of the Past*, XII (1913), 23-41.
701. Thompson, R. C., & R. W. Hutchinson. *A Century of Exploration at Nineveh.* London: Luzac & Co., 1929.
702. Valle, Pietro Della. *Viaggi.* Brighton: G. Gancia, 1843 (reprint of the 1653 edition). 2 vols.

Archeology

703. Arne, T. A. J. *Excavations at Shah Tepe, Iran.* Stockholm: Elanders, 1945.
704. Botta, Paul Emile. *The Buried City of the East*: Nineveh. London: National Illustrated Library, 1851.
705. Braidwood, Robert J. "From Cave to Village in Prehistoric Iraq," *BASOR*, No. 124 (1951), 12-18.
706. Delougaz, P., H. D. Hill & Seton Lloyd. *Private Houses and Graves in the Diyala Region*, Vol. LXXXVIII of *OIP*. Chicago: Oriental Institute, 1966.
707. Dyson, Robert H., Jr. "Digging in Iran: Hasanlu, 1958," *Expedition*, I (1958-59), 4-18.
708. ———. "The Death of a City," *Expedition*, II (1959-60), 2-11.
709. ———. "Hasanlu and Early Iran," *Archaeology*, XIII (1960), 118-129.
710. ———. "Ninth Century Men in Western Iran," *Archaeology* XVII (1964), 3-11.
711. *Expedition*, XIII (1970-71), 1-72 (Pts. 3-4 of this volume are entirely devoted to Iran and the work of The University Museum there).
712. Frankfort, H., S. Lloyd & T. Jacobsen. *The Gimilsin Temple and the Palace of the Rulers at Tell Asmar*, Vol. XLIII of *OIP*. Chicago: Oriental Institute, 1940.
713. German Oriental Society. "Excavations of the Ruins of Babylon," *Records of the Past*, II (1903), 3-15, 149-151, 185-189, 273-285.
714. Haines, Richard C. "A Report of the Excavations at Nippur During 1960-61, *Sumer*, XVII (1961), 67-70.
715. Hansen, D. P., & G. F. Dales. "The Temple of Inanna, Queen of Heaven at Nippur," *Archaeology*, XV (1962), 75-84.
716. Knudstad, James. "A Report of the 1964-1965 Excavations at Nippur," *Sumer*, XX (1966), 111-114.
717. Kramer, S. N., F. R. Steele & D. McCown. "The New Nippur Excavations," *Univ. Museum Bulletin, Univ. Penn.*, XVI (1951), 1-39.
718. Lamberg-Karlovsky, C. C. *Excavations at Tepe Yahya, Iran 1967-1969*, Bulletin No. 27 of *American School of Prehistoric Research, Peabody Museum* (Monograph No. 1 of *The Asia Institute of Pahlavi University*). Cambridge, Mass.: Harvard Univ. Press, 1970.
719. Langdon, Stephen H., & D. B. Harden. "Excavations at Kish and Barghuthiat 1933," *Iraq*, I (1934), 113-136.
720. Layard, A. H. *Nineveh and Its Remains.* New York: G. P. Putnam, 1850. 2 vols.
721. ———. *Discoveries in the Ruins of Nineveh and Babylon.* London: John Murray, 1853.
722. Lloyd, Seton. *Foundations in the Dust: A Story of Mesopotamian Exploration.* New York: Penguin Books, 1955.
723. ———. *Mounds of The Near East.* Edinburgh: Edinburgh Univ. Press, 1963.
724. McCown, Donald E. "Recent Finds at Nippur, A Great City of Ancient Mesopotamia," *Archaeology*, V (1952), 70-75.
725. McCown, Donald E., & Richard C. Haines. *Nippur I: Temple of Enlil, Scribal*

        Quarter, and Soundings, Vol. LXXVIII of *OIP.* Chicago: Oriental Institute, 1966.
726. Perkins, Ann L. *Comparative Archeology of Early Mesopotamia,* No. 25 of *SAOC.* Chicago: Oriental Institute, 1949.
727. Pinches, T. G. "Discoveries in Babylonia and the Neighboring Lands," *Records of the Past,* IX (1910), 95-112.
728. Rassam, Hormuzd. *Asshur and The Land of Nimrod.* New York: Eaton & Mains, 1897.
729. Smith, George. *Assyrian Discoveries: An Account of Exploration and Discoveries on the Site of Nineveh, During 1873 and 1874.* London: Low, Marston & Seale, 1875.
730. Speiser, E. A. "Closing the Gap at Tepe Gawra," *Ann. Rept. Smithsonian Inst. for 1939* (1940), 437-445.
731. Steele, Francis R. "Esarhaddon Building Inscription From Nippur," *JAOS,* LXX (1950), 69-72.
732. Tobler, Arthur J. *Excavations at Tepe Gawra,* Vol. II of *Univ. Penn. Museum Monographs.* Philadelphia: Univ. Penn. Press, 1950.
733. Wilber, Donald N. *Persepolis: The Archaeology of Parsa, Seat of The Persian Kings.* New York: Thos. Y. Crowell, 1969.
734. Woolley, C. Leonard. *Ur of The Chaldees.* New York: Chas. Scribner's Sons, 1930.
735. ———. *Excavations at Ur: A Record of Twelve Year's Work.* London: E. Benn, 1954.

Philology and Linguistic

736. Alexander, John B. *Early Babylonian Letters and Economic Texts,* Vol. VII of *Babylonian Inscriptions In The Collection of James B. Nies.* New Haven, Conn.: Yale Univ. Press, 1943.
737. Bezold, Carl. *Catologue of Cuneiform Tablets in The Kouyunjik Collection,* London: British Museum, 1889-99. 5 vols.
738. Booth, A. J. *Discovery and Decipherment of The Trilingual Cuneiform Inscriptions.* London: Longmans, Green, & Co., 1902.
739. Budge, E. A. Wallis *Assyrian Texts.* London: Trubner & Co., 1880.
740. Cameron, George G. "The Old Persian Text of the Bisitun Inscription," *Journal of Cuneiform Studies (JCS),* V (1951), 47-54.
741. ———. "Persepolis Treasury Tablets Old and New," *JNES,* XVII (1958), 161-172.
742. ———. "The Elamite Version of the Bisitun Inscriptions," *JCS* (1960), 59-68.
743. ———. "The Monument of King Darius at Bisitun," *Archaeology,* XIII (1960), 162-171.
744. ———. "New Tablets From the Persepolis Treasury," *JNES,* XXIV (1965), 167-192.
745. Crawford, Vaughn E. *Sumerian Economic Documents From The First Dynasty of Isin,* Vol. IX of *Babylonian Inscriptions In The Collection of James B. Nies.* New Haven, Conn.: Yale Univ. Press, 1954.
746. Delitzsch, Friedrich. *Assyrian Grammar,* trans. A. R. S. Kennedy. New York: B. Westermann & Co., 1889.
747. Gadd, C. J. A. *A Sumerian Reading-Book.* Oxford Univ. Press, 1924.
748. Gelb, Ignace J. "Reorganization of the Chicago Akkadian Dictionary," *Orientalia,* n.s., XVIII (1949), 376-377.
749. ———. *Morphology of Akkadian, A Comparative and Historical Sketch.* Chicago: Privately printed, 1952.
750. ———. *Sargonic Texts From the Diyala Region,* No. 1 of *Materials For The Assyrian Dictionary (MAD),* Chicago: Oriental Institute, 1952.

751. ——. "Present State of the Akkadian Dictionary," *Orientalia*, n.s., XXI (1952), 358-359.
752. ——. *Standard Operating Procedure For The Assyrian Dictionary*. Chicago: Oriental Institute (Mimeographed), 1954.
753. ——. *Glossary of Old Akkadian*, No. 3 of *MAD*. Chicago: Oriental Institute, 1957.
754. ——. *Old Akkadian Writing and Grammar*, 2d ed., No. 2 of *MAD*. Chicago: Oriental Institute, 1961.
755. ——. *Sequential Reconstruction of Proto-Akkadian*, No. 18 of *AS*. Chicago: Oriental Institute, 1969.
756. Gelb, I. J., P. M. Purves & A. A. MacRae. *Nuizi Personal Names*, Vol. LVII of *OIP*. Chicago: Oriental Institute, 1943.
757. Gelb, I. J., & E. Sollberger. "The First Legal Document From the Later Old Assyrian Period," *JNES*, XVI (1957), 163-175.
758. Goetze, Albrecht. *Old Babylonian Omen Texts*. New Haven, Conn.: Yale Univ. Press, 1947.
759. Heidel, Alexander. *The System of The Quadriliteral Verb in Akkadian*, No. 13 of *AS*. Chicago: Oriental Institute, 1940.
760. Kent, Roland G. "Old Persian Studies," *JAOS*, LXII (1942), 266-277.
761. ——. "Old Persian Texts," *JNES*, III (1944), 232-233.
762. ——. "The Oldest Old Persian Inscriptions," *JAOS*, LXVI (1946), 206-212.
763. ——. "On Some Old Persian Inscriptions of Darius I," *JAOS*, LXVII (1947), 30-33.
764. ——. "Cameron's New Reading of the Old Persian at Behistan," *JAOS*, LXXII (1952), 9-20.
765. ——. *Old Persian Grammar, Texts, Lexicon*, rev. ed. New Haven, Conn.: Amer. Oriental Soc., 1953.
766. Kraetzschmar, Richard. "The Sign of the Breath at the End of Words in the New-Babylonian and Achaemenian Inscriptions," *Hebraica*, VII (1890-91), 149-151.
767. Kramer, Samuel N. "The Oldest Literary Catalogue: A Sumerian List of Literary Compositions Compiled About 2000 B. C.," *BASOR*, No 88 (1942), 10-19.
768. ——. "Sumerian Literary Texts from Nippur in the Museum of the Ancient Orient at Istanbul," *AASOR*, XXIII (1944), 1-46.
769. ——. "The Tablet Collection of the University Museum," *JAOS*, LXVII (1947), 321-322.
770. Lacheman, Ernest R. *Palace and Temple Archives*, Pt. 2, Vol. V of *Excavations at Nuzi*, Vol. XIV of *Harvard Semitic Series*. Cambridge, Mass.: Harvard University Press, 1950.
771. ——. *The Administrative Archives*, Vol. VI of *Excavations at Nuzi*, Vol. XV of *Harvard Semitic Series*. Cambridge, Mass.: Harvard Univ. Press, 1955.
772. ——. *Economic and Social Documents*, Vol. VII of *Excavations at Nuzi*, Vol. XVI of *Harvard Semitic Series*. Cambridge, Mass.: Harvard Univ. Press, 1958.
773. ——. *Family Law Documents*, Vol. VIII of *Excavations at Nuzi*, Vol. XIX of *Harvard Semitic Series*, Cambridge, Mass.: Harvard Univ. Press, 1962.
774. Lenormant, Charles Francois. *Lettres Assyriologiques, Seconde Série: Etudes Accadiennes*. Paris: Maisonneuve, 1873-79. 3 vols.
775. Lutz, Henry F. "A Neo-Babylonian Debenture," *Univ. Calif. Publ. Semitic Philology*, X (1940), 251-256.
776. Menant, Joachim. "Oriental Cylinders of the Williams Collection," *AJA*, II (1886), 247-260.
777. Oppenheim, A. L. "Notes to the Harper Letters," *JAOS*, LXIX (1944), 190-196.
778. ——. *Letters From Mesopotamia*. Chicago: Univ. Chicago Press, 1967.

779. Oppert, Jules. *Das Lautsystem des Alterperischen.* Berlin: J. Springer, 1847.
780. Pfeiffer, Robert H., & Ernest R. Lacheman. *Miscellaneous Texts From Nuzi,* Vol. IV of *Excavations at Nuzi,* Vol. XIII of *Harvard Semitic Series.* Cambridge, Mass.: Harvard Univ. Press, 1942.
781. Rawlinson, Henry C. "The Persian Cuneiform Inscriptions at Behistun," *JRAS,* X (1847), 1-349; XI (1849), 1-192.
782. ———.*The Cuneiform Inscriptions of Western Asia.* London: British Museum, 1861-80. 6 vols.
783. ———. "The Behistun Inscription," *Records of the Past,* I (1902), 327-350.
784. Reiner, Erica. *A Linguistic Analysis of Akkadian.* The Hague: Mouton, 1966.
785. Sayce, A. H. *A Primer of Assyriology.* New York: Fleming H. Revell Co., 1894.
786. Speiser, E. A. "Comments on Recent Studies in Akkadian Grammar," *JAOS,* LXXIII (1953), 129-138.
787. Stephens, Ferris J. *Old Assyrian Letters,* Vol. VI of *Babylonian Inscriptions in the Collection of J. B. Nies.* New Haven, Conn.: Yale Univ. Press, 1944.
788. von Weidner, Ernst F. "Ein Babylonisches Kompendium der Himmelskunde," *AJSL,* XL (1923-24), 186-208.
789. Winckler, Hugo. "The Cuneiform Inscriptions in the Tunnel of Negub," *Hebraica,* IV (1887-88), 52-53.
790. ———. "Nebuchadnezzar's Artificial Reservoir," *Hebraica,* IV (1887-88), 174-175.
791. ———. "The Laws of Hammurabi, King of Babylonia," *Records of the Past,* II (1903), 67-98.
792. ———. "The Code of Hammurabi, Pt. I," *The Independent,* LV (1903), 67-70.
793. ———. "The Code of Hammurabi, Pt. II," *The Independent,* LV (1903), 127-132.
794. ———. "The Code of Hammurabi, Pt. III," *The Independent,* LV (1903), 183-190.

Religion, Culture, and Mythology

795. Delitzsch, Friedrich. "The Religion of the Kassites," *Hebraica,* I (1884-85), 189-191.
796. Heidel, Alexander. *The Babylonian Genesis: The Story of The Creation.* Chicago: Univ. Chicago Press, 1942.
797. Hooke, Samuel. *Babylonian and Assyrian Religion.* Norman: Univ. Oklahoma Press, 1963.
798. Hyde, Thomas. *Historia Religionis Persarum.* Oxford Univ. Press, 1700.
799. Jacobsen, Thorkild. "Primitive Democracy in Ancient Mesopotamia," *JNES,* II (1943), 159-172.
800. ———. "Sumerian Mythology: A Review Article," *JNES,* V (1946), 128-152.
801. Kramer, Samuel N. *Lamentations Over The Destruction of Ur,* No. 12 of *AS.* Chicago: Oriental Institute, 1940.
802. ———. "Ishtar in the Nether World according to a New Sumerian Text," *BASOR,* No. 79 (1940), 18-27.
803. ———. "Langdon's Historical and Religious Text from Nippur—Additons and Corrections," *JAOS,* LX (1940), 234-257.
804. ———. "Sumerian Literature: A Preliminary Survey of the Oldest Literature in the World," *Proc. Amer. Philosophical Soc.,* LXXXV (1941-42), 293-323.
805. ———. *Sumerian Mythology,* Vol. XXI of *Memoirs.* Philadelphia: American Philosophical Soc., 1944.
806. ———. "Corrections to 'The Epic of Gilgames and its Sumerian Sources,'" *JAOS,* LXIX (1944), 83.
807. ———. "The Death of Gilgamesh," *BASOR,* No. 94 (1944), 2-12.
808. ———. "Dilmun, the Land of the Living," *BASOR,* No. 96 (1944), 18-28.
809. ———. "The Epic of Gilgames and its Sumerian Sources," *JAOS,* LXIV), 7-23.

810. ———. "Death and Nether World according to the Sumerian Literary Texts," *Iraq*, XXII (1960), 59-68.
811. ———. *Sumerian Mythology*, rev. ed. New York: Harper, 1961.
812. ———. *The Sacred Marriage: Aspects of Faith, Myth, and Ritual in Ancient Sumer*. Bloomington: Indiana Univ. Press, 1969.
813. Mendelsohn, Isaac. "Free Artisans and Slaves in Mesopotamia," *BASOR*, No 89 (1943), 25-29.
814. Sayce, A. H. *Social Life Among the Assyrians and Babylonians*. New York: Fleming H. Revell Co., 1893.
815. ———. *Babylonians and Assyrians: Life and Customs*. New York: Chas. Scribner's Sons, 1899.
816. Smith, George. *The Chaldean Account of Genesis*. New York: Scribner, Armstrong & Co., 1876.
817. ———. "The Chaldean Account of the Deluge," *Records of the Past*, I (1902), 363-380.

Biography

818. Burrows, Millar. "A Sketch of C. C. Torrey's Career," *BASOR*, No. 132 (1953), 6-8.
819. Fletcher, James P. *The Autobiography of a Missionary*. London: Hurst & Blackett, 1853. 2 vols.
820. Haines, Richard C. "Erich F. Schmidt, September 13, 1897—October 3, 1964," *JNES*, XXIV (1965), 145-147.
821. Kubie, Nora B. *Road to Nineveh*. Garden City, N. Y.: Doubleday, 1964.
822. Lamb, Harold. *Cyrus the Great*. Garden City, N. Y.: Doubleday, 1960.
823. Layard, A. H. *Autobiography and Letters From His Childhood Until His Appointment As H. M. Ambassador at Madrid*, ed. by W. N. Bruce. London: John Murray, 1903. 2 vols.
824. Rawlinson, George. *A Memoir of Major-General Sir Henry Creswicke Rawlinson*. London: Longmans. Green & Co., 1898.
825. Waterfield, Gordon. *Layard of Nineveh*. London: John Murray, 1963.

Chronology

826. Albright, William F. "Stratigraphic Confirmation of the Low Mesopotamian Chronology," *BASOR*, No. 144 (1956), 26-30.
827. Buchanan, Briggs. "The Date of the So-Called Second Dynasty Graves of the Royal Cemetery at Ur," *JAOS*, LXXIV (1954), 147-153.
828. Cameron, George G. "Darius and Xerxes in Babylonia," *AJSL*, LVIII (1941), 314-325.
829. Dubberstein, Waldo H. "Assyrian-Babylonian Chronology (699-612 B.C.)," *JNES*, III (1944), 38-42.
830. Goetze, Albrecht. "Additions to Parker and Dubberstein's Babylonian Chronology," *JNES*, III (1944), 43-46.
831. ———. "The Chronology of Sulgi Again," *Iraq*, XXII (1960), 151-156.
832. ———. "The Kassites and Near Eastern Chronology," *JCS*, XVIII (1964), 97-101.
833. Neugebauer, O. "The Chronology of the Hammurabi Age," *JAOS*, XLI (1941), 58-61.
834. Nylander, Carl. "Old Persian and Greek Stonecutting and the Chronology of Achaemenian Monuments," *AJA*, LXIX (1965), 49-55.
835. Parker, R. A., & W. H. Dubberstein. *Babylonian Chronology 626 B.C. — A.D. 45*, No. 24 of *SAOC*. Chicago: Oriental Institute, 1942.

836. Poebel, Arno. *The Second Dynasty of Isin According To A New King-List Tablet*, No. 15 of *AS*. Chicago: Oriental Institute, 1955.
837. Rowton, M. B. "The Date of Hammurabi," *JNES*, XVII (1958), 97-111.
838. ——. "The Date of the Sumerian King List," *JNES*, XIX (1960), 156-162.

Art and Architecture

839. Babelon, Ernest. *Manual of Oriental Antiquities, Including the Architecture, Sculpture, and Industrial Arts of Chaldaea, Assyria, Persia, Syria, Judaea, Phoenicia, and Carthage*, trans. B. T. A. Evetts. New York: G. P. Putnam's Sons, 1889.
840. Crawford, Vaughn E. "Nippur, the Holy City," *Archaeology*, XII (1959), 74-83.
841. de Morgan, Jacques. "The Temple of Susinak," *Harper's Monthly Magazine*, CX (1905), 875-884.
842. Muller, Valentine. "Types of Mesopotamian Houses," *JAOS*, LX (1940), 151-180.
843. Porada, Edith. "Seal Impressions of Nuzi," *AASOR*, XXIV (1947), 1-138.
844. ——. *The Art of Ancient Iran: Pre-Islamic Cultures* New York: Crown Publishers, 1965.
845. Schmidt, Erich. *Persepolis*, Vols. LXVIII & LXIX of *OIP*. Chicago: Oriental Institute, 1953-56. 2 vols.
846. Starr, R. F. S. "A Rare Example of Akkadian Sculpture," *AJA*, XLV (1941), 81-86.

INDEX

Abbas I, 5
Abbott, Jacob, 19
Abu Hatab, 142
Abu Khazaf, 115
Achaemenids, 7
Adab, 48, 51, 66-70, 142
Adler, Cyrus 32-33, 43, 44, 79
Afghan War, 9
Age of Materialism, 24
Age of Realists, 23-27
Age of Reason, 17
Age of Romanticism, 17-23
Agrab, See Tell Agrab
Akkad, 48, 107
Akkadians, 2, 70
Albright, William F., 87, 121, 137
Aleppo, 50
Alexander the Great, 4, 118
Allen, Edgar P., 33
Allen, George, 103
American Institute for Persian Art & Archaeology, See Iranian Institute of America
American Oriental Society, 22-23, 26-27, 43, 49, 52, 79, 89, 125-126
American Philosophical Society, 44, 89, 126
American School of Archaelogy at Jerusalem, 71
American School of Classical Studies at Athens, 94
American Schools for Oriental Research, 131
American Schools of Oriental Research at Baghdad, 96-97, 108-110, 112-113, 131-133
American Schools of Oriental Research at Jerusalem, 131
Amorites, See Babylonians
Amurru, 85
An (god), 48
Andrae, Walther, 119
Antiquaries Society of London, 118
Archaeological Institute of America, 46, 49, 131-132
Artaxerxes, 4
Ashur, 3
Ashurbanipal, 48

Ashurnasirpal, 21
Asmar, See Tell Asmar
Assyrian Dictionary, 97-101, 137-138
Assyriological Studies, 104
Assyriology (definition), 1-2

Babylon, 3-4, 5, 6, 13, 14, 55, 118
Babylonian Exploration Fund, 53, 54, 56, 58, 61
Babylonian Expedition of the University of Pennsylvania, The, 59, 80
Babylonian Expedition Series, 36
Babylonians, 2, 48, 107
Bache, Charles, 109
Bacon, Leonard W, 21
Baghdad, 9, 47, 50, 51-52, 54-55, 57, 58, 60, 67, 69, 131-133
Baltimore, 32
Banks, Edgar J., 66-70
Barbaro, Giosafat, 4
Barton, George A., 39, 78, 84, 87-88, 122, 128, 131-133
Behistun, 7, 8, 9, 11, 81
Belser, Carl W., 40-41, 78
Bembo, Ambrogio, 7
Berry, George R., 38, 77
Bey, Bedry, 55
Bey, Haidar, 68
Bey, Hamdy, 54, 57, 59
Bezold, Carl, 16
Billah, See Tell Billah
Birs Nimrud, See Borsippa
Bismya, See Adab
Blackwell, James S., 37
Blake, Frank R., 76, 87, 121
Bodine, Mrs. S. T., 73
Bombay, 8
Borsippa, 51, 67
Boston, 22, 23, 27
Botta, Paul E., 13, 14, 19, 116
Breasted, Charles, 117
Breasted, James H., 65, 90-92, 97-98, 102-103, 114, 117
Brewster, David, 21
Brinton, Daniel G., 44
Briggs, C. A., 52
Brown, Charles R., 43
Brown, Francis, 28-30, 49, 79

Bryant, William C., 17
Buckingham, James S., 6
Budge, E. A. W., 15, 50
Bushire, 119
Byron, Lord, 1

Cameron, George G., 96, 101, 122, 130-131, 136
Cartwright, John, 5
Chaldeans, 2, 3
Chardin, Jean, 5
Chiera, Edward, 77, 87, 100-101, 112, 116, 121-122, 127-128
Childe, Gordon, 128
Clark, Clarence H., 53
Clark, Edward W., 35, 53, 59
Clark, Hyde, 26
Clay, Albert T., 36-39, 71-72, 73, 77, 79-80, 83, 85, 89, 90, 123, 128, 131, 132
Clemens, Samuel L., 24
Colleges:
 Amherst, 21
 Bowdoin, 19, 21
 Bryn Mawr, 39, 78, 87, 122
 Central Turkey, 50
 Dropsie, 108-110
 Middlebury, 21
 Roberts, 68
 Union, 21, 26
 Williams, 21
Columbia Univ. Contributions to Oriental History & Philology, 82
Columbia Univ. Oriental Studies, 82, 86
Constantinople, 50, 51, 56, 58, 59, 62, 67-68
Cooper, James F., 17
Craig, James A., 41, 53, 45, 78
Ctesias of Cnidus, 4
Ctesiphon, 55, 113
Cuneate, 5
Cyaxares, 3
Cyrus the Great, 26, 130

Dair, 119
Damascus, 57
Damghan, 114
Darius the Great, 7, 8, 11, 118
Davis, Asahel, 20
Debevoise, Neilson, 96
Delaporte, Louis J., 128

Delitzsch, Friedrich, 16, 40, 41, 46, 64, 98
Dickinson, Emily, 24
Diodorus Siculus, 4
Diyala, 110, 115
Dougherty, Raymond P., 89, 99, 123-124
Drehem, 143
Dubberstein, Waldo H., 96, 135
Duncan, George S., 86-87
Dur-Sharrukin, See Khorsabad

East India Company, 9
Ecbatana, 118
Edgerton, William F., 124
Effendi, Mohammed S., 57
Edur, 48
Elamites, 48, 107
Eldred, John, 5
Eliot, Charles, 50
Emerson, Ralph W., 18
Enlil, 48, 63
Ensi, 48
E-nunmah, Temple of, 106
Erech, 119
Eridu, 48
Esarhaddon, 3
Eshnunna, See Tell Asmar
Etana, 48

Fara, 31, 63, 114, 142
Farnsworth, Wilson A., 21
Field, Perez H., 53, 56
Figueroa, Don Garcia de Silva, 5
Fischer, Clarence S., 61-63, 73
Fletcher, James P., 18-19
Frankfort, Henri, 115-116
Fraser, James B., 18
Furlani, Giuseppe, 119
Furness, William H., 73

Gadd, C. J., 106
Gardner, Francis, 22
Gasur, See Nuzi
Gawrah, See Tepe Gawra
Geere, H. V., 61, 63
Geers, F. W., 99
Gelb, Ignace J., 101, 135, 138
Genouillac, Henri de, 110, 118
Ghirshman, Roman, 119
Girumu, 145
Goetze, Albrecht, 124
Goodsell, Daniel A., 21

Gordon, Cyrus H., 109
Gottheil, Richard J. H., 41, 78, 79, 81, 88
Gouvea, Antoine de, 5
Greenough, William W., 22
Grice, Ettaline M., 89
Grotefend, Georg F., 8-10
Guti, 48

Hadley, James, 26
Halevy, Joseph, 16
Hall, I. H. 49
Hamilton, R. W., 118
Hammurabi, 70, 115
Hammarabi, Code of, 66, 83, 87
Harper, Robert F., 39-40, 43, 53-56, 64-66, 69, 78, 88
Harper, William R., 39-40, 42, 64-65, 67-68
Harris, Joel C., 24
Harris, Joseph S., 73
Harrison, Charles C., 72-74
Harte, Bret, 24
Harvard Semitic Series, 82, 121
Hasanlu, 137, 147
Hashmargalshu, 131
Haskell, Caroline E., 65
Haskell, H. B., 21
Haupt, H. H. Paul, 32-34, 42, 44, 46, 73, 76, 79, 86-87, 121
Hawthorne, Nathaniel, 18
Haynes, John H., 50-51, 53, 57, 59-63
Heidel, Alexander, 135
Herzfeld, Ernest E., 117-118, 134-135
Hieroglyphs, 6
Hilprecht, Hermann V., 34-37, 39, 44, 53-57, 59, 61-63, 71, 73-76, 77, 121
Hincks, Edward, 9-12, 14
Hissar, See Tepe Hissar
Hitti, Philip K., 122
Holmes, Oliver W., 18
Hopkins, E. W., 80
Houston, Samuel F., 73
Howells, William D., 24
Hutchinson, R. W., 118
Hyde, Thomas, 5-6
Hystaspes, 8

Iranian Institute of America, 131
Iraq Expedition, 114-116
Irving, Washington, 17
Ischali, 115, 146
Isin, 48

Istakhr, 146
Ives, Edward, 6

Jackson, Abraham V. W., 41-42, 45, 78, 85, 123, 129
Jacobsen, Thorkild, 101, 115
James, Henry, 24
Jarmo, 147
Jasm, 51
Jastrow, Morris, Jr., 35-37, 44, 45, 73-74, 79, 81, 84, 87, 121, 131-132
Jemdet Nasr 111-112, 143
Jenks, William, 22
Jeremiah, 3
Jerusalem, 21
Jerwan, 116, 131-132, 145, 146
Jewish Institute of Religion, 38
Johnson, Edwin L., 85
Johnston, Christopher, Jr., 33-34, 76, 86
Jonah, 3
Jones, J. L., 73
Jordan, Julius, 119
Journals:
American Antiquarian, 25
American J. of Archaeology, 46, 137
American J. of Semitic Languages and Literature, 46, 86, 136
Archaeology, 137
Beiträge zur Assyriologie, 34, 46
Hebraica, 34, 46
J. of the American Oriental Society, 22, 31, 86
J. of Cuneiform Studies, 137
J. of Near Eastern Studies, 136
J. of the Society of Oriental Research, 85
Museum J., 82
Records of the Past, 81

Kaempfer, Englebert, 5-6
Kakzu, 19
Karim Shahir, 147
Kassites, 2, 48
Keiser, Clarence E., 72
Kent, Roland G., 90, 136
Kermanshah, 7
Khafajeh, 109-110, 115-116, 144-145
Khorsabad, 13, 14, 19, 116, 144
Kidder, Daniel P., 19-20
King, Leonard W., 85
Kinneir, J. McDonald, 6
Kirkuk, 112

Kish, 48, 110-112, 142-143
Knudson Albert C., 77
Koldewey, Robert, 67
Kouyunjik Collections, 65
Kramer, Samuel N., 101, 134, 136-137
Kut-al-Amara, 69

Lagash, 48, 118
Langdon, Stephen, 111-112
Larsa, 48, 119
Lassen, Christian, 9, 11
Lau, Robert, 74
Lawrence, A. W., 106
Layard, Austen H., 13-14, 15, 19, 20, 22, 26, 49
Le Conte, Robert G., 73
Legrain, Leon, 122
Leipzig, 16, 30
Lenormant, Francois, 15
Lenox, James, 22
Loftus, William K., 14, 20
London, 9, 10, 13, 50, 54, 67
Longfellow, Henry W., 18
Longperier, Henri, 11
Lowell, James R., 18
Lowell Lectures, 135
Lowenstern, Chevalier I., 11
Luckenbill, Daniel D., 78, 88, 97-100, 122
Lugal, 48
Lutz, Henry L. F., 89, 124-125
Lyon, David Gordon, 30-32, 39, 40, 49, 76, 86, 120-121

MacCurdy, John F., 38
Mackay, Ernest, 111
McKinley, President, 66
Mallowan, M. E. L., 118
Malyun, See Tepe Malyun
Marsh, Dwight W., 21
Mason, Otis T., 25
Maynard, John A., 98-99
Medes, 3
Meek, Theophile J., 130
Melville, Herman, 18
Menant, Joachim, 16, 50
Mercantile Library Assn., 21
Mercer, Samuel A. B., 85-86, 99
Merrill, Selah, 21, 25, 26-27
Meyer, Joseph A., 60
Miller, O. D., 25-26
Missione Archeologica Italiana di Mesopotamia, 119

Mitchell, Hinckley G., 38-39, 77
Mosul, 5, 6, 13, 14, 18, 23, 50, 108, 116
Mugheir 67
Munter, Frederik, 7, 8
Museums:
  Bibliotheque Nationale, 50, 81
  British, 25, 32, 45, 50, 65, 67, 81, 105-108, 118
  Chicago Field, 110-112
  Cleveland Mus. of Art, 113
  Fogg Art, 112
  Harvard Semitic, 31-32, 76, 86, 112
  Haskell Oriental, 65, 89, 99, 102
  Imperial (Constantinople), 54, 59, 68
  Louvre, 50, 67, 81, 119
  National Mus. at Baghdad, 106, 110
  Oriental Institute, 102-103
  Peabody, 32, 112
  Toledo Mus. of Art, 113
  University (Pennsylvania), 36, 63, 72, 105-108, 112, 113, 122, 134, 137
Muss-Arnolt, Wilhelm, 40-41, 98

Nabopolassor, 3
Nahum, 3
Naksh-i-Rustam, 11, 146
Naram-Sin, 48
Nebuchadnezzar, 4
Neo-Classic Age, 17, 23
New Haven, 23, 26
Newman, John P., 25
Newton, F. G., 106
New York, 26, 44, 56, 58, 59, 67
New York Historical Soc., 21, 22
New York Independent, 25, 50
Nidnusha, 131
Niebuhr, Carsten, 6-8
Nies, James B., 123
Nimrod, 25
Nineveh, 3-6, 13-15, 19-23, 25, 116, 118
Nippur, 36, 40, 44, 47-49, 51-63, 65, 137, 141-142
Noorian, Daniel Z., 51, 53, 57
Norris, Edwin, 10, 11, 14, 98
Notgemeinschaft der Deutschen Wissenschaft, 119
Nuzi, 112-113, 143

Oliver, G. A., 6
Olmstead, Albert T., 84-85, 93-97, 122, 126, 136

Oppenheim, A. L., 137, 138
Oppert, Jules, 10-12, 14, 15, 110
Oriental Clubs:
　New Haven, 79, 90, 127
　New York, 44, 79, 90, 126
　Philadelphia, 44, 79, 89-90, 126
Oriental Exploration Fund, 66, 68
Oriental Institute, 90-92, 93-104, 114-118, 122, 134, 137
Oriental Institute Communications, 104
Oriental Institute Publications, 104
Ottoman Empire, 93, 105

Paige, Jason, 69
Palmyra, 52
Paris, 9, 67
Parker, Richard A., 135
Parrot, André, 119
Parthians, 49, 113
Pepper, William, 53-54, 59
Persepolis, 5, 7, 8, 81, 117-118, 145
Persepolitan Inscriptions, 7-10
Persian Expedition, 117-118
Persians, 2
Peters-Hilprecht Controversy, 73-76
Peters, John P., 35, 43, 44, 49, 52-58, 59, 67, 73-75
Petrie, Flinders, 60, 105
Pfeiffer, Robert H., 112, 120-121, 130
Philadelphia, 34, 44, 56, 62, 89
Pickering, John, 22
Piepkorn, Arthur, 96, 101
Pinches, Theophilus, 50
Place, Victor, 14, 116
Poe, Edgar A., 18
Poebel, Arno, 76, 101, 122
Porter, Robert K., 13
Price, Ira M., 40, 78, 88, 99, 122
Prince, John D., 34, 42, 53-54, 74, 78, 79, 88, 123

Ragozin, Zenoide A., 45
Ranke, Hermann, 73-74
Rassam, Hormuzd, 25
Rauwolff, Leonhard, 4-5
Rawlinson, Henry C., 8-12, 14, 22, 26, 54
Rayy, 146
Rhages, See Rayy
Rhyn, G. A. F. van, 26
Rich, Claudius, 13
Riley, F. B., 132
Rishahr, 119

Riza Shah Pahlevi, 113, 117
Robinson, Edward, 19, 22
Rockefeller, John D., 68
Rockefeller, John D., Jr., 91-92
Rogers, Robert W., 33, 44, 80, 83-84, 95, 129
Royal Asiatic Society, 9, 12
Royal Danish Society of Sciences, 7
Royal Irish Academy, 10, 12

Saggs, H. W. F., 137
Salisbury, E. E., 23
Sargon the Great, 48, 70, 107, 115
Sargon II, 3, 11, 93-94, 116
Sayce, A. H., 15, 26, 45, 50, 54
Schmidt, Erich F., 114
Schmidt, Nathaniel, 38, 42, 78, 88-89, 93, 123
Schrader, Eberhard, 16, 28, 64
Scoggin, Gilbert C., 77
Seleucia, 4
Seleucids, 49
Seminaries:
　Andover Theological, 19, 21, 43, 50, 71
　Auburn Theological, 21
　Baptist Theological, 43
　Episcopal, 21
　Union Theological, 19, 28-29, 50, 52
　Western Theological, 85
Semitic Study Series, 81
Sennacherib, 3, 94, 116
Shenshi, See Tepe Shenshi
Sippar, 119
Smith, Azariah, 20
Smith, Edgar F., 73
Smith, George, 14, 24
Smith, Sidney, 106
Smyrna, 51
Société Asiatique, 9
Speiser, Ephraim A., 108-109, 129
Starr, Richard, 112
Stephens, Ferris J., 124, 131, 137
Sterrett, John R. S., 51, 54
Stevenson, Mrs. Cornelius, 73
Stevenson, James H., 42-43, 78, 89
Stuart, Moses, 22
Studies in Ancient Oriental Civilization, 104
Sumer, 48, 107
Sumerians, 2, 47-48, 70
Sumerology, 2
Summer School of Hebrew, 43

Sunday School Times, 35, 54
Susa, 81, 118, 119

Taintor, Edward C., 26
Takht-i-Jamshid, 4
Talbot, W. H. F., 12, 98
Tal-i-Bakun, 146
Taylor, J. E., 14, 105
Taylor, John P., 33, 43
Teheran, 114
Tell Agrab, 116, 146
Tell al-Ubaid, 106-107, 142
Tell Asmar, 115, 144
Tell Billah, 109-110, 144
Tell Ibrahim, 67
Tell Umar, 113, 144
Telloh, 51
Tepe Gawra, 108-110, 143-144
Tepe Hasanlu, See Hasanlu
Tepe Hissar, 114, 145
Tepe Malyun, 137, 147
Tepe Shenshi, 116, 145
Tepe Yahya, 147
Thompson, R. C., 85, 105, 118
Tolman, Herbert C., 45, 78-79, 80-81, 85, 89, 123
Torrey, Charles C., 71-72, 90
Toy, Charles H., 49
Tremayne, Arch, 89
Trumbull, H. C., 54
Tudela, Benjamin de, 4
Tureng Tepe, 145
Twain, Mark, 24
Tyschen, Oluf G., 7, 8

Ubaid, 70
Umar, See Tell Uman
Universities:
  Berlin, 10, 28, 32, 38, 53, 64, 79, 88, 90
  Boston, 38, 77
  California, 124-125
  Chicago, 39-40, 42, 46, 64-66, 68, 70, 78, 88, 93-104, 114, 122, 134-135, 137
  Colgate, 38, 42, 77, 87
  Columbia, 41-42, 78, 88, 123
  Cornell, 42, 78, 88, 93-94, 123
  Harvard, 30-32, 50, 66, 76, 86, 120-121
  Illinois, 94
  Johns Hopkins, 32-34, 46, 54, 76, 86-87, 121

Leipzig, 31, 32, 35, 39, 40, 41, 64
Madison, See Colgate
Michigan, 40-41, 78, 88, 123
Missouri, 37, 77, 87, 94
New York, 42, 78
Oxford, 15, 110-112, 116
Pennsylvania, 32-33, 34-37, 47-63, 64, 65, 71, 73-76, 77, 87, 105-108, 109-110, 112, 134, 137
Princeton, 37-38, 77, 87, 122
Vanderbilt, 42-43, 45-46, 78-79, 89, 123
Yale, 21, 45, 64-65, 71-72, 79, 89, 123-124
Univ. of Calif. Publications in Semitic Philology, 82
Ur, 14, 48, 67, 105-108, 142
Ur-Nammu, 48
Uruk, See Erech

Valle, Pietro della, 5, 7
Vanderbilt Oriental Series, 86
Vanderburgh, Frederick, 88, 123

Ward, William H., 25, 49-52, 67, 79, 81, 132
Warka, See Erech
Watelin, Louis C., 111
Waterman, Leroy, 88, 99, 113, 123, 129-130
Weld, Herbert, 110
Wells, Calvin, 73
Westergaard, Niels L., 11
Whitman, Walt, 18
Whitney, William D., 26
Whittier, John G., 18
Williams, W. F., 21
Wilson, John A., 95, 97
Winckler, Hugo, 16
Wolfe, Catherine L., 49
Wolfe Expedition, 29, 49-52, 54
Wooley, C. Leonard, 106-108
Wright, Austin H., 21

Xerxes, 7-9

Yahya, See Tepe Yahya
Yale Oriental Series, 82, 86

Ziggurat, 58, 60, 63, 106
Zoroaster, 45

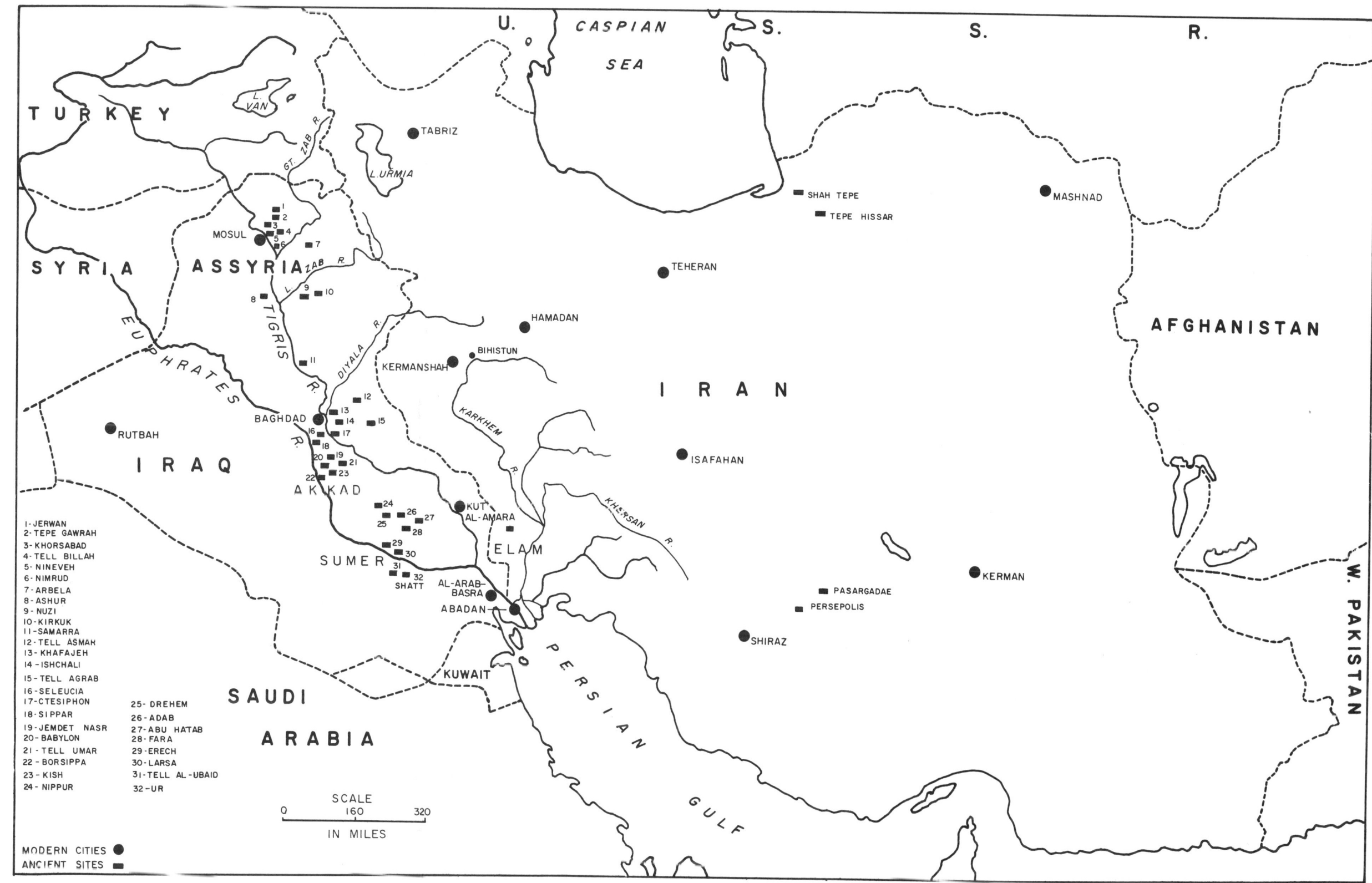

Map of Iraq and Iran

LIBRARY OF DAVIDSON COLLEGE